AMERICA SECOND

AMERICA SECOND

How America's Elites
Are Making China Stronger

Isaac Stone Fish

Alfred A. Knopf · New York · 2022

THIS IS A BORZOI BOOK
PUBLISHED BY ALFRED A. KNOPF

www.aaknopf.com

Knopf, Borzoi Books, and the colophon are registered trademarks of
Penguin Random House LLC.

Library of Congress Cataloging-in-Publication Data
Names: Stone Fish, Isaac, author.
Title: America second : how America's elites are making China stronger /
Isaac Stone Fish.
Description: First Edition. | New York : Alfred A. Knopf, 2022. |
Includes bibliographical references and index.
Identifiers: LCCN 2021024242 (print) | LCCN 2021024243 (ebook) |
ISBN 9780525657705 (hardcover) | ISBN 9780525657712 (ebook)
Subjects: LCSH: Political leadership. | Friendship—Political aspects. |
United States—Foreign public opinion, Chinese—History. |
Public opinion—China—History. | United States—Relations—China. |
China—Relations—United States. | United States—Foreign economic
relations—China. | China—Foreign economic relations—United States. |
United States—Race relations. | Chinese—United States—History.
Classification: LCC JC330.3 .S86 2022 (print) | LCC JC330.3 (ebook) |
DDC 303.3/4—dc23
LC record available at https://lccn.loc.gov/2021024242
LC ebook record available at https://lccn.loc.gov/2021024243

Front-of-jacket photograph © Peter Dazeley / The Image Bank /
Getty Images
Jacket design by Tyler Comrie

Manufactured in the United States of America
First Edition

To my grandma Sandy,
who taught me that sharks don't sleep

Contents

AMERICA SECOND

Introduction

★

CONSIDER GRINDR. YES, THAT GRINDR, THE DATING AND HOOKUP app that revolutionized gay culture in America. In January 2018, the private Chinese technology firm Beijing Kunlun acquired Grindr. "The Chinese government will not have access to your account," Grindr said in a May 2017 blog post. "Beijing Kunlun is not owned by the Chinese government." Indeed, Kunlun is a private company, and its founder, Zhou Yahui, is known in China mostly for having amassed enough wealth to have spent $1.1 billion on a divorce. He's not seen as especially beholden to the ruling Chinese Communist Party.[1]

But Grindr was lying. Because a Chinese company owned all of Grindr's data, photographs, and messages, the Party could access all of that information, regardless of where it's stored. And that data includes compromising photos and messages from some of America's most powerful men—some openly gay, and some closeted. Couple this with China's continued innovations in facial recognition, an industry more advanced there than in the United States, and there are some fascinating and concerning national security implications. Crudely put, Beijing could now access the dick pics of millions of Americans. In 2011, the then U.S. congressman Anthony Weiner tweeted a lewd photograph, setting off a chain of events that led to his 2017 imprisonment. Beijing can blackmail a closeted congressman who does not want to be Weiner 2.0.[2]

In many ways, Grindr under Chinese ownership was a disaster. Grindr's new president, Scott Chen, was a terrible fit for the culture;

he even announced on Facebook that he opposed gay marriage. While it's unknown if the Chinese government has accessed Grindr data, Reuters found that Grindr gave Beijing-based engineers access to the personal information—including private messages and HIV status—of millions of Americans. In March 2019, amid growing unease about Beijing's influence in America, the government body, the Committee on Foreign Investment in the United States (CFIUS), ordered Kunlun to unwind the deal. A year later, Kunlun sold Grindr to an American investment firm. National security types rejoiced.

But the story doesn't end there. Grindr's ties to Beijing still jeopardize the privacy of everyone who uses the app. An investment group called San Vicente Acquisition LLC, formed just weeks before the Kunlun deal, now runs Grindr. James Lu, the chairman of the board of Grindr, as of August 2021 is also the chairman of a Chinese investment firm majority owned by a Chinese city government. A recent Norwegian government report found that Grindr still shares data with the tech giant Tencent, a Chinese company with close ties to Beijing. Meanwhile, Grindr's user base keeps growing: from 3.8 million active daily users in 2018 to more than 4.5 million in 2020. Kunlun, which had paid $245 million for its 98 percent stake in Grindr, sold the firm less than three years later, for $608 million: an impressive gain. All of this is despite Grindr's abysmal privacy controls. "Not going to sugar coat this," Mozilla Foundation researchers wrote in a February 2021 review of twenty-four popular dating apps' privacy and security. "Of all the dating apps we reviewed, Grindr is the worst of the worst."[3] Unlike TikTok, the Chinese-owned viral video app, Grindr collects information about its users that couldn't be more personal.

Grindr in 2022—wholly owned by an American firm and vetted by CFIUS—is more of a security threat than it was several years ago.

Questions like those raised by the Grindr saga are being asked in boardrooms, Hollywood studios, government offices, and universities across America. How much access to the American market should Chinese firms get? Are private Chinese firms more or less dangerous than state-owned ones? How did American entities get so entangled into the Chinese system? How worried should we be about those who willingly or unwillingly aid the Party in America? Grindr's chairman is Chinese American. How does one address the issue of problematic ties to Beijing without stigmatizing or discriminating against Asian Americans? How do we stop Americans from spreading Party propaganda without impinging on their freedom of speech? Does the economic benefit of partnering with Chinese institutions outweigh the political and national security costs? And most important, where should we draw the line?

America Second is a book about the pernicious aspects of the Party's influence in America. And it's a book about how to fight back without being Trumpian or racist: tactics like exposing unethical and illegal U.S. corporate behavior in China, partnering with American allies, educating Americans about threatening Party ministries like the United Front, restricting American institutions' ability to support the genocide in Xinjiang, and not stigmatizing Chinese Americans. For decades, Beijing successfully incentivized many elite Americans to strengthen China at the cost of America. In targeted and sophisticated ways, American policy needs to remove those incentives. And it needs to contain China, and weaken the Party's global influence.

I'm pro-China (inasmuch as one can be for or against any country, especially one as massive and multifaceted as China). I lived in China for six years: mostly in Beijing, but also in Shanghai, Hong Kong, and the northeastern city of Harbin. I've visited all of its twenty-two provinces, its four municipalities, its five (questionably named) autonomous regions, including Xinjiang and Tibet, the "special" administrative regions of Hong Kong and Macau, and the country of Taiwan, which Beijing has long disingenuously claimed. But I am anti-Party. I would love to live in China again, and when the Party is finally excised from leadership, perhaps I will.

Chinese officials love to remind Americans that "China has five thousand years of history." But the Party has ruled for only seventy-two of those years, far less time than many of the dynasties that preceded it. One of the many tricks the Party plays is convincing both Chinese and Americans that its rule over China is inevitable. It's not.

The Party exercises its influence over America quite differently than the Russian president Vladimir Putin's regime does. Instead of engendering chaos to weaken America, the Party works in quieter ways, in ways that attract less attention and intrigue. More than anything else, it speaks the soft language of *corruption*. For many years, the Party has seduced and corrupted certain individual Americans and their companies and agencies. The list of individuals is long and unfortunately distinguished: Jimmy Carter, Madeleine Albright, the Disney CEO Bob Iger, and the former Chicago mayor Richard M. Daley have all advanced the Party's interests in America.

In early 2017, U.S. counterintelligence officials warned Trump's aide and son-in-law, Jared Kushner, that Wendi Deng Murdoch, a naturalized American citizen and the former wife of the press baron, may be working "to further the interests of the Chinese government."[*4] People like Carter, Albright, and Iger further the interests of Beijing, but they almost certainly do so unintentionally, which makes it more effective and more dangerous.

This is a book about greed and compromises and the strange forms that influence can take. This is a book about how the Walt Disney Company helped destroy the Tibet movement and how Steven Seagal and Mike Tyson spread Party propaganda.

Perhaps most surprisingly, I focus on one major figure in the American establishment and how well he served the Party. In his decades-long reign as America's most famous statesman, Henry Kissinger has been called many things. Senator John McCain called him the world's most respected individual. The novelist Joseph Heller called him an "odious schlump who made war gladly." Xi Jinping, China's leader, calls him an "old friend of the Chinese people."

But the most accurate way to describe Kissinger, from the time he started his consulting company in 1982 to the present, is as an agent of Chinese influence. He may be one of the most brilliant Americans of the twentieth century—and a former intelligence agent himself—but he should have been more careful. (When reached for comment, a Kissinger representative denied that Kissinger was an agent of Chinese influence and called the allegation libelous. Kissinger's rela-

---

* At the time, a spokesman for Mrs. Murdoch said she "has no knowledge of any FBI concerns or other intelligence agency concerns relating to her or her associations."

tionship with China, he said, "is in the highest and best tradition of American statesmanship.")

Just how vigilant should Americans be about Beijing? What does the Party *want* from America? It's important to recognize the limits of our understanding of Chinese leaders: we know about as much about the top of the Party today as we did about Soviet leaders during the 1950s. Does Xi wish to destroy or subvert American democracy, or coexist peacefully with it? There is no known plan of Chinese dominance, no "hundred-year marathon" to overtake the United States by 2049. Chinese leaders can't see into the future: they are mortals, just like the rest of us. I don't believe Beijing is pursuing a grand strategy to defeat America or render it powerless. It cannot be emphasized enough just how intertwined our economy is with China's—even after years of decoupling under Trump and President Joe Biden.

But evidence suggests that the Party wants America to yield. It wants Americans to recognize their mistakes and apologize. Beijing wants America as a reliable and pliant Second to China's First. A friend.

THROUGHOUT THE BOOK, I ADDRESS SOME OF THE ETHICAL COM-promises that I have made throughout my twenty years of interacting with China. I'm not including my own experiences and transgressions because I rank along with the prominent people I describe here. I'm doing it for four reasons. First, the set of compromises I'm most familiar with are my own, and the writing of this book has provoked reflection on the decisions I have made.

Second, journalists and pundits gleefully uncover hypocrisy: whether it's a homophobic congressman with a Grindr account or the Trump critic LeBron James advocating self-censorship on Hong Kong. The Chinese expression is "those who retreat fifty steps scorn those who retreat one hundred steps." I've made many of the errors I criticize others for making.

Third, throughout my career I have craved guidance on these issues. What is appropriate behavior? In 2009, as a struggling freelance journalist in my mid-twenties living in gray Beijing, paying $350 a month for an apartment where the showerhead hovered over the toilet, I would have written for *China Police*, the magazine for the Ministry of State Security, if it had paid at least thirty cents a word. Hopefully the younger journalists, businesspeople, and thinkers coming up in the field can avoid the potholes that shook me.

Yes, the Party appeared more benign when I lived in China from 2006 to 2011, before Xi and before the concentration camps. But that's a lousy excuse for facilitating unethical behavior. And if intentionality matters, then my lack of opportunity doesn't absolve me. Ten years later, I can afford to be choosier with the funding I take and the work that I do. But the gray area is vast, and I have certainly stumbled. I hope to do better in the future and that my examples are illustrative.

And fourth, my incentives differ from those of many of the people I write about and from many other China watchers: my career would almost certainly benefit in the short term, and possibly in the long term, if Beijing scorns me or denies me a visa. I'd get a "dissident bump": this symbol of Party disapproval would help convince Americans that I'm a valid critic.

Despite my publicly critical stance, I've never had visa problems (though I never applied for one in COVID-era China). Why have the China visa gods smiled on me? Perhaps I'm seen as nonthreatening. Perhaps another arm of the Party besides the Ministry of Foreign Affairs thinks I deserved a visa. Perhaps the New York consulate believes I'm a supporter, or perhaps I'm not important enough to have triggered a ban, or even a hassle. (I know they've never confused me with another Isaac Stone Fish.)

The poet Louis Jenkins describes an "agent of Fate, capricious and blind."[5] I see the China visa gods the same way. Placate them with praise of China's One Belt One Road initiative, or blather about China's five thousand years of history, or offer justification of the imprisonment of a million Muslims, and they might still reject you. But one can state, as I do, that the Party should not rule China and still wait only three days for a visa.

Honestly, I would prefer to maintain my access to China. I wrote these words in August 2019, from a ritzy coffee shop in the central business district in Beijing, the city where I lived for most of my twenties. The sky is a crisp blue. Last night I drank a perfect cocktail at a Japanese whiskey bar, and riding the subway, which formerly felt as crowded and as charming as Times Square at New Year's Eve, was calm and pleasant. The Hong Kongers fighting for their rights seem a world away. The luxury brands, seamless mobile payment, and clean streets that now characterize Beijing feel on a gut level incompatible with genocide, and yet the Party is committing crimes against humanity in Xinjiang.

How responsible are we? From 2013 until 2021, Merit E. Janow ran the School of International and Public Affairs, the prestigious graduate program at Columbia University. A longtime trade lawyer, she served as the deputy assistant U.S. trade representative (USTR) for Japan and China in the George H. W. Bush administration. Since 2009, Janow has also served on the international advisory council of the China Investment Corporation, the Party's sovereign wealth fund, which manages assets worth roughly $1 trillion.[6] Is it inappropriate for a dean at a major American university to advise the Party on how to invest its money? I'm not sure. Janow doesn't believe so. In an October 2019 panel, she said the suggestion that her annual attendance at the advisory council meetings has "tainted" her judgment is "just plainly objectionable." What are we supposed to do, she said, put "our head in the sand with a country like China"? In an email, Janow called any idea that she is compromised "unfounded and unfair." She added that, besides her hotel and travel being covered, CIC does not compensate her.[7]

Many prominent Americans and their family members serve and have served as advisers and board members of Chinese government institutions. Kissinger served on the international advisory council of the state-owned China Development Bank.[8] Angela Chao and James Chao, the sister and father of Trump's transportation secretary, Elaine Chao—and the CEO, and founder, respectively, of the U.S. shipping company Foremost Group—both served on the board of the China State Shipbuilding Corporation, which makes ships for the military. Ten days after Trump's election, the state-run Bank of China elected Angela to its board.[9] Is that appropriate?* (It's not just

---

* Foremost thinks so. A spokesperson told me that Chao was publicly nominated for the Bank of China position in June 2016—recommended, the spokesperson noted, by an outgoing American board member and fellow Harvard

China, of course. Saudi Arabia and the United Arab Emirates are also particularly pernicious.)

The Dole Amendment, named for the senator turned Taiwan lobbyist Bob Dole, bars former USTRs or deputy USTRs from advising foreign governments. That doesn't apply to Janow, a former deputy assistant USTR. But it does apply to Robert Zoellick, the former president of the World Bank, deputy secretary of state, and, from 2001 to 2005, the U.S. trade representative. In 2013, a year after leaving the World Bank, Zoellick joined the board of Temasek Holdings, the sovereign wealth fund owned by the government of Singapore. The Dole Amendment is written too narrowly to prohibit Zoellick's Temasek board seat. Should we consider that board seat—or his consulting work with the public relations firm the Brunswick Group, where he is a senior counselor, or even his board seat on Twitter—when he discusses how to improve the U.S.-China relationship, as he did in an influential December 2019 speech?[10]

For these edge cases like Zoellick, perhaps I'm being too critical. "If you show me a situation with no conflicts," said the then American Express chairman, James Robinson, a Kissinger client, "I'll show you a level of mediocrity and incompetence that means nothing will ever happen."[11] Powerful people face an adjusting series of incentives and norms that constrain and inform their behavior. Hypervigilance is exhausting and counterproductive. In the 1950s, the Soviet leader Nikita Khrushchev bemoaned that the United States wouldn't even sell buttons to the Soviet Union.[12] "Buttons can hold up a soldier's trousers," he groused.

It's not that Janow's participation on a Party board compromises her. Rather, it's that both Janow and those who engage with her should be aware that her board seat and her relationship with the Party are two of the many factors that inform how she speaks and thinks about China and its place in the world.

As people advance in their careers, they often enmesh themselves into networks of institutions, reducing their desire and incentive to criticize the places that support them. In late 2019, I joined the advi-

---

alumnus—and served on the CSSC board at a time when "bilateral relations were better than they are in 2021."

sory board of a project at the think tank Center for Strategic and International Studies (CSIS) studying Russian and Chinese disinformation. I'm not bragging: mid-career professionals in D.C. join these projects more often than they attend parent-teacher conferences. They paid me $500 for the two one-hour sessions: a high hourly rate but a modest sum. I felt warmer toward CSIS, because they validated me. In a barely perceptible way, I shared brand equity with them, and to tarnish them would be to tarnish myself. (I also now run a consulting company, which presents other ethical concerns: more on that later.)

An influential May 2017 study in the medical journal *JAMA* found that hospitals which limited visits and gifts from drug company representatives ordered significantly fewer of those medications, and a 2016 ProPublica investigation demonstrated that the more money doctors receive, on average, from pharmaceutical companies, "the more brand-name medications they prescribe."[13] Even a single meal with a pharma rep can increase the likelihood that a doctor prescribes more expensive drugs. In a June 2017 article, the physician Nicole Van Groningen writes about her experiences as a medical resident, when a pharma rep invited her to a "trendy" Manhattan restaurant for an "educational" dinner: "The drug that was promoted that evening, which cost roughly 500 percent more than a dirt-cheap (and just as effective) alternative, still sticks out in my mind as a go-to treatment option for a common disease in my field. I'm sure this isn't a coincidence."[14] Most doctors aren't compromised.

But if a single steak dinner can steer a doctor to prescribe more expensive medicine, what about, as the Sinologist John K. Fairbank called it, the "full blast of Chinese friendship"?

PART ONE

HOW TO WIN FRIENDS AND
INFLUENCE PEOPLE

CHAPTER ONE

The History of America's Influence on China

★

ALTHOUGH AMERICA ONLY RECENTLY STARTED GRAPPLING WITH Beijing's influence, China's worry about American influence stretches back to the mid-nineteenth century, when the country entered a period of decline and decay that didn't end until the 1990s.

It was a new direction for a proud and often isolated civilization. Before the mid-nineteenth century, China had largely ignored America. Chinese elites believed that foreign countries were necessarily inferior to China—literally the Middle, or Central, Kingdom. "The location of the United States is in the Far West," wrote the diplomat Qiying to the emperor in 1844.[1] "It is the most uncivilized and remote of all countries . . . an isolated place outside the pale, solitary and ignorant. Not only are the people entirely unversed in the forms of edicts and laws, but if the meaning be rather deep, they would probably not even be able to comprehend. It would seem that we must make our words somewhat simple."

This diplomat's views of China's superiority were not that uncommon. After all, Christopher Columbus sailed to the New World in 1492 to find a shorter route to the fabled riches of the Far East, and London sent colonists to Jamestown in the early seventeenth century in part to find a route linking the Atlantic to the riches of the Pacific. To these early European explorers and colonialists, the Americas were a waypoint.

As a European civilization took root in the United States, the European image of China as an exemplar of refinement and progress remained. The pamphleteer Thomas Paine called the Chinese "people of mild manner and good morals," Thomas Jefferson flirted with the idea of imitating China and remaining isolated from Europe, and Benjamin Franklin described China as the "wisest of nations," and even once argued that the Chinese, and not the Europeans, served as a better model for America.[2] George Washington owned hundreds of luxury Chinese products, including a fine collection of porcelain, while the tea dumped into the harbor during the Boston Tea Party all came from China. Many Americans saw China as a "storied source of wealth and wisdom, and a country from whom the young republic might learn," the historian Gordon H. Chang writes in his book *Fateful Ties: A History of America's Preoccupation with China*. Until the mid-nineteenth century China was the world's richest nation and the tea merchant Wu Bingjian, who invested in railroad construction in the United States, probably the world's richest man.[3]

Several major factors changed that dynamic and, with it, the image of China in America. Before the industrial age, the size of a country's economy basically reflected the size of its population; so China was seen as wealthy, even if millions of Chinese lived in serf-like conditions and regularly faced famines. "China has been long one of the richest, that is, one of the most fertile, best cultivated, most industrious, and most populous countries in the world," the Scottish economist Adam Smith wrote in *The Wealth of Nations*, but "the poverty of the lower ranks of people in China far surpasses that of the most beggarly nations of Europe"—a characterization that remained accurate until the 1990s.

Throughout the nineteenth century, America followed the European path and industrialized and urbanized, while China remained deeply agrarian. Corruption and widespread opium addiction weakened both the country and the Qing dynasty, which had ruled China since 1644.

The philosophy of Manifest Destiny and America's westward expansion, and America's massive economic growth in the mid-nineteenth century, ended the period in which China served as a moral inspiration for some Americans. Perhaps the best description of the mid-century shifting of power and perceptions between the two nations came from Commodore Matthew Perry, who in 1853 famously "opened up" Japan to the world by sailing a threatening squadron of ships into Tokyo's harbor.[4] "With our territory spreading from ocean to ocean, and placed midway between Europe and Asia," Perry wrote in a book about his trip, published in 1856, eight years after the discovery of gold and six years after California obtained statehood, "it seemed that we might with propriety apply to ourselves the name by which China has loved to designate herself, and deem that we were, in truth, 'the Middle Kingdom.'"[5]

AS POWER SHIFTED FROM CHINA TO THE UNITED STATES, SO TOO did the direction of anxiety. In the eighteenth century, some elite American observers fretted whether their remote outpost could ever aspire to the greatness of China. But in the second half of the nineteenth century it was the turn of the Chinese to look to Americans and wonder about their future. Much of these Chinese anxieties concerned Christianity: thousands of American missionaries, influenced by a millenarian strand of Christianity that believed the second coming of Jesus Christ required global conversion, saw China as the key to fulfilling the "manifest destiny of the Christian Republic," in the words of one missionary. "Look where we may, beneath the wide expanse of the heavens, we can find no distinct enterprise so laudable, so imperious, so inconceivable in its results, as the conversion of China," wrote another.[6] More so than merchants and the military, missionaries shaped the country's nineteenth century.

Christianity's biggest influence on China was, in a word, disastrous. Inspired by missionary texts translated into Chinese, the failed Confucian scholar Hong Xiuquan believed he was the brother of Jesus Christ. And so he wandered the countryside in the 1840s, preaching about the one true god Ye-huo-hua, baptizing converts, and raising an army of the faithful. Wielding his "sword for exterminating demons," Hong and his army captured the city of Nanjing and established New Jerusalem, the de facto capital of their Kingdom of Taiping, or Heavenly Peace, governed by a prime minister who called himself the Holy Ghost.[7] In the roughly two decades it took the Qing to destroy the movement, the fighting led to the death of more than twenty million people from violence or famine—one of the most devastating rebellions the world has ever seen. Hong died of illness or suicide in 1864 in New Jerusalem, after exhorting his faithful to follow the book of Exodus and, like the Israelis in the desert, eat manna to stay alive.

Besides raising an army to fight the Taiping, the Qing waged a propaganda battle to stop the spread of Christian ideas. "A Record of Truth to Ward Off the Cult," published in 1861 under the name "the Most Heartbroken Man in the World," is an astonishing invective, more graphic than the notorious 1903 Russian anti-Semitic text *The Protocols of the Elders of Zion,* which concocted a Jewish plot for global domination. Probably written by a Qing general, the text warns of a dangerous religion where men marry their daughters, "practice sodomy with the priests without restraint," and seek to obtain the organs of children.[8]

American missionaries in China remained divided on whether Hong was a Christian or a blasphemer. But besides the astonishing impact of the Taiping rebellion, Christianity suffered a vanishingly low rate of actual converts. ("What infatuation to embrace such a religion as this!" the "Record of Truth" exhorts.) And so late in the nineteenth century, a group of American and British Protestant missionaries tried a new tact, packaging Christianity "together with Western education, science, capitalism, and political theory, offering the combination as a remedy that would strengthen China," writes the journalist John Pomfret in his 2016 book, *The Beautiful Country and the Middle Kingdom: America and China, 1776 to the Present.* "With their Chinese partners, they built China's modern education system, introduced Western medicine, print media, science, and sports, fought foot-binding and female infanticide, organized antipoverty and rural reconstruction efforts, and nurtured generations of Chinese modernizers," Pomfret writes.[9]

This new approach was more effective than sheer proselytizing, but it engendered another round of backlash. Incited by their resentment of Christian and foreign influence and supported by the Qing, in 1898 a secret sect by the name of the Society of Righteousness and Harmony (called the Boxers, in English) started attacking foreigners throughout the country. In a move that embarrassed many local reformers, in June 1900 the de facto ruler of China, the empress dowager Cixi, declared war on the foreigners. They "blaspheme our gods," she wrote in her war declaration.[10] "Thus it is that the brave followers of the Boxers have been burning churches and killing Christians." The foreigners fought back against the Boxers and the Qing dynasty, forming a partnership called the Eight-Nation Alliance—the only time in history that Russia, Japan, the United States, and Germany all fought on the same side. The New York *Sun* called the Boxer Rebellion "the most exciting episode known to civilization."

The Boxer Rebellion worsened relations between China and the West. After the Eight-Nation Alliance defeated the Boxers and the Qing army in August 1900, some of the victorious soldiers rampaged across Beijing, looting, raping, and burning. "A great spirit of fear still holds this vast city of ruins," wrote the British journalist George Lynch, who visited Beijing after the foreign powers won.[11] "There are the things that I must not write, and that may not be printed in England, which would seem to show that this Western civilization of ours is merely a veneer over savagery." The victors demanded an indemnity over four decades of 450 million taels of silver—an imperial Chinese currency—and the government ended up paying the equivalent of billions of dollars over that period, further impoverishing a country where millions lived on the cusp of starvation.

The crushing defeat of the Boxers and the Qing was sobering. The Boxers had "dreamed of creating a China cleansed of the injustice of foreign ways, and they set out to free their region and their country from its humiliation by blood and fire," writes the historian Odd Arne Westad.[12] They hastened the collapse of the Qing Empire—a dynasty often considered foreign by many Chinese, because the rulers were of the Manchu ethnicity—but did nothing else to purge China from outside influence.

There were a few constructive aftereffects of the calamity. Part of the Boxer indemnity went back to China in the form of scholarships and the building of Tsinghua University in Beijing. Like Harvard for American politicians, Tsinghua later became the school for Communist Party elite; the Chinese chairman Hu Jintao graduated in 1965 with a degree in engineering, while his successor, Xi, received both a bachelor's in chemical engineering and a graduate degree in Marxist theory and ideological education.

But generally speaking, the rebellion failed miserably. It humiliated the Qing government and became an odious reminder for the Chinese about the modern weakness and irrelevance of their country. "More fully than any event before it, the Boxer War had placed China outside the Western-led international system, a pariah state, the center of a 1900 axis of evil," Westad writes.

A decade later, in 1911, the Qing fell, ushering in another period of chaos, where China was a failed state. Beijing today calls the period from the first Opium War in 1839, when the United Kingdom prevented China from limiting its imports of the drug, to the 1949 establishment of the People's Republic of China the century of humiliation. It was this miasma of weakness that "produced" Mao Zedong, the leader who reunified the country in the 1950s and returned it to its earlier state of isolation.*

THAT PERIOD BETWEEN THE FALL OF THE QING DYNASTY AND THE rise of Mao was the zenith of American influence within China, as well as Chinese esteem for America.

It was a time of political unrest but extraordinary intellectual ferment. In 1919, a twenty-five-year-old Mao decried the "total emptiness and rottenness of the mental universe of the entire Chinese people."[13] Some Chinese intellectuals believed that American-style democracy was the key to save China from its troubled interregnum. "We must sweep away millennia of despotism in all its forms," wrote Zou Rong, a revolutionary who died in prison in 1905, in a popular text, so "the descendants of the Yellow Empire all become Washingtons."[14]

Perhaps unsurprisingly, many Americans agreed. Unlike the governments in Germany, Britain, and Japan, which saw China's chaos as an opportunity to increase their colonial holdings, some U.S. government officials supported the Chinese people's struggle for democracy and regrowth. "Never has one nation had a greater opportunity to act as counsellor and friend to another and to help a vast and lovable people to realize its striving for a better life," Paul Reinsch, minister, or ambassador, to China from 1913 to 1919, wrote in his memoirs.[15]

---

* "The East is red / the sun is rising / and China has produced a Mao Zedong."

The historian Chang explains, "It was America's fate, many believed, to be China's friend, protector, benefactor, and savior."

Granted, this often came from a place of condescension, both because of the widespread American belief in the inferiority of Chinese people and because of the instability of the Chinese empire. We seek to live in "peace and friendship" with the Chinese, Secretary of State John Hay wrote in 1900, even though Beijing finds itself in "virtual anarchy."

Into this political vacuum stepped the physician and political philosopher Sun Yat-sen, the most prominent of voices calling for a "democratic" China free from foreign rule. (The Qing rulers were Manchus, a northern people whom the majority Han considered non-Chinese.) Today, Sun is revered by many as a founding father; in China and Taiwan, his given name Zhongshan graces universities, streets, and plazas. "Yat-sen," the Cantonese pronunciation of his name "the Tranquility of the Immortals," actually comes from an American preacher, who baptized the seventeen-year-old Sun. Sun graduated from high school in Honolulu (not far from the school Barack Obama attended roughly one hundred years later). "This is my Hawaii," reads a plaque at Sun Yat-Sen Memorial Park in that city.[16] "Here I was brought up and educated; and it was here that I came to know what modern civilized governments are like and what they mean." Sun's wife, Song Qingling, who outlived her husband by fifty-six years and who later served several prominent roles in China's Communist government, spoke fluent English and graduated from Wesleyan College in Georgia.

Throughout the first decade of the twentieth century, Sun led a series of uprisings against the Qing. When the Qing dynasty finally collapsed in October 1911, some Americans believed that Sun's relationship with America had inspired the Chinese overthrow of the last dynasty. "America is responsible for the revolution," the New York City journal *The Independent* wrote. "Its leaders are largely young men educated in the United States or in the American mission schools. They have imbibed from us the spirit of freedom." (Sun was on a fundraising tour in Denver when he heard the news of the fall of the Qing; he rushed back to China.) On January 1, 1912, Sun announced the founding of the Republic of China as its first president but just forty-five days later yielded power to General Yuan Shikai, a former Qing military commander.[17]

On April 17, 1913, Yuan asked all churches in China to set aside April 27 as a day of prayer for the new republic, winning praise from American observers. It represented "the most remarkable official document that had been issued in a generation," Secretary of State William Jennings Bryan said in an April 18 cabinet meeting, while President Woodrow Wilson said he "did not know when he had been so stirred and cheered as when he read that message in the paper."[18] And Wilson, before yielding to America's separation of church and state, even considered asking American churches to pray for China. Thousands did anyway. The organizing body the Federal Council of Churches asked 150,000 Protestant churches to hold services for China, and in May 1913 the United States became the first great power to formally recognize the Republic of China.

It's striking how many Americans served key roles in early twentieth-century China. The minister to China, Reinsch, met regularly with Chinese leaders. "As I represented the Republic upon which it had been largely modeled, whose spirit the Chinese were anxious to follow, it fell to me to counsel with Chinese leaders as if I had been one of their number," he wrote. In 1913, the scholar Frank Goodnow, soon to be president of Johns Hopkins University, served as Yuan's chief legal adviser.[19] He wrote a constitution for Yuan without "vexatious restrictions" on his power, providing international and domestic cover for him to consolidate control.[20] Yuan did not wait long to use his new American-authored powers. In December 1915, he proclaimed himself emperor. His death six months later from kidney failure ended the restoration of empire in the Middle Kingdom, and it fell back to Sun to try to modernize China.

Sun needed American advice. A Stanford University dropout named Homer Lea served as a key military adviser to Sun, who called the Coloradoan—a five-foot-tall hunchback from being dropped on his back as a baby—"the greatest military theorist under Heaven." (Lea had other admirers. Lenin praised Lea's 1909 book, *The Valor of Ignorance*, which predicted future Japanese aggression: "[Lea] understood more about world politics than all the cabinet ministers now in office.") Sun had apparently offered Lea the position of chief of staff of China's military, but in February 1912, while inspecting Chinese troops, Lea suffered a stroke; he died nine months later, at the age of thirty-five. Sun himself died of cancer in 1925, at the age of fifty-eight, and his aide Chiang Kai-shek soon took over.[21]

Sun had appeared to genuinely want to mold China after America, or at least what he perceived America to be. His successor, Chiang, had a more authoritarian vision for his country, even though he maintained a close relationship with America and saw the need to work with and learn from the United States. This couldn't have been more different from the views of his great rival.

MAO HAD LONG DISTRUSTED AMERICA AND DETESTED ITS MED-dling in the Middle Kingdom. In 1921, he deemed America "the most murderous of hangmen" for allegedly supporting an enemy of the Party, even though the European powers still held "concessions" of territory in his country.[22]

Instead, Mao looked to the Russians, who after their 1917 revolution became the world leaders of the Communist movement. China's government today remains Leninist and still maintains many of those Soviet imports from the 1920s: the Politburo runs the country; Party secretaries run provinces, cities, and universities; and political commissars ensure that military officers remain loyal to the Party.

After Sun died, American observers began to worry. Americans like the former ambassador Reinsch had desperately wanted China to become an "Asiatic United States"; Secretary of State Bryan even sent Yuan an encyclopedia about Thomas Jefferson, because he hoped it might help him "produce a United States of China." But what worked for America in the late eighteenth century didn't work for China in the early twentieth. With some assistance from a belligerent Japan, China slid into anarchy, warlordism, and, eventually, a civil war between Chiang's Nationalists and Mao's Communists. The United States backed the Nationalists. They lost, and Mao established the People's Republic of China in 1949.

The Chinese government never again countenanced American-style democracy, despite the attempt of some protesters in Tiananmen Square in 1989 and in Hong Kong in 2019. As the prominent early twentieth-century intellectual Kang Youwei said, reflecting the views of those who felt China's salvation lay elsewhere, copying America "would be like a blind man riding a horse to the edge of a deep pit at midnight."[23]

AS LENIN PONDERED GLOBALIZING COMMUNISM IN 1920, HE WROTE about the tactics necessary for success. The "more powerful enemy can be vanquished only by exerting the utmost effort, and without fail, most thoroughly, carefully, attentively and skillfully using every, even the smallest, 'rift' among the enemies," he wrote.[24] The proletariat must exploit "every, even the smallest, opportunity of gaining a mass ally even though this ally be temporary, vacillating, unstable, unreliable and conditional. Those who fail to understand this," he added, "fail to understand even a particle of Marxism." Some loyal Soviets, for example, could join with British dockworkers to overthrow British imperialism. Lenin, and his colleague Leon Trotsky, called this the United Front. Both friends and enemies were to be found in every corner of the globe.

In 1924, embracing Lenin's strategy, the Party founded the United Front Work Department; Mao put it to work "mobilizing friends to strike at enemies."[25] Through international delegations and trainings, sophisticated intelligence targeting, and carefully calibrated propaganda, the United Front worked to convert Chinese and foreigners to the Party's vision of China.

Their work on Americans focused on undermining popular support for Chiang and his Nationalists. In the 1930s and 1940s, the United Front infiltrated and weakened Nationalist-supporting groups both in China and in America, just as today it subverts and co-opts Chinese Christians, businesspeople, and intellectuals, as well as their American counterparts. "The bottom line," according to a United Front publication, "is to increase as many people that support us and reduce as many people that oppose us."[*26]

For Mao and his Party, winning the civil war was never just about

* "Who are our enemies? Who are our friends?" Mao wrote in an influential 1925 essay. "This is a question of the first importance for the revolution. The basic

military maneuvers; it was also a clash over which ideas would follow the marching armies and stay after the battles had ended. His disruption of Nationalist groups through subterfuge and propaganda was a continuation of warfare by other means.

Mao and Zhou suffused Lenin's principles with the Chinese strategic tradition of "political warfare," a concept championed by the fifth-century B.C.E. philosopher Sunzi. "The highest realization of warfare is to attack the enemy's plans. Next is to attack their alliances; next to attack their army; and the lowest is to attack their fortified cities," he wrote in *The Art of War*. Political warfare and United Front work aim to win battles, in other words, without firing a shot.

This strategy continues to inform the Party's activities today. War should "overwhelm the enemy's will" through "public opinion warfare" that "attacks hearts and takes over morale," the People's Liberation Army (PLA) analyst Zhang Changjun wrote in a 2007 article in a Chinese journal called *Military Correspondent*.[27] In a 2017 article, two Chinese professors explained that "physical warfare is the method, and psychological warfare is the goal. Physical warfare must serve and support psychological warfare—they're not opposed."[28] Psychological warfare, they wrote, includes diplomatic, public opinion, legal, and ideological warfare, as well as political ideology work—disseminating "correct" political opinions. What are these "correct" opinions? In January 2021, the adviser to a pro–Hong Kong government think tank wrote an op-ed about how one of the city's media outlets was too critical of the government. The solution? "Hiring experts to wage the publicity and psychological warfare against its inflexible political opposition and critics who are not amenable to facts and reason."[29]

THE UNITED FRONT HAD SOME CRUCIAL EARLY SUCCESSES WITH Americans. For decades, the Communists' most effective American friend was Edgar Snow, who in 1936 got the scoop of a lifetime when he became the first foreign journalist to interview Mao; an experience he recounted in his best-selling 1937 book, *Red Star over China*. In

---

reason why all previous revolutionary struggles in China achieved so little was their failure to unite with real friends in order to attack real enemies."

the weeks he spent with Mao—at the time, the leader of an isolated band of rebels, fighting a quixotic battle for survival—Snow produced a biographical sketch that introduced the Chinese Communists to the world.

Mao struck Snow as "a gaunt, rather Lincolnesque figure" who ruled with a "ritual of hero-worship built up around him." One feels, Snow writes, "that whatever extraordinary there is in this man grows out of the uncanny desire to which he synthesizes and expresses the urgent demands of millions of Chinese." What readers of Snow's book didn't know is that he allowed Mao and his team to edit and "correct" the roughly twenty-thousand-word-long interview.*[30]

It wasn't just Snow. At times coordinating with Joseph Stalin, Mao convinced many of the Americans he met of his commitment to Western-style democracy and "genuinely free general elections." While fooling Western journalists, he was denouncing Americans in Chinese-language texts; the lack of bilingual journalists and diplomats facilitated Mao's strategy of spreading different messages to different audiences. (A trend that continues today, with businesspeople like Alibaba co-founder and Party member Jack Ma sounding more like a Silicon Valley tech entrepreneur in English and more like a Party apparatchik in Chinese.[31])

World War II brought the Chinese Civil War to a convoluted new phase. After Japan invaded China in 1937, the Nationalists turned to fighting the Japanese, allowing the Communists to regroup. In August 1944, while the United States was working with the Nationalists to expel Japan from China, an American delegation visited the Communist headquarters in the tiny northern Chinese city of Yan'an.

---

* Snow stars in the historian Julia Lovell's excellent 2019 book on Maoism, "because without him both a domestic and an international cult of Mao would be hard to imagine." Snow was far from the only American journalist in pre-Communist China who blurred the line between reporter and advocate. Theodore H. White, who later went on to write a best-selling book about China, as well as a series on American presidential elections, got his start as a propagandist for the Nationalists—a job he didn't quit until months after joining *Time* magazine. Few were as egregious as the *Nation* and the *New Republic* contributor Agnes Smedley, as skilled a public brawler as Trump's aide Kellyanne Conway, though Smedley did, in fact, work as a Russian spy. "I may not be innocent," she said in 1932, "but I'm right."

"Chinese and American interests are correlated and similar," Mao told them.[32] "We will not be afraid of democratic American influence. We will welcome it." Though it may sound surprising now that the fiercely independent revolutionary would claim to be fine fighting on behalf of an American commander, he had effectively timed his remarks.

A month earlier, the U.S. president, Franklin Delano Roosevelt, had demanded Chiang allow the American general Joseph Stilwell to command Chinese troops. Chiang, who didn't want to give up control of his army, had stalled in response, and FDR soon moved on. "We would serve with all our hearts under an American general," Mao told the visiting Americans. "That is how we feel towards you." He sensed a chance to seem the willing collaborator, as opposed to the United States' actual partner in the war, the recalcitrant Chiang. To Americans and Europeans, Mao communicated a message of internationalism and support for America. Stalin played his part in pretending that Mao approved of America.

A few years later, when victory over the Nationalists was imminent, Mao sensed the time was right to shift his tone. In August 1949, several months before his troops captured Beijing, Mao wrote a famous screed against the outgoing American ambassador, John Leighton Stuart, who had lived much of his life in China and who, Mao wrote, "pretended to love both the United States and China and was able to deceive quite a number of Chinese."[33] Mao called the 1945–1949 civil war against the Nationalists "the war to turn China into a U.S. colony," and stated that "the prestige of U.S. imperialism among the Chinese people is completely bankrupt."

When the Communists took over in 1949, many of the tens of thousands of Americans living in China fled, and Mao expelled the vast majority of the rest. For the next two decades, Chinese propaganda excoriated American values and ideals, and the Party tortured and killed thousands of Chinese with connections (real or imagined) to America. By the time the United States started fighting the Chinese in the Korean War in 1950, there were only dozens of Americans living in China, a number that would remain roughly constant until the late 1970s.

Beijing called the Americans and other foreigners living in China, and those outside who wanted to engage with the Party, "foreign friends." At the time, most friends were from outside the American sphere of influence. The Peruvian philosophy professor Abimael Guzmán, who later founded the Maoist group the Shining Path, spent several months in China in the 1960s, taking classes with other revolutionaries from across the global south. After Cambodian rebels deposed King Sihanouk in 1970, he took up residence in the former French embassy in Beijing, where he plotted his return to power and wrote propaganda songs praising Mao. (When he died, in Beijing in 2012, Xi expressed "shock" at the death of an "old friend of the Chinese people.")[34]

The small group of American friends include Sidney Rittenberg, a former U.S. soldier who became the first American to join the Party and who translated messages for the top leadership, and George Hatem, a doctor who had joined Snow on his first trip to Mao and then stayed in China for decades, helping to fight the spread of venereal diseases and leprosy.[35]

Snow, who moved to Switzerland in 1959 after McCarthyist harassment, remained a friend. In 1960, the Party gave Snow the chance to spend five months in China, a journey Snow recounted in his 1962 book, *Red China Today: The Other Side of the River.* "I saw no starving people in China, nothing that looks like old-time famine," Snow wrote amid the greatest famine of the twentieth century, which killed tens of millions of people.[36] "I do not believe there is famine in China."

After Mao consolidated his power over China, he treated the United States with nearly unremitting hostility. The Party's most important foreign relationships in the 1950s and 1960s were with enemies and critics of the U.S. government. In America during the Mao years, the Party's biggest source of influence, and its biggest propaganda success, was with the black community. The Party convinced some American blacks, understandably disaffected by a country that was struggling through an often bloody movement for basic civil rights, that Beijing embraced the worldwide anticolonial, anti-imperialist, and antiracist struggle.

In 1959, the Party invited the writer and activist W. E. B. Du Bois to celebrate his ninety-first birthday in Beijing. Long frustrated with the despicable way many Americans treated him—"in my own country for nearly a century I have been nothing but a nigger," he said—Du Bois praised Beijing. "Come to China, Africa, and look around," he said in a speech in Beijing that the Party broadcast over the radio.[37] "China is flesh of your flesh and blood of your blood. China is colored, and knows to what the colored skin in this modern world subjects its owner." In April 1968, just days after the assassination of Martin Luther King Jr., Mao proclaimed, "On behalf of the Chinese people, I hereby express resolute support for the just struggle of the Black people in the United States."[38]

The Party's embrace of revolution endeared it to some radical groups, in America and globally. French, Italian, and West German leftists embraced Mao and the anarchy of the Cultural Revolution. The Black Panthers' founders sold copies of *Quotations from Mao Zedong* on the Berkeley campus to raise money to buy guns; better known in English as the *Little Red Book,* the book was a common sight in Harlem in the late 1960s and early 1970s.[39]

Beijing's lip service to the black community in the United States, and in certain African countries, helped it paint itself as a global underdog allying with the racially oppressed against the imperialists. And by successfully courting some of the most critical voices on racial discrimination, like Du Bois, Beijing provided itself with international cover for the mistreatment and slaughter of its own minorities, such as the Tibetans and Uyghurs.

But despite the occasional visit from intellectual celebrities like Du Bois and the Italian filmmaker Michelangelo Antonioni, China under Mao was as cut off from the West as North Korea is today. This isolation and antagonism of Mao's China was an opportunity for Chiang and Taiwan, the island that he ruled over as a dictator until his death in 1975. Taiwan's close relationship with the United States—and its vital strategic value—meant that it had a surprising amount of influence over its Western ally.* People began to speak of the "China Lobby" as an informal nexus of intensely powerful interests representing Taiwan in the United States. In 1949 the United

---

* America's influence over Taiwan, and the security relationship that helped prevent a Chinese attack, were far more profound.

States had recognized Taiwan's capital, Taipei, as the legitimate seat of government for all of China, and continued to do so until Washington reestablished diplomatic relations with the People's Republic in 1979. Throughout the 1950s and 1960s, "no foreign lobby in Washington has ever been so rich or so powerful, or interfered so insidiously in the American governmental process," two journalists wrote in a 1977 book about lobbying.[40] In 1960, Taipei even successfully pressured the publishing house Macmillan to remove from circulation for fourteen years a critical book called *The China Lobby in American Politics*, which argued that Taipei silenced American critics of Taiwan.[41]

Adding to this state of affairs in the late 1960s—China's intense isolation from and antagonism to the United States, as well as Taiwan's influence there—were rapidly deteriorating relations with the Soviet Union. China and Russia fought a border skirmish in 1969, and Mao worried about a war with its more powerful northern neighbor.

Luckily for Mao, Richard Nixon thought the United States needed China to balance against the Soviets. Moreover, he feared China's isolation. "We simply cannot afford to leave China forever outside the family of nations, there to nurture its fantasies, cherish its hates and threaten its neighbors," Nixon wrote in a 1967 *Foreign Affairs* article, two years before he assumed the presidency.[42] By the late 1960s, the United States and China had started sending feelers to each other. Once again, Mao reached out to Snow, who in October 1970 returned to China for the last time. Mao told Snow that he welcomed a Nixon visit to China "as a tourist or as President"—a message that the U.S. side overlooked.

When Zhou finally met Kissinger in July 1971, the first high-level contact between the two sides in decades, Zhou opened the conversation by asking about Snow.[43] "Thirty-five years ago he became a friend with us," Zhou said. "Now he is an old friend." Snow—whom Mao referred to in their last meeting together as "Friend Snow," "Friend" playing the role of a title, just like Chairman Mao or President Nixon—died on February 15, 1972.[44] Six days later, Nixon and Kissinger landed in China for Nixon's historic trip, ending the first era of relations between the two countries and establishing the basic framework for our relations to this day.

CHAPTER TWO

Friends with Benefits

★

"THE ARC OF THE MORAL UNIVERSE IS LONG," MARTIN LUTHER King Jr. said, "but it bends toward justice." That was in 1967, however, when a shambolic China barely managed to exert global influence. Today, the wealthy and powerful country that China has become exerts a powerful force on the world and on America. In sophisticated ways, Beijing persuades, cajoles, and cudgels some American companies, institutions, and individuals to promote the values of the Party, parrot the Party's views, and enshrine self-censorship about China in their corporate and individual cultures. A pattern of acceptance of Chinese influence has emerged, with variance more in degree than direction. The arc of the moral universe remains long, but it now bends toward accommodation.

This book explores how this accommodation—or "friendship," as the Party and its allies call it—is widespread across America. It has a clear origin story: one that helps illuminate the China problems the United States faces today and how to address them. Before Disney thanked a Chinese public security bureau that rounded up Muslims and sent them to concentration camps, before LeBron James criticized the Houston Rockets' general manager for supporting democracy in Hong Kong, before Marriott fired an employee for supporting Tibet, before Boeing ran ads praising Beijing, before Sheldon Adelson personally lobbied to kill a bill condemning China's human rights record, before Ronald Reagan called China a "so-called Communist country," the man whose relationship became a blueprint for everything that came after sat with Zhou in a Chinese government guest-house in July 1971, discussing philosophy.[1]

BY HIS FLATTERY, PERSISTENCE, AND CHARM OVER DOZENS OF hours of conversation over five years, Zhou initiated Kissinger as a friend of China. The relationship wasn't merely diplomatic, or coldly strategic. A former assistant secretary of state, in a formerly classified study about Chinese negotiating behavior, described Kissinger's memoirs of the time as "replete with almost awestruck recollections of the personal escorts, elaborate tours, and lavish banquets meticulously arranged by his Chinese hosts during his nine visits between 1971 and 1976," the year that Mao and Zhou died. It was during these years that Kissinger helped bring isolated China back into the world order, and it's when he became known as a reliable friend by Zhou. Kissinger's admiration persisted. "In some sixty years of public life," he writes in his 2011 book, On China, "I have encountered no more compelling figure" than Zhou.*[2]

Kissinger's trips to China in the early 1970s were monumental not only for reestablishing a relationship between the two countries. They also inaugurated two distinct but interrelated phenomena that still shape America today. First Beijing employed United Front tactics, cultivating friends and weakening enemies, to shape American politics and business. The second is the rise of what could be called diplomat consultants, who fit into the long-standing Chinese tradition of trading access for accommodation.

Increasing exposure to China did bring immense benefits to America's economy and helped encourage millions of Americans to spend time in China. These are very real upsides, and they should not be ignored. At the same time, these diplomat consultants are the field agents of Party influence, especially in the business world, where they help American firms compete and cohere to Party standards while instructing these same firms on how to chill anti-Party speech.

---

* Zhou's views on Kissinger are unknown. In 1973, Mao told a British visitor that Kissinger was "just a funny little man who shudders all over with nerves every time he comes to see me."

All intelligence agencies recruit foreign agents. But the Party's relationship with its American friends, Kissinger included, is different because of the Party's expansive attitude toward espionage. There are two major differences between Washington's and Beijing's views on intelligence gathering. The first involves the deeply political nature of the Party's intelligence and security services. In China's intelligence agencies, like in many branches of its government, political commissars and Party secretaries work with their more technocratic counterparts to ensure the agency and its staff follow the correct political lines. "The Ministry of State Security People's Police are red troops loyal to the Party," a ministry spokesperson said in January 2021, in reference to an internal Chinese police force.[3]

The second is Beijing's reliance on a wide range of nontraditional allies—including students, academics, businesspeople, and employees of nonprofits, both Chinese and foreign—to further its intelligence goals. During the Cold War, the CIA helped fund the literary magazine *Encounter*, co-founded by the influential neoconservative Irving Kristol.[4] Edward Snowden's 2013 revelations showed some of the links between the National Security Agency and American companies like Verizon. In China, these links are the rule, not the exception.

Beijing still conducts normal espionage and spycraft: infiltrating enemy organizations, hacking into rival governments, and cultivating foreign agents—sometimes by sending them messages on LinkedIn.[5] But it does a whole lot else, too.

In 2018 the Party History Research Center, an important institution that helps drive the Party's view on history, published an essay on Zhou's views on spying.[6] Zhou believed the Party had a "remarkably" different stance toward espionage from that of other countries, because it linked espionage with United Front work. "Zhou advocated making many friends, using United Front work to drive intelligence work, and nestling United Front work within intelligence work," the essay said.*[7] Before running the Chinese government as its premier, Zhou founded the Party's intelligence unit and built its first espionage

---

* One United Front publication called Zhou "the master artist of United Front work."

cells.[8] Zhou, in other words, was the Party's first spymaster. And in this Chinese sense of "espionage," Kissinger was Zhou's most important American asset. In Chinese parlance—a friend.

The annals of spycraft are replete with people who likely had no idea they were being fooled. "Any unwitting agent is more effective when left in the belief that they are genuinely holding the moral high ground, not representing an authoritarian intelligence agency," Thomas Rid, a professor of security studies at King's College London, testified to Congress in March 2017.[9] The best agents, in other words, are the ones who don't know they are agents.

Because of the mismatch between the Party's expansive view of espionage (that includes what American targets often perceive simply as friendship) and the more constrained Western view, Americans often don't understand the deal they are taking when they "accept" the friendship. Indeed, few friends have ever expressed any public awareness of what friendship actually means: support not of China but of the Party. The Party expects friends to silence their criticism, so as not to "embarrass" or "offend" China, and to praise and advance the Party's policies. "Being a 'friend' of China means you're politically in tune with the Communist Party," said the longtime China scholar Perry Link, "whether you know it or not."*[10]

LEAVING OFFICE AFTER THE DEMOCRAT JIMMY CARTER'S 1976 VICtory, Kissinger spent the next five years adrift. While in government, he was stunningly influential. National security adviser from 1969 to 1975 and secretary of state from 1973 to 1977—the first person to jointly hold both roles—Kissinger had overseen the secret bombing of Cambodia, masterminded America's opening to China in 1972, and won the 1973 Nobel Peace Prize for negotiating with the Vietnamese.

He survived the Watergate scandal and Nixon's 1974 resigna-

---

* The longtime China scholar Edward Friedman on old friends of China: "Usually, it is the CCP side that labels some international visitor or another as a friend. To me, the term was an insult, a claim to your face that you were a lap dog." And the scholar Anne-Marie Brady: "Friendship terminology is a means to neutralize opposition psychologically and to reorder reality."

tion mostly unscathed and, under President Gerald Ford, mediated between the Arab and the Israeli worlds and supervised anti-Communist interventions in Latin America. "Kissinger, with his thick glasses and even thicker accent, hardly had the look of a superstar," Walter Isaacson writes in his 1992 biography of Kissinger. "Indeed, it seemed more likely that he would be mistaken for a prosperous deli owner from Brooklyn than an international sex symbol." But Kissinger, who famously quipped that "power is the ultimate aphrodisiac," had astonishing appeal. In 1972, Playboy Club bunnies ranked Kissinger as the man they would most like to go out with.[11] A 1973 Gallup poll even found him to be the most admired man in America.[12] Kissinger once said that Mao "had the quality of being at the center of wherever he stood . . . It moved with him whenever he moved." While in government, Kissinger had learned to create a similar type of aura.

Leaving office was a hard transition from being at the center of power. Kissinger moved to New York City and considered entering the 1980 Senate race in New York. He consulted for Goldman Sachs and declined an offer to join the firm as a partner.[13] He taught at Georgetown. He wrote two best-selling memoirs about his time in the White House and gave hundreds of speeches, some paid and some for free. He joined NBC as a commentator and consultant. He tried to enter the Reagan administration, but Reagan scorned him. He even got paid to promote gold and silver medallions of historical figures, sold by a corporation called Franklin Mint. "This was not an exercise I would care to repeat," he said about his medallion work.

Kissinger almost accepted a professorship at Columbia but withdrew after students protested his hiring because of his role in the Vietnam War. "Hiring Kissinger would be like hiring Charles Manson to teach religion," one demonstrator said, while the leftist linguist Noam Chomsky, speaking at a Columbia protest, said Kissinger should instead be appointed to "the Department of Death."[14]

Academic life wouldn't have suited Kissinger, anyway. His top salary in government was $63,000, and he said he was "deeply in debt" after leaving office.[15] "I'm a world figure," he told a Harvard dean who courted him to join the university. "I can't just lead a normal professor's life." Indeed, in the waning days of the Ford administration, while hosting friends aboard his Boeing 707, he mused, "What university would give me an airplane like this?"[16]

What, then, could he do after leaving office that was sufficiently lucrative and statesmanlike? In 1982, Kissinger settled on a solution. He founded Kissinger Associates, a firm that advised American and foreign businesses on strategy, business development, and geopolitical risk, and occasionally acted as a door opener, arranging meetings between top officials and business executives. "With no legal training and little financial acumen, he could not follow the usual revolving-door practice of returning to a law firm or bank," Isaacson writes. "So he set himself up as a statesman for hire, one who would, for a hefty fee, purvey foreign policy expertise to private corporations, undertake diplomatic assignments for them, and serve as a personal national security adviser to their chairman." Kissinger described the firm as a provider of "geopolitical-economic advice."[17] In 1986, for example, American Express paid the firm $420,000 for services that included quarterly speeches by Kissinger and occasional calls and meetings between top American Express executives and Kissinger staff, which at the time included Kissinger's replacement as National Security Adviser Brent Scowcroft and the firm's president, Lawrence S. Eagleburger, who had served as Secretary of State Kissinger's executive secretary.*

There was continuity between his old job and the new. Once again, Kissinger worked globally, this time as a consultant, negotiator, and general font of diplomatic savoir faire. In the 1980s, Kissinger mediated between the insurance agency AIG and the government of Argentina. He helped the CEO of Heinz, Tony O'Reilly, meet the presidents of Turkey, Ivory Coast, and Zimbabwe. "It's like traveling with someone who is still a secretary of state," said Robert Day, a Kissinger client and the then chairman of the investment firm Trust Company of the West. Eagleburger said the firm "acted as a mini State Department."[18]

Kissinger's greatest calling card was China, which in the early 1980s was just beginning its transition to state capitalism. "Kissinger and

---

* "You have to remember that the fee is not compulsory," Kissinger said in 1986, "so you have to assume that if it isn't worth their while, they wouldn't pay it."

his associates make a real contribution, and we think they are particularly helpful in countries with more centrally planned economies, where the principal players and the dynamics among the principal players are of critical importance," said O'Reilly in 1986.[19] "This is particularly true in China, where he is a popular figure and is viewed with particular respect."*[20] O'Reilly's comments go right to what Kissinger offered American businesses above all else: that vaunted friendship that he had cultivated with Zhou and other top leaders (and vice versa). This type of personal relationship is much more valuable in a country like China, where there is a widespread perception that personal relationships, or *guanxi,* are required to get things done and where individuals constrain the laws—as opposed to in liberal democracies, where the laws constrain individuals.

In other words, with the creation of Kissinger Associates, Kissinger began to monetize his friendship with China. This, in turn, changed the way he spoke about the country—regardless of what he really thought. "Once China becomes strong enough to stand alone, it might discard us. A little later it might even turn against us, if its perception of its interests requires it." Kissinger wrote presciently in his 1979 memoirs. But then his public stance shifted. Throughout the 1980s, Kissinger frequently adopted a reverential tone toward China, and one out of character for someone known for his starkly unsentimental views of the world. "The question is, could China be a possible ally of the United States in the future?" Kissinger said in a 1980 speech to the Northeastern Retail Lumbermen's Association. "Well, I, of course, have a strong personal and maybe even sentimental feeling about China."

In a 1985 speech to the Economic Club of Detroit, Kissinger said, "The most sophisticated, clearheaded, unsentimental, unemotional analysis of foreign policy that I have seen is to be found in Beijing. They demonstrate that a country that has survived with uninterrupted independence for 3,000 years did not do so by accident." That first

---

* Kissinger brought Day to China in late 1987. In May 1988, he brought his client David Rockefeller, the Chase Manhattan Corporation chairman, to Beijing to meet with China's then leader, Deng Xiaoping.

statement carried weight for the assembled heavies of Detroit, coming from a famed realist and a man considered the most brilliant foreign policy thinker and practitioner in the United States. But Kissinger would often undercut the credibility of his own analysis by describing an emotional response. "Nobody," Kissinger wrote in a draft of a 1985 speech to the think tank CSIS, "is more sentimental about China than I am or more dedicated to close relationships." Despite this frank confession of bias, Kissinger's praise of China—regardless of whether he believed what he was saying—not only helped shape the American debate about China as a country America could partner with but also ensured Kissinger's access to China's leadership.

Kissinger is one of the most brilliant thinkers of the twentieth century and has more experience dealing with the Party than any American, alive or dead. Why not just take what he says about China at face value? In other words, why not assume that Kissinger's words and actions reflect his intellect and experience? To answer that, it's helpful to quote some of Kissinger's contemporaries about his character. A man as powerful as Kissinger will always create enemies. But Kissinger incited an astonishing amount of invective, especially from those who worked with him directly. "I admire Henry," said Richard V. Allen, who served as Ronald Reagan's first national security adviser.[21] "What is troubling about him is why he needs to be so devious and manipulative—he's so brilliant, he works so hard. He sees connections before everyone else. He could rise just as high if he played straight. But for some reason, he just can't play straight. He *has* to manipulate." His former mentor at Harvard, Bill Elliott, at his 1963 retirement dinner called Kissinger "the most arrogant man I've ever met."[22] In a January 1989 phone call with the Soviet leader, Mikhail Gorbachev, George H. W. Bush thanked him for meeting with Kissinger and said he looked forward to the briefing on the meeting.[23] But "they would not necessarily believe everything because this was, after all, Henry Kissinger," Bush said, according to a transcript of the meeting. Some of the men who worked closest with Kissinger spoke frankly about his tendency to deceive. "Kissinger doesn't lie because it's in his interest," said his close aide Helmut Sonnenfeldt, whom *The New York Times* called "Kissinger's Kissinger" in his 2012 obituary.[24] "He lies because it's in his nature."

In elite Chinese politics, the most talented practitioners of guanxi blend a modest dissembling with extravagant hospitality and a skillful cultivation of the friend's sense of importance. And Kissinger's personality—his brilliance, his cravings for power, his obsession with intense games of strategy and manipulation—made him an ideal target.

By the late 1980s, Kissinger had increased his exposure to China. In December 1988, he launched a fund called China Ventures, for which he served as chairman, chief executive, and general partner.[25] The fund partnered with China International Trust and Investment Corporation (CITIC), a state-owned investment firm tasked with serving as the Party's "window to the outside world."[26] Kissinger's archives feature photographs of a May 1989 signing ceremony with Rong Yiren, the founder of CITIC.[27] According to an offering memorandum, the fund raised $75 million to invest in projects that "must enjoy the unquestioned support of the relevant PRC authorities." It's unclear if Kissinger actually believed this partnership would benefit China or the United States, but it's fair to assume he thought it would benefit Kissinger.

IT'S IMPORTANT HERE TO PAUSE AND DISCUSS HOW THE PARTY interacts with the economy of China. This will be a simplification, but major points need to be made legible for the rest of Kissinger's story to make sense.

The Party oversees and owns state-owned enterprises (SOEs): companies that are officially part of the government. Versions of SOEs also exist in the United States, such as the famous Tennessee Valley Authority, established by Franklin Roosevelt in 1933, and the passenger rail line Amtrak. But SOEs are far more common, powerful, and integrated into China's government than they are in the United States. Those who run SOEs are almost always Party members, and the Party expects them to implement its policies. Several months before Rong and Kissinger partnered, for example, the Party appointed Rong the deputy head of the National People's Congress Standing Committee, a symbolically important Party role.[28] There are countless examples of Chinese officials seamlessly transitioning between running SOEs and running cities or provinces. Some lament what they see as a similar dynamic in the United States—the "revolving door" between government and big business, such as when Dick Cheney moved from the Pentagon to Halliburton, and then from Halliburton to the vice presidency. But Cheney was not in government when he ran Halliburton, and Washington does not control Halliburton. By going into business with Rong, Kissinger was partnering with the Party.*[29]

KISSINGER'S TIMING WITH CHINA VENTURES WAS UNLUCKY. WHEN Deng Xiaoping became China's ruler in the years following Mao's 1976 death, he had inherited a brutalized nation. Mao had launched two disastrous campaigns of social and economic reformation that had resulted in tens of millions of deaths.

Deng, who ruled China from the late 1970s until the early 1990s, radically liberalized the country's economy and grudgingly reformed the political system. "Open the windows, breathe the fresh air and at the same time fight the flies and the insects," Deng said, signaling his willingness to embrace change while admitting the risks to the Party's grip on power.[30] Eventually, Mao's fervent paranoia about American influence gave way to a modicum of openness. In 1987, KFC became the first American fast-food restaurant to open in China, with a hugely popular shop near Tiananmen Square. Chinese people could start traveling abroad again, and they discovered just how far behind the Party had kept them. In 1988, the state network China Central Television aired *River Elegy*, a hugely popular documentary that was surprisingly critical about China's decline and the West's success, contrasting images of China's poverty with Manhattan skyscrapers.[31] The series argued, according to one of its writers, "that the solution for China was democracy and human rights."[32]

Chinese politics in the 1980s jerked between different directions. Similar to how the U.S.S.R. had undergone periods of openness and closure, sometimes tied to the whims of its leaders and sometimes

---

* Rong also served as vice-chairman of the Chinese People's Political Consultative Conference, an important United Front organization.

reflecting their perceptions of political and economic necessity, Beijing in the 1980s moved between liberalization and autarky.

By the late 1980s many in the Party concluded that China's windows had opened too wide. With more minor fluctuations, that's the stance the Party has held from the late 1980s to the present. Indeed, the Party would never again allow as much openness to America as China had experienced in the first half of the twentieth century or the mid-1980s. "Some of our people, having taken a few glimpses of the skyscrapers and freeways abroad," the conservative leader Chen Yun said dismissively, have concluded "that socialism is no match for capitalism."[33]

If China's leaders needed another reminder of the perils of American influence, they got it in the spring of 1989, when hundreds of thousands of students massed on Tiananmen Square and began advocating for American values like liberty and democracy. On May 30, a brave student read a statement about how democracy is "the hope for which we thirst, we Chinese who have suffered decades of repression under the feudal autocracy."[34] Protesters then unveiled the Goddess of Democracy, a plaster statue modeled on the Statue of Liberty. Soon after the crackdown began, late in the evening of June 3, 1989, a tank toppled the statue, and soldiers destroyed it with iron bars.[35]

On June 4, while Chinese soldiers massacred unarmed protesters in and around Tiananmen Square, ABC News interviewed America's most famous statesman from his weekend home in Kent, Connecticut. "What should America do, Dr. Kissinger?" the ABC News host, Peter Jennings, asked on June 4, 1989. "I wouldn't do any sanctions," Kissinger replied. In a July 30 column for the *Los Angeles Times*, Kissinger decried the "brutality" of the massacre but wrote, "To avoid any misunderstanding, let me summarize my own response to the events in Beijing. No government in the world would have tolerated having the main square of its capital occupied for eight weeks by tens of thousands of demonstrators who blocked the area in front of the main government building," implying that then president Bush would have ordered soldiers to open fire if an Occupy-style movement massed in front of the White House.[36]

Television viewers might have seen Kissinger as an elder statesman and realist, with a disinterested stake in simply seeing order prevail.

But Kissinger, via his board seats on companies that saw him as a gatekeeper to China, his Kissinger Associates clients, and especially China Ventures, had both a financial stake in China—and an incentive to speak positively about the Party.

"If I knew then what I know now, I would not have wanted him on that broadcast, plain and simple," Jennings said later. "And I think my management would have understood that perfectly."

KISSINGER WASN'T THE ONLY ONE MORE ACCOMMODATING THAN their reputations might have augured. President George H. W. Bush, onetime head of the CIA, condemned the massacre, suspended weapons sales to China, and ordered a "sympathetic review" of requests by Chinese students who wanted to stay in America.[37] But by June 5, he was ready to announce that "now is the time to look beyond the moment to important and enduring aspects of this vital relationship for the United States."[38] In a June 23 letter to Deng, Bush announced his "great respect for what you personally have done for the people of China and to help your great country move forward," and pleaded for help in "preserving this relationship that we both think is very important." Bush believed his status as a friend of China and his relationship with Deng meant that the United States needed to maintain a close relationship with the Party. As he later told a biographer, "Had I not met the man, I think I would have been less convinced that we should keep relations with them going after Tiananmen Square."[39] Once more, the practice of statecraft with China seemed to melt away in favor of enigmatic personal relations.

This may seem like just another chapter in American presidents' long history of coddling dictators when it serves their interests—from Franklin Delano Roosevelt's relationship with "Uncle Joe" Stalin, to George W. Bush's protection of Saudi Arabia after 9/11.

The issue is only clear in hindsight: today, Beijing threatens U.S. power more than any country since Nazi Germany. Actions like Bush's—especially at pivotal points in history—helped foster this threat. Bush prided himself on his foreign policy knowledge: he had served as the ambassador to the United Nations and as CIA director before winning the vice presidency in 1980. Could Bush have guessed that he was paving the way for the desperately poor country of China to jeopardize U.S. dominance? Perhaps that's an unfair standard. Still, one hopes for more discernment. Pressed in a TV interview to name the greatest leader he'd ever met, Bush first demurred but then praised, solely, Deng.[40]

Bush had first encountered Deng while running America's liaison office in China from 1974 to 1975. The two maintained a good enough relationship that Bush had sent his wife, Barbara, to tell Deng that he planned to run for president. In October 1988, Deng had even taken the extraordinary step of endorsing Bush, saying that he hoped his "old friend" would "be victorious in the elections."[41]

And so, in July 1989, Bush sent his national security adviser, Brent Scowcroft, and deputy secretary of state, Lawrence Eagleburger—two men who had worked at Kissinger Associates in the 1980s—on a secret trip to Beijing to meet his friend Deng and repair the relationship after Tiananmen.[*42]

Bush also sent Nixon and Kissinger on secret trips, in October and November 1989, respectively. Nixon brought Michel Oksenberg, a China specialist who served in the National Security Council under Carter. Kissinger brought his client Maurice Greenberg, chairman of AIG—Kissinger served as chairman of AIG's international advisory board—and the lawyer Judith Hope, with whom he served on the board of the railroad Union Pacific. (Greenberg denied that the trip was improper. While "economic questions were raised," said Greenberg, "there were no business discussions.")[43] In his book On China, Kissinger writes that he "accepted an invitation from China's leaders to come to Beijing that November to form my own views."[44] He doesn't mention Greenberg, Hope, or his partnership with CITIC.

Nixon told Chinese leaders that "many in the United States, including many friends of China, believe the crackdown was excessive and unjustified."[45] Kissinger told them to do more propaganda. "The problem," Kissinger said during his November 1989 trip, "came

---

* Beijing's response was, as Ambassador James Lilley wrote at the time, "close the door and beat the dog": in other words, punish demonstrators without the prying eye of the United States. (Eagleburger died in 2011, and Scowcroft died in 2020.)

because there was a disagreement within the Party, and not because of opposition between the students and the government. But because China hasn't done enough propagandizing, its international image has suffered huge damage."[46] That is to say, Kissinger took the opportunity to meet with his old Chinese counterparts to advise them on obscuring their massacre of students.

As for Beijing, it thought that the Party's friendship with Bush and Kissinger would be enough to stabilize the U.S.-China relationship. Kissinger's trip might have made it more confident in that assessment. The United States has checks and balances, however, and Congress cared little that Bush saw himself as an "old friend" of China, and even less for Kissinger's business interests. Congress felt the United States should punish the Party and protect Chinese students studying in America, and in November 1989 it adopted legislation protecting Chinese students—which Bush promptly vetoed, instigating a fight with Congress so intense that it prompted Senator Pete Wilson (R-Calif.) to leave his sickbed and fly to D.C. in order to vote against Bush. But Bush prevailed.[47]

Bush also advocated an idea that would reverberate throughout the 1990s and the first decade of the twenty-first century: that China would inevitably democratize. "I am convinced that the forces of democracy are going to overcome these unfortunate events in Tiananmen Square," he said during his June 5 press conference, hours after the massacre.[48] And, in an idea that seemed rational and even likely at the time, Bush claimed the United States would work with the Party to help it democratize.

In the aftermath of this messy recalibration of relations, Kissinger closed China Ventures. The Tiananmen massacre had sent China's economy into a tailspin, and the country had once again withdrawn inward. William E. Simon, a Treasury secretary under Nixon and a board member of China Ventures, put it succinctly: "I would say, to put it mildly, that the thing is on hold."*[49]

---

* A column Kissinger published in the *Los Angeles Times* in October 1989 included this note: "Kissinger says that in early June, China Ventures was still not operational and had made no investments. On June 6, China Ventures canceled the announcement of its formation planned for June 15 and on July 24

SIMON COULD HAVE BEEN SPEAKING ABOUT THE RELATIONSHIP IN general. In the early 1990s, few Americans wanted to be friends with China. The Party and its interests mattered little in D.C., especially among the business community. Until the late 1990s, Chinese officials and businesspeople in the D.C influence game often found themselves in a distant second place behind Taiwan. The reasons were part political and part economic. Tiananmen caused the country to be a global pariah, and images of the army massacring unarmed students remained seared in the minds of Americans. Although China's population was roughly forty times larger, in 1995 America's exports to Taiwan were $26.9 billion, to China, just $11.8 billion.[50] "Where China was the dream of the future for American business," the journalist James Mann writes in his 1999 history of the U.S. relationship with China, "Taiwan represented the profits of the present day."[51]

Furthermore, Taiwan was an ally, by history, shared values, and affinity. Taiwan's civil society was flourishing, and its people loved baseball. Taiwan's de facto embassy owned and hosted events in the mansion known as Twin Oaks—built by Alexander Graham Bell's father-in-law in 1888 and one of the largest estates in Washington.[52] In February 1997, President Clinton, Vice President Al Gore, and their wives went to a Lunar New Year's party in Chinatown attended by Jason Hu, Taiwan's chief representative in the United States. Meanwhile, a Chinese diplomat complained to *The New York Times,* "Why didn't the President come to our party?"

Still, there were challenges inherent in a situation where the United States was attempting to balance relations with two enemies. It led to some embarrassing moments. In May 1994, a Taiwanese government plane carrying President Lee Teng-hui and his top aides on their way

---

its board voted not to consider any investments 'at the present time.' Further, Kissinger canceled a speech to an investment conference in Beijing sponsored by CITIC, scheduled for Oct. 2. He remains a partner in the investment group. 'The reason for these actions,' Kissinger said, 'was to enable me to comment free of any implication of self-interest on events in China. I have a special regard for this relationship, which I helped to establish and which has been supported by five administrations of both parties.' "

to Nelson Mandela's inauguration landed for a refueling stop in Honolulu.[53] The State Department, mindful of the delicacy of ties among
the United States, China, and Taiwan, declined to grant Lee a visa to
leave the airport, and instead offered him a reception in an airport
transit lounge. Lee refused to leave the plane. He scornfully told an
American official who boarded to greet him, "I can't get too close to
the door of the plane, I might slip and enter America."*[54]

Ever aware of their delicate strategic position, the Taiwanese
wanted to remind Washington—and show Beijing—the strength of
the relationship between Taipei and the American people's representatives in Congress. The 1994 Republican Revolution, which led to the
Republicans gaining control of both the House and the Senate for the
first time in more than four decades, buoyed Taipei's case by empow-
ering three Taiwan supporters—Newt Gingrich, Bob Dole, and Jesse
Helms, who became the Speaker of the House, the Senate majority
leader, and the chairman of the Senate Foreign Relations Committee,
respectively. And Taipei, via the Taiwanese think tank the Taiwan
Research Institute, signed a three-year, $4.5 million contract with
Cassidy & Associates, one of D.C.'s top lobbying shops. Cassidy came
up with a plan based on President Lee's having received a PhD in
agricultural economics from Cornell in 1968: In 1994, Cornell alumni
from Taiwan had donated $2.5 million for a chair named for Lee.[55]
Cornell responded with an invitation for Lee to address a reunion in
1995. The invitation had massive implications.

Secretary of State Warren Christopher assured Beijing that the U.S.
government would not let Lee attend. But Cassidy began persuading
members of Congress to let Lee speak at Cornell. "We started raising
the question of why America was kowtowing—we deliberately used
that expression all the time—to China regarding its relationship on
Taiwan," said Gerald S. J. Cassidy, the firm's CEO and co-founder.
"Why on matters so small as whether President Lee could visit this
country, we could be so influenced by China, and was this not in fact
weakening our standing with China? And did this meet America's
principles regarding our support of democracy around the world?"[56]

---

* Fredrick Chien, Taiwan's foreign minister, told an American official in Taiwan
  that Americans were "a bunch of spineless jellyfish."

Beijing thought its friends would persuade Congress not to "hurt" China and the relationship by supporting Taiwan. It was wrong. In February 1995 testimony, Gingrich supported the idea of Lee's visiting America, and even advocated Taiwan rejoining the United Nations.[57] In May, the House and the Senate passed nonbinding resolutions supporting Lee's visit to Cornell. The House vote passed 396 to 0, the Senate's 97 to 1. The longtime Taiwan supporter Dole, amid a successful campaign to secure the 1996 GOP presidential nomination, even considered organizing a plane to fly members of Congress to Cornell to see Lee. Not wanting to battle both houses of Congress, and mindful of the potential public relations disaster, the Clinton administration grudgingly granted Lee a visa.

The Taiwanese assured the Clinton administration Lee's Cornell speech would be apolitical. It wasn't. "Communism is dead or dying," Lee said, "and the peoples of many nations are anxious to try new methods of governing their societies." He added, "I believe that the Taiwan Experience has something unique to offer the world in this search for a new direction"—a subtle call for the democratization of the mainland and a stirring piece of campaign rhetoric for Taiwan's first democratic election, less than nine months away. "He totally double-crossed us," the then assistant secretary of state for East Asia, Winston Lord, said.[58]

The speech sparked what became known as the Third Taiwan Strait Crisis. Beijing canceled arms control talks and official visits to and from the United States, recalled its ambassador, and fired missiles into the Taiwan Strait. It sought to communicate to the Taiwanese that electing a politician like Lee would threaten their safety and that the United States should refrain from meddling in Taiwan's relationship with China.*

As the crisis raged, China's friends like Kissinger worked to ameliorate it. In early July 1995, Kissinger led a delegation to Beijing on a trip organized by the America-China Society (which he founded in 1987 to lobby for deeper financial and cultural ties between the two countries). Kissinger brought the former secretary of state turned consultant Al Haig, the former deputy secretary of state John C. Whitehead,

---

* The first two happened in 1954–1955 and 1958.

and, once more, the AIG chairman Greenberg. Kissinger met with top leaders like Premier Li Peng, who told him that the Clinton administration had "shaken the foundations" of bilateral relations and "hurt the feelings of the entire Chinese people."*[59]

On the morning of July 13, Kissinger told the Senate Foreign Relations Committee that America should calm down and wait. Give Beijing "some opportunity to reflect about the strong feelings expressed by many Americans," he said. "They should try to avoid too much of a confrontation in the immediate future." That afternoon, the group of China friends met in the White House with Clinton and Vice President Al Gore and their national security team. According to a declassified transcript of the meeting, all four men urged Clinton and Gore to soften their stance on China. "If the administration can move in the direction of improving relations with China, we will do what we can to help with the Republicans in Congress, who I believe are behaving very irresponsibly on this issue these days," Kissinger said.†

In early July 1995, Gingrich had called for the United States to resume diplomatic ties with Taiwan.[60] Speaking on CBS's *Face the Nation*, Gingrich said the Clinton administration should tell Beijing it must "live with the reality that the people of Taiwan are a free people and deserve it."

Meanwhile, Kissinger was working behind the scenes. "Henry called me and said, 'This is not good,'" Gingrich told *The New York*

---

* In October 1989, Beijing had difficulty finding foreign dignitaries to celebrate the fortieth anniversary of the founding of the People's Republic of China—in part because it required them to sit on a rostrum on Tiananmen Square, four months after the massacre. Even Kissinger declined. Beijing rustled together a senior Pakistani legislator, a Czech Politburo member, North Korea's minister of finance, the vice-chairman of the Sino-Soviet Friendship Association—and Haig, who just eighteen months ago had mounted an unsuccessful campaign for the Republican nominee for president.

† The four men, along with the former U.S. trade representative Carla Hills, had just come back from a trip to Beijing. No major media, however, said that the America-China Society had organized the trip; nor did any of them mention Greenberg's appearance on it. In 1993, Hills had founded Hills & Company International Consultants; that year she also joined AIG's board. Kissinger was appointed chairman of AIG's international advisory board in 1987. It was classic Kissinger.

Times, about his Taiwan remarks. "I said 'I wanted their attention.' He said, 'You have their attention.'" And so Gingrich retracted his comments. "I was trying to rattle their cage, to get their attention," he said, referring to Beijing. "I don't think we should recognize Taiwan." Gingrich told the *Times,* "In the case of China, I'm frankly puzzled. My conclusion after talking to Henry is that I'm just going to have to spend a lot of time thinking about China and studying China." Kissinger said, "I think he would be the first to admit that he is just beginning to educate himself on foreign policy." Kissinger, Gingrich told the *Times,* "likes me a lot."[61]

THE THIRD TAIWAN STRAIT CRISIS ENDED IN MARCH 1996, AFTER the U.S. government sailed two aircraft carrier groups into the area. "Beijing should know, and this US fleet will remind them, that while they are a great military power, the strongest, the premier military power in the Western Pacific is the United States," explained Clinton's defense secretary, William Perry.[62] On March 23, 1996, Taiwanese went to the polls for the first time in history and elected Lee with roughly 55 percent of the vote—more than twice that of any of his opponents.

Beijing concluded that it was neither active enough in nor informed enough about U.S. politics. In 1995, it created a central leading group, an important top Party body, to study U.S. congressional affairs.[63] "We certainly haven't done enough lobbying of the U.S. Congress," Jiang Zemin, China's then chairman, told *U.S. News & World Report.*[64] "I always welcome U.S. senators and congressmen to visit China. I believe it is unlikely that those American friends who have met me could form the impression that I am a dictatorial tyrant," he said.

Party leaders became focused on influencing America during the 1996 U.S. presidential election, with a clear preference for reelecting Clinton. Even though Clinton, as governor of Arkansas, had visited Taiwan four times, and China never, he was certainly better than Dole, who had said in March 1996 that he supported the island nation rejoining the United Nations.

In supporting the Democrats, Beijing was trying a different tack than its Leninist game of influence and attempting to engage in typical D.C. horse-trading—without the experience or expertise to pull it off. Though mostly forgotten today, the fundraising scandal known as Chinagate preoccupied the White House for months, until the Monica Lewinsky affair broke in 1998.* It wasn't the first China failure to meddle in U.S. affairs (and wouldn't be the last), but it was a particularly embarrassing one: and one that taught Beijing a crucial lesson about the relationship among power, money, and influence in D.C.

The scandal had its roots in Clinton's obsession with fundraising. Concerned about the power of the Republican-controlled Congress in the 1996 election, the Clinton team prioritized raising money: Clinton held an astonishing 237 fundraising events in 1996. In exchange for raising money, the Clinton administration gave unprecedented access to the White House—for the fundraisers, donors, and their contacts. Johnny Chung, a previously obscure Taiwanese-born entrepreneur and one of the main players in the scandal, was allowed into the White House forty-nine times.[65] In April 1996, Vice President Al Gore held a fundraising event at a Buddhist temple in Los Angeles. A Taiwanese-born immigration consultant helped arrange for roughly $55,000 of donations from monks and nuns, many of whom had taken vows of poverty.

In August 1996, Chung visited an abalone restaurant in Hong Kong and met with General Ji Shengde, the then head of China's military intelligence. "We hope to see him re-elected," Ji said of Clinton, according to Chung's 1999 House testimony.[66] He continued, "I will give you 300,000 U.S. dollars. You can give it to the president and the Democratic Party." (It is illegal for American political parties to accept money from foreign donors.)

Beijing felt the need to ingratiate itself with the White House after the Taiwan Strait Crisis and, seeing Taipei's largesse, thought that

---

* It's hard to find nonpartisan information about that period. Most of the books about the scandal have titles like *Year of the Rat: How Bill Clinton and Al Gore Compromised U.S. Security for Chinese Cash* and *Deception: How Clinton Sold America Out to the Chinese Military*. In March 1997 the magazine *National Review* published a cover story about the scandal titled "The Manchurian Candidates," which featured the strikingly offensive image of the Clintons with buckteeth.

spending money was helpful. It saw Congress as merely a rubber-stamp body beholden to the president. "Into the 1990s, Beijing labored under a deficient understanding of the U.S. political system," writes the China scholar David Lampton. "After all, neither President Nixon nor President Carter had consulted Capitol Hill before dramatically changing policy toward China in the 1970s."*[67] Why couldn't Beijing just directly influence the White House?

But the donations just made things worse for Beijing. As the scandal grew, the *New York Times* columnist Thomas Friedman wrote in March 1997:

> Every major decision the Administration now makes on China is going to be scrutinized for links, real or imagined, to campaign donations. Administration China experts will be reluctant to take chances. And the prospects for bipartisanship on China will be diminished, since the China bashers in Congress are going to have a field day using China's own ham-fisted efforts at influence-peddling to discredit anyone who tries to engage Beijing on the urgent, serious agenda that needs addressing.[68]

The scandal also served as a reminder of just how strong the Taiwan lobby remained. Although all four of the main Asian American players had Taiwan connections, Congress focused on their linkages to Beijing: the first major report, March 1998's *Investigation of Illegal or Improper Activities in Connection with 1996 Federal Election Campaigns*, emphasized how a variety of Chinese "entities were acting to influence U.S. elections."[69]

Just fourteen months after losing the 1996 presidential election, Dole registered as a foreign agent for Taiwan, earning his law firm a monthly retainer of $30,000.[70] In July 1998, Dole appeared on the *Late Show with David Letterman*. Clinton had just visited Beijing, a trip that distracted from his domestic scandals, and during which he stated that the United States didn't support Taiwanese independence.

---

* There's still so much we don't know because relevant archives in Beijing remain inaccessible. Though it's possible Beijing might have donated money to discredit the Democrats, Chinagate was likely just a blunder.

"Let's forget the Monica Lewinsky stuff for a second here, and let's just talk about President Clinton in China," Letterman said.

Dole responded, "Well, I think overall, you know, I think his trip was very good until he made the statement about Taiwan. I think that did—probably raised it from about an A to a C, or lowered it from about an A to a C. I think that was a mistake. Taiwan should—and China should determine their relationship; the president sort of said that there should not have independence [*sic*], there can't be one China, one Taiwan, and they can't belong to any world organizations, which I think was a mistake, and I expect next week when Congress meets, and I'm not there any longer, there'll probably be a big firestorm."[71] Not once did Dole mention that Taiwan was paying him to praise it. (Through a spokesperson, Dole declined to comment.)

The investigation into Chinagate dragged on for years. In May 1999, Congress hauled in the four Asian Americans to testify. Chung's testimony was the most contentious. "You have had your 15 minutes of fame, and it's sort of obvious that you are a very minor and insignificant puppet" of Beijing, said Representative Tom Lantos (D-Calif.).[72] Chung denied acting as an agent of the Chinese government and castigated Congress for the pay-to-play nature of U.S. politics.

Chung's simple message still resonates today: if U.S. politicians didn't need so much money to win elections, it would be harder for Beijing to influence American politics. He added, "Please keep in mind that I didn't create this system, you did."

Chung and Beijing were not wrong about the corruptibility of the executive branch. Trading money for access, *The New York Times* wrote in an August 1997 editorial titled "The White House Turnstile," "continues to poison American politics [and] deepen the cynicism of Americans."[73] In a notorious line from a July 1997 interview, Chung said, "I see the White House is like a subway. You have to put in coins to open the gates."[74] Beijing learned from its failures trying to buy its way in that it was both illegal and ineffective to insert the coins itself; far better for American corporations and for its American friends to do it for Beijing.

THE DESIRE FOR ACCESS ALSO FLOWED IN THE OTHER DIRECTION. While in the early twentieth century, missionaries and politicians drove American interest in China, by the late twentieth century, businesspeople led the charge.

The desire of American corporations to invest in China had grown in the 1980s, not least of all because the U.S. government, eager to use the relationship with China to counterbalance the Soviet Union, encouraged them to do so. But after the 1989 Tiananmen massacre and the 1991 fall of the Soviet Union, there was little U.S. appetite for investing in China. Meanwhile, some American businesses began worrying about offshoring to China and competition with Chinese companies.

Indeed, the early 1990s were a bad time for American business interests in China. After Tiananmen, and the Taiwan-sympathetic Republican takeover of Congress in 1994, Congress and the White House started threatening to remove China's most favored nation (MFN) trading status, a designation that extended to China the trading benefits the United States gave every country—except North Korea, Syria, Libya, Iran, Cuba, and Iraq.[75] In May 1993, Clinton issued an executive order stating that China's "overall, significant progress" on human rights would dictate renewal. As Chinese officials continued to arrest prominent dissidents, force some women who violated the one-child policy to have abortions, and suppress protests in Tibet, corporations recognized they couldn't argue that China was actually making progress on human rights. They needed a different justification for increasing trade with China and for permitting it to enter the World Trade Organization (WTO), which would make its MFN status permanent.

And so a propaganda battle was fought in America. Starting in the mid-1990s, some prominent corporations and U.S. officials began loudly arguing that trade with China would both benefit Americans and democratize China. Allowing American businesses to invest in China, in other words, would alleviate the human rights concerns impeding trade, because the investments themselves would improve China's political system. Spearheaded by Boeing and several other major multinationals like Motorola, Exxon, and IBM, American businesses launched one of the largest lobbying efforts in history.

They spent hundreds of millions of dollars to normalize trade relations with China and to bring it into the WTO. "Economic liberalization in China is ultimately going to lead to political liberalization," the presidential candidate George W. Bush's chief foreign policy adviser, Condoleezza Rice, said in 1999, voicing a view that many Republican and Democratic politicians and businesspeople espoused. "That's an iron law."[76]

The strategy was naive, at best.*[77] "Everyone who knew China didn't see seeds of liberalization," Stapleton Roy, who served as the American ambassador to China from 1991 to 1995, told me in a July 2019 interview. So no one important in the government believed China was going to democratize? I asked him. "Absolutely not," he said. That idea "was used to sell policy, not formulate it."

Meanwhile, Beijing in the mid-1990s began learning that punishing and rewarding American companies for Washington's behavior was an effective strategy to force them to lobby for its interests. The prime target for this was Boeing, the world's largest airplane manufacturer. When America upsets Beijing, "we are the designated hostage," complained Boeing's then CEO, Philip M. Condit, in 1996.[78] In the mid-1990s, Boeing sold roughly 10 percent of its planes to China and dreamed of that percentage skyrocketing. Because of the Party's control over the Chinese airline sector, Beijing could more easily coordinate purchases of planes than, say, computers. And because the global airline market was a duopoly, with the European consortium Airbus competing with Boeing for Chinese purchases, Beijing could reward Airbus and punish Boeing for Washington's actions—and vice versa. Lawrence Clarkson, Boeing's chief international strategist, put it succinctly. If we don't deliver for China, he said in 1996, "we're toast."[79]

Boeing's relationship with China stretches back to the company's 1916 founding: its first engineer was a Chinese student studying in America—a fact of which Boeing officials and supporters are fond of reminding their customers in Beijing.[80] The company co-founded

---

* In his January 1993 confirmation hearing to be secretary of state, Warren Christopher said that the United States would "seek to facilitate a peaceful evolution of China from communism to democracy by encouraging the forces of economic and political liberalization in that great country."

China's first aircraft manufacturer in the 1930s; in 1932, Japanese pilots shot down the Boeing representative Robert M. Short while he was in a fighter plane defending the city of Suzhou; he earned a hero's funeral in Shanghai, with more than one million public mourners.[81] In 1972, Nixon helped broker Boeing's first sale of ten planes to the Communist Party; the company opened an office in Beijing in 1980.[82]

Boeing had a head start against Airbus, which didn't sell its first plane to China until 1985. But in April 1996, amid the pro-Taiwan wave then cresting in D.C., Premier Li Peng gave Airbus a $1.5 billion order for planes that Boeing had widely expected to receive.[83] European leaders, Li said, "do not attach political strings to cooperation with China, unlike the Americans who arbitrarily resort to the threat of sanctions or the use of sanctions."[84] (Note how Li himself is attaching political strings to a business decision.) This is the reason, he said, that China cooperates with the Europeans. "There's no doubt we are being punished," said Ronald B. Woodard, then president of Boeing Commercial Airplane Group.[85]

Boeing emphasized to Beijing that the company was working to improve China's standing in America. It had three major cards to play in this effort, and it played them well. First, as America's largest exporter, Boeing helped prevent the trade deficit with China—$39.5 billion in 1996, and growing sharply, a concern for policy makers even before Trump's presidency—from growing even more lopsided.[86] Second, the company could argue that trade brought jobs: not only for Boeing, but for its many suppliers, which at the turn of the century numbered roughly ten thousand and were spread across an astonishing 420 of the 435 congressional districts.[87]

Third and most important, Boeing knew how to mobilize its massive influence network. In March 1996, the U.S. ambassador to China, James Sasser, spoke at a meeting of the U.S.-China Business Council in Beijing. "Nothing," Sasser said, "makes an impression on a member of Congress like a visit or phone call from a CEO from the member's district or state."[88] No one implemented that strategy as successfully as Boeing. In 1996, for example, a Boeing representative showed up at Square Tool & Machine Corporation in El Monte, California, and asked the company's owner and Boeing supplier Jolinda Resa to lobby Congress on China.[89] She said yes. She contacted her congresswoman and invited local business leaders to attend a lunch featuring a speaker arranged by Boeing. "In order to keep my 70 employees working," she said, "I felt I should do everything I could."* Condit, the CEO, said, "Every one of those suppliers is an exporter and should understand the importance of China, and we think they do."[90] He described the process as an "all-out campaign."

Like with any successful manipulative relationship, there were rewards to counterbalance the punishments. In a culmination of years of lobbying—both for the planes and for China's interests—Boeing signed a $3 billion deal during an October 1997 state visit by the Chinese chairman, Jiang Zemin. "That's always a wonderful feeling," Condit said.

Another industry that salivated over the market opportunity created by China's WTO entry was insurance. "When the actuaries think about 1.2 billion lives, their mouths water," MetLife's chairman emeritus Harry Kamen said in 1999. And so insurance companies began lobbying, in both the United States and China. Sandra Kristoff, the former director for Asian affairs at the National Security Council, joined New York Life as its executive vice president: in a six-month period in 1999, she saw nearly a hundred members of Congress. Ian Lancaster, who ran the China office of the U.S. insurance giant Chubb for much of the 1990s, met constantly with government officials in Beijing and D.C. "Basically, my job for eight years was government affairs and lobbying," he told me.

The case of AIG, for decades the world's largest insurer, taught other insurance companies the importance of American friends with high-level Chinese contacts. Perhaps unique among major American corporations, AIG's origin story traces back to China directly, where the company's founder, C. V. Starr, opened an agency in Shanghai in 1919; he didn't open an office in the United States until 1926. Like practically every other foreign business, the company left China after the 1949 Communist takeover. But it reentered in 1980, earlier than

---

* "The corporate campaign has no financial limits, be it political contributions or wining and dining or paying for lobbyists," said the California representative Nancy Pelosi. "The companies don't care what they spend because the payoff to them is so enormous."

most. After 1989's Tiananmen massacre, its then CEO, Greenberg, refused to pull AIG out of China, sending a powerful signal globally that the country remained open for business. In 1987, Greenberg had appointed Kissinger chairman of AIG's international advisory board; Kissinger had introduced Greenberg to Deng and regularly brought him to meetings with Chinese leaders.[91] In 1990 the then mayor of Shanghai, Zhu Rongji, appointed Greenberg chairman of an international business advisory council, and in 1992, Beijing granted AIG a license to sell insurance, the first for a foreign company since 1949. Greenberg said that "Li Peng, Zhu Rongji, and Jiang Zemin had a lot to do" with AIG's receiving the license.*[92]

Beijing empowered its senior American friends—especially Kissinger and former president Bush, who became a consultant after leaving office in 1993, but also people like Scowcroft and the former secretary of state Haig—to facilitate other insurance deals in China. Struggling to receive a license to sell insurance in China, Lancaster persuaded Chubb's CEO, Dean O'Hare, to take a similar approach as AIG and to hire Bush. "He's a natural," Lancaster recalls telling O'Hare in the mid-1990s. "Him coming here will get us access to the senior level"—crucial in a political system that prioritized top-down decision making. Chubb also hired Scowcroft's consulting firm the Scowcroft Group, through which, Lancaster said, they communicated with Bush. In April 1996, Chubb paid for Bush and Scowcroft to visit Beijing.[93] Bush introduced Chubb's CEO, O'Hare, to Jiang Zemin and brought O'Hare to meetings with the state investment firm CITIC.[94] In June 1998, several weeks before Clinton's first presidential trip to China, the Chubb group helped sponsor another trip by Bush and Scowcroft.[95] O'Hare so badly wanted a Chinese operating license, writes the journalist Joe Studwell in his 2002 book, *The China Dream*, "that his firm paid for Mr. Bush to visit Beijing twice, Mr. Scowcroft six times and former under-secretary of state Arnold Kanter many more times." (European friends, like the former British prime minister Edward Heath, participated as well.)[96]

The persistence helped. In April 1999, Chubb finally received its

---

* As for the other companies that left after the massacre? "They all came back," Greenberg said, "like we knew they would."

license, and in September 2000, Chubb opened its first China branch in Shanghai.[97] Scowcroft cut the ribbon. "When you went to the Chinese and said, 'I have Brent Scowcroft and Arnie Kanter coming out, they would make sure you could see them. If I, as Lancaster, wanted to see some of the senior people, there was no way," Lancaster told me. "If you're unknown in China and trying to get known and you're trying to get a license there, having a former president at a reception might get people to come who might not come otherwise," said Mark Greenberg, Chubb's senior vice president, in 2000, when explaining why the company hired Bush.[98] "We get to rub shoulders with them and get to know them better."

Beijing took a different approach from other countries like Japan, or the United Kingdom, or Saudi Arabia. In 1997, Taiwan had retained fourteen U.S. law firms and countless PR firms: Beijing had just one law firm, and one public relations firm, working directly for it in Washington.[99] Why did Beijing need to hire public relations firms, when American corporations, nonprofits, and former government officials, in exchange for preferential treatment in China, would do the lobbying for them?

What Beijing most wanted from the United States in that period— and what U.S. corporations abetted—was entry into the WTO. American corporations and trade associations spent more than $113 million on their WTO campaign—$31.2 million in the first half of 2000—with Boeing alone spending $4.24 million on lobbying in that period. Representative Merrill Cook (R-Utah) said he was offered $200,000 in corporate campaign donations to change his vote to yes.[100] "If somebody's on the margin and they screw up this vote," the U.S. Chamber of Commerce president, Thomas Donohue, said, "they'd better not look to me for money." Jock Nash, Washington counsel for the textile company Milliken & Company that objected to China's entry into the WTO, said, "There is no way on God's earth that you can mount a grassroots effort to bring popular pressure on Washington that will overcome the pressure being put on them by the Fortune 500."[101]

The Party had refined its tactics. Several years earlier, it had invited international blowback (and real strategic losses) by crudely handing over a $300,000 cash payment to the DNC to reelect Clinton. That kind of outlaw financing was no longer necessary. Now the Party had friends serving on the boards of major American companies. And those companies had similar interests with the Party: increased investment in China, and a desire to not let the U.S. government's frustrations with Beijing interfere with business. "Did [the Chinese] ask us to do it? Never!" Cindy Smith, a Boeing spokeswoman, said in 1997. "Are they happy and pleased? Of course."

ON DECEMBER 19, 2001, EIGHT DAYS AFTER CHINA JOINED THE WTO, Chairman Jiang hosted a private dinner for the businessman Neil Bush, the son of the former president and the brother of the current one. Held from 6:00 to 8:00 p.m. in Zhongnanhai, the Chinese leadership compound, the dinner was intimate. The only other guests were a vice foreign minister; the U.S. ambassador to China, Clark Randt Jr., a lawyer and one of George W. Bush's fraternity brothers at Yale; and an interpreter. "You look remarkably like your brother, the president, with whom I had good meetings in Shanghai," Jiang said, according to a declassified State Department cable that describes the dinner in detail.

"Why does China have such a poor image in the United States?" Bush asked.

"We need better PR," Jiang said. "Formerly, we called this the 'Propaganda Department' but that term had a bad connotation. Now, we call this department the PR department."

"The term 'Communist' does not have a positive connotation in the United States," Bush said.

"Communism. What does it mean?" Jiang mused. "We have spent a lot of time debating this."

Jiang described his September 2000 interview with the CBS journalist Mike Wallace: "Mr. Wallace suddenly asked me if I was a 'dictator,'" Jiang said, and then made a face of mock terror. "Of course not, I am a 'strong leader.' People said my interview was good." At one point during the dinner, Jiang, the vice foreign minister, and the interpreter all broke into song. "We would rather fight and die than live in shame and servitude at the hands of these invaders," they crooned.

Just days after the dinner, Neil spoke at Tsinghua, one of the country's most prominent universities. When President Bush himself spoke at the university in February 2002, a student mentioned Neil's December talk and said that Neil explained how many American politicians "have a lot of misunderstandings about China." What, the student asked, would President Bush do about it? "It's important for our political leaders to come to China," Bush replied. "And when I go back home, I [*sic*] describe a great nation, a nation that has not only got a great history, but an unbelievably exciting future."[102]

It's worth examining the word "misunderstanding." In the United States, the word is expansive and intimates a kind of gentleness, an honest mistake. But for the Party, "misunderstanding" often means something much narrower: it simply refers to explaining the country differently than the Party does.

After the acrimonious March 2021 meeting between top U.S. and Chinese officials in Alaska, Chinese media blamed U.S. "misunderstanding" of China's benign intentions, for example. The Party chief of Xinjiang blames false information for people "misunderstanding" Xinjiang, while in January 2020 the chief executive of Hong Kong promised that her subjects could still enjoy freedoms unavailable in the rest of China unless they allowed "misunderstandings" to get in the way. "Misunderstanding," in other words, means contradicting the Party.

Mentioning "misunderstanding" in his speech was an incredibly subtle, tentative step for Neil, and one that he almost certainly didn't realize he was taking. But it was the first of many and marked the beginning of a long and successful campaign that turned him into one of the Party's most successful American agents. (Neil Bush responded, "I categorically disagree with your assessment; your assertion is absolutely false.")

Soon after the December 2001 dinner, Neil met Jiang's son Mianheng in Shanghai. "Please tell him that my English is good," Jiang had told Neil at the dinner. "He thinks it is not." Mianheng, who earned a PhD in engineering from Drexel University in Philadelphia, had co-founded the company Grace Semiconductor Manufacturing in Shanghai with Winston Wong, the son of one of Taiwan's most powerful businessmen. In August 2002, Grace hired Neil as a consultant. The company would pay him $400,000 in stock annually over five years,[103] plus $10,000 every time he attended a board meeting.[104] "He is very good at helping us with the macroeconomic situation, especially in the U.S.," Wong said about Neil Bush.[105] In 1999, Neil had founded the education company Ignite!, to help teach children who, like himself, had learning disabilities. Wong and his sister invested roughly $2 million.[106]

For Neil, China represented a great opportunity amid a tough time. After twenty-two years of marriage, he had fallen in love with another woman, and in the summer of 2002 he sued his wife, Sharon, a former elementary school teacher, for divorce. It was a nasty split, and Sharon went to the press. In July 2003, a Houston TV station obtained a videotape of Neil Bush's deposition. Among the many unsavory details that came out of the divorce proceedings was Neil's relationship with Grace Semiconductors, which had previously been private.

"Now, you have absolutely no educational background in semiconductors, do you, Mr. Bush?" Sharon's lawyer asked.

"That's correct," Neil responded. He added later, "But I know a lot about business and I've been working in Asia quite a long time. . . . I feel I've had pretty extensive business interaction over there and that's what I would bring, just general business knowledge," he said.

The deposition also revealed that Neil on business trips to Asia slept with women who came to his hotel rooms in Thailand and Hong Kong. "You have to admit that it's a pretty remarkable thing," his wife's attorney said in the deposition, which caused a major scandal when it was leaked, "for a man just to go to a hotel room door and open it and have a woman standing there and have sex with her."[107]

"It's very unusual," Bush replied. He added that it happened at least three or four times, that he didn't know if the women were prostitutes, and that he didn't pay them.

I asked a former high-ranking Western intelligence official who covered China at the time whether he thought Beijing had orchestrated the women in Hong Kong to entrap and blackmail the president's brother. "It's impossible to say," he said. Perhaps it was pure dumb luck, he added, or perhaps it was a detailed operation to turn Bush. In other words, it may have simply been a gesture of hospitality, typical of the etiquette of business partners in the region, or a honeypot operation to compromise Bush. "The only way to be sure is to have someone on the inside" intimately familiar with the workings of the Chinese Ministry of State Security or the military, he said, and declined to comment any further. While we can't know the inner workings of the Party's security apparatus, we can see the success of the campaign to turn the Bushes into friends of China.

Though it was George H. W. Bush who first met senior Party officials in the 1970s, it was Prescott junior, the brother of George H. W. Bush and a former insurance executive, who initiated the Bush family's business relationship with China. Prescott began consulting in China in the mid-1980s, while his brother served as Reagan's vice president. In September 1989, Prescott joined an early wave of American businessmen returning to the capital after the Tiananmen massacre. "We aren't a bunch of carrion birds coming to pick the carcass," he told *The Wall Street Journal* in Beijing.[108] "But there are big opportunities in China, and Americans can't afford to be shut out." (Both George H. W. and his brother repeatedly denied any inappropriate financial links with China; George H. W. passed away in 2018, his brother Prescott in 2010.)

In 1993, Prescott co-founded the United States of America–China Chamber of Commerce and, as chairman of its board of directors, earned fees for recruiting corporate clients. In January 1994, he signed on behalf of the chamber an agreement with St. Louis to help market local businesses in China and with Hebei province to help it negotiate contracts with Missouri companies.[109] In a speech that month, Prescott said, "I don't think you can ignore the human rights aspects, but I don't think we should link trade with human rights." He added, "Cutting off trade with China will only hurt the U.S." In a speech to business executives in Chicago in January 1995, Prescott recommended working closely with the Party. "You want to be sure you've got the party bosses working with you," he said. "They're pretty good guys now, the ones I've met."[110] In November 1999, the Chinese automotive components manufacturer Wanxiang Group hired Prescott as its senior economic adviser.[111] "He doesn't have set responsibilities. When we need his help, we will contact him," said a Wanxiang spokesman. "He has many friends."

Sixty-eight and spry after losing to Clinton in 1992, George H. W.

Bush returned to Houston to plan his future. His predecessors had a variety of different post-presidencies: Carter had committed himself to humanitarian concerns after leaving office, while Ford had enriched himself with board seats and speeches—in 1992, Nixon accused him of "selling the office"—but Ford's business was almost entirely domestic.[112] Reagan, who before Trump was the oldest president ever elected, was seventy-seven when he left office in January 1989. Eight months later, he accepted roughly $2 million from Japan's then-largest media group, Fujisankei, to spend eight days in the country giving speeches and interviews.[113] Alzheimer's soon precluded future business.

The elder former president Bush, who had more foreign policy experience than any of his twentieth-century predecessors, decided to take a global remit for his post-presidency career. In May 1995, he became a senior adviser to the international board of the Canadian gold-mining giant Barrick.[114] A year later, he wrote a letter to the Indonesian dictator, Suharto, praising the company, which was fighting to get a stake in an Indonesian gold mine worth tens of billions of dollars.[115] He also delivered a paid speech to roughly twenty thousand people in Tokyo—many of whom were members of the Reverend Sun Myung Moon's Unification Church—about "family values." And in 1998, he personally lobbied the Kuwaiti oil minister on behalf of Chevron. (Responding to a March 1997 *Fortune* magazine article titled "George Bush, Corporate Shill," a spokesman for George H. W. said, "We don't speak to any company that falls off the turnip truck." The spokesman added, "He is very much in demand these days, and I think he's grateful for that, since he has no other means of income.")

But China loomed largest. Though little noticed at the time, the United Front was expanding its ties with the Bush family. George H. W.'s first known postpresidential encounter with the organization came in June 1998, when Chubb co-organized a seminar Bush headlined with the Chinese People's Association for Friendship with Foreign Countries (CPAFFC). Founded in 1954 and for a long time run by the powerful Li Xiaolin, CPAFFC hides its United Front connections. It calls itself a "nongovernment organization" that builds friendship with people around the world.[116] In fact, it is a Party organization, overseen by the Foreign Ministry, which implements

United Front work: "to increase as many people that support us and reduce as many people that oppose us."[117]

Li organized George H.W.'s meetings with the top leaders in Beijing, said Chubb's Lancaster. "I always found her a delightful, charming lady who had been an insider because of her father," Li Xiannian, who had served as China's head of state in the 1980s, said Lancaster. The United Front, which managed the relationships between retired U.S. officials, their families, and top Party leaders, was mostly run by princelings: the children of the Party elite. Like Xi, Li grew up among the red aristocracy; the two were childhood friends.[118] "If you were with her," Lancaster said, "you could get access to just about anyone."

When George W. Bush took office in January 2001, he had planned to toughen America's policy toward China. During his campaign, he called the country a "strategic competitor" and excluded the Chinese chairman, Jiang, from the list of leaders he called after his inauguration.[119] Meanwhile, Jiang sought to remind Americans that George H. W. approved of China. "The father of President Bush, Bush Sr., came over to China many, many times and had many meetings with me in the seat you are now occupying," Jiang told *The Washington Post* in March 2001. "We believe Bush Sr. will definitely push Bush Jr. to bring U.S.-China relations to a new level." A few weeks later, George W.'s uncle Prescott spoke with a reporter from the *Tampa Bay Times*.[120] The countries had just resolved a crisis over a collision between a Chinese fighter jet and an American spy plane, and Prescott was optimistic. In China, he said, having a brother who served as a president, and a nephew as the current president, is a "big asset." He added, "People don't run out and give us business because of that. . . . But they certainly are willing to talk." On April 14, his United States of America–China Chamber of Commerce posted a letter on its website. "China has a special place in my heart. I have been personally involved in China for over 15 years. My brother, George has been instrumental in the development of U.S. and China relations since 1974," Prescott wrote.[121] "As we are marching into the 21st Century, the interaction between the U.S. and China has created a sea of opportunities: dynamic growth and endless possibilities for profits."

Chapter Three

America Consents

★

CHAIRMAN HU JINTAO WAS NOT A MAN TO SHOW EMOTION. I SPENT almost six years living in Beijing during the 2002–2012 Hu era, and outspoken Chinese would occasionally call him a wooden puppet. In his memoirs, George W. Bush diplomatically described him as a man with an "unexcitable demeanor," while a source familiar with the British government told me that Queen Elizabeth II of England called him the most boring person she's ever met.[1]

That made his behavior all the more shocking. During an April 2006 state visit, Hu hugged Kissinger.[2] Several days later, on a tour of a Boeing plant in Seattle, he hugged Paul Dernier, a systems installation supervisor who had just presented Hu with a Boeing cap. "I was totally and emotionally caught off guard," Dernier said, calling it a highlight of his career. China and the United States working together, Hu said, would help "maintain world peace, promote common development, and create a brighter future for mankind." It would be, Hu said, "win-win."[3]

Indeed, until the second half of the Trump administration, it seemed to many Americans as if Kissinger was right about China's rise. "Ever since Richard Nixon's trip to China, every president, Republican or Democrat," the government official turned consultant Scowcroft said in 2007, "has decided to deepen engagement with China, which is the central thrust of our policy." Binding America with China would only benefit both countries—or so the thinking went. (It wasn't until later that U.S. officials started to privately joke that "win-win" meant China wins twice.) "It was so pervasive. There was such a strong conventional wisdom about China," the Princeton University professor Aaron Friedberg, who served as an Asian affairs adviser for Vice President Dick Cheney from 2003 to 2005, told me in October 2019. "We were doing well by doing good. We are all going to make money, and we were promoting a process that will eventually lead to their liberalization and peace in our time. Who's going to question it? It's like the oxygen that you breathe."

AT FIRST, THE SPY PLANE INCIDENT OF APRIL 2001 SEEMED TO AUGUR a bleak new era of U.S.-China relations. But a cataclysm on the other side of the world wiped that incident from the international stage. After the planes hit the Twin Towers and the Pentagon on September 11, 2001, Jiang quickly expressed solidarity with Bush. When the two leaders met for the first time several weeks later, Bush praised Jiang for standing "side by side with the American people as we fight this evil force."[4] In February 2002, Bush took his first presidential trip to Beijing, planned to coincide with the thirtieth anniversary of Nixon and Kissinger's trip. "Our ties are mature, respectful," Bush said.[5] "We discussed a lot of issues, starting with terrorism."

The 9/11 attacks also saw the return to the political arena of the Party's oldest and dearest American friend. In November 2002, Bush appointed Kissinger to chair the 9/11 Commission, tasked with the pivotal role of investigating the worst terrorist attacks in American history.

But Kissinger's baggage from the Vietnam War and the bombings in Cambodia, the conflicts of interest from his consulting firm, and his penchant for secrecy raised concerns. "If you want to get to the bottom of something, you don't appoint Henry Kissinger. If you want to keep others from getting to the bottom of something, you appoint Henry Kissinger," the New York Times columnist Maureen Dowd wrote.[6]

The question of conflict of interest had dogged Kissinger Associates from his China Ventures during Tiananmen Square and throughout the 1990s, most pointedly in 1997 amid the Chinagate scandal. "I happened to be at a dinner in Los Angeles with you a couple of days after Tiananmen," said Arianna Huffington, then a conservative commentator and activist, in an October 1997 debate with Kissinger on the TV show *Firing Line*.[7] Even then, she said, you refused to "condemn what China did." And some critics of yours, Huffington continued, "suggested that it is because of your financial interests, after all, you do have a lobbying consulting firm which does represent many companies that do business in China." Kissinger replied that "less than 5 percent of my income has anything to do with China." He added, "I think that our national debate has reached a sorry point when somebody who has attempted to serve his country that saved him, for forty years, can be accused of doing it for financial reasons." Kissinger would sometimes coyly and sometimes aggressively downplay his China connections to journalists. "We do have a reputation for a special arrangement with China," Kissinger told the *Financial Times* in March 2000. "But it is wrong."[8]

That conflict-of-interest debate intensified after Kissinger's appointment to chair the 9/11 Commission. Though overlooked at the time, Kissinger did have massive conflicts of interest—with Boeing, Blackstone, and the state-owned energy firm China National Offshore Oil Corporation, among others—that would have prevented him from ethically and responsibly serving. While China was his lodestar, Kissinger did in fact have a special relationship with several other nations. In February 2000, he even took the extremely unusual step of becoming an official "political adviser" to the president of Indonesia, an unpaid position that he took while serving on the board of Freeport-McMoRan, a mining company with extensive concerns in the country.[9]

Throughout the winter of 2002, the attacks on Kissinger's integrity mounted. On December 5, former secretary of state Madeleine Albright also called on Kissinger to release his client list (eighteen months after she had established her own consulting firm, with a private client list).[10] "I do think it is important to know who his clients are," she said.*[11]

The next day, Kissinger resigned from the commission. In March

---

* Public debate about Kissinger's conflicts of interest was not new. The first push came in 1983, when Congressman Henry B. González (D-Tex.) claimed that Kissinger, who chaired the government's Bipartisan Commission on Central

2003, he bitterly told a journalist that enemies trying to "settle scores" fueled the questions about his client list.[12] But his December 2002 resignation letter was more polished. "For over half a century, I have never refused to respond to the call from a president," he wrote, "nor have I ever put my personal interests ahead of the country's interests."[13]

DESPITE THIS 9/11 IMBROGLIO, KISSINGER PLAYED A LARGER ROLE in the Bush administration than he had in any government since Ford's, where he served as secretary of state. "Of the outside people that I talk to in this job," Vice President Dick Cheney told Bob Woodward in the summer of 2005, "I probably talk to Henry Kissinger more than I talk to anybody else. He just comes by and I guess at least once a month, [Chief of Staff] Scooter [Libby] and I sit down with him."[14] In an email Donald Rumsfeld released in his archives, the then secretary of defense described a June 2005 conversation he had with Kissinger. "The question is how do you develop a strategy for the PRC for the next 10 years. . . . The PRC plays all over the board. It isn't checkers, and it isn't even chess. It is a totally different game, and they're good at it, and they're doing it."

It is clear in hindsight that one piece of the "totally different game" involved United Front work to shift the perception of Taiwan among the American elite. In November 2003, Kissinger had brought his client William B. Harrison Jr., the CEO of JPMorgan Chase, to Beijing. JPMorgan wanted to advise and underwrite the IPO of the state-owned China Construction Bank, one of the country's four biggest banks. Photographs from Kissinger's archives show the former ambassador to China Stapleton Roy—who joined Kissinger Associates as a vice-chairman in December 2000—shaking hands with Jiang, while Harrison looks on excitedly.[15] "Dr. Kissinger is an old personal friend, and he has introduced me to many of his old friends in China," Harrison said at a November 12 press conference in Beijing.[16] "This kind of friendship is extremely important."

America, financially benefited from the companies he consulted for that did business in the region.

On November 11, Kissinger and Roy brought Harrison to meet with the Beijing Party secretary, Liu Qi, and to a meeting with the state councillor Tang Jiaxuan at Zhongnanhai.[17] Tang told Kissinger and Harrison to oppose Taiwanese independence. "The Taiwan problem remains the biggest factor influencing the development of U.S.-China relations," Tang told them.[18]

Why did Tang tell the CEO of JPMorgan Chase to oppose Taiwanese independence? Because it reminded Harrison that pushing against Taiwan would please the Party. There is no evidence Harrison acted against Taipei in any way. But he didn't need to do anything: he just needed to understand what Beijing expected of him. Indeed, the issue is not Harrison's behavior but the immense effort Beijing spent to make the American elite understand the "correct" position on Taiwan. These constant reminders helped weaken the standing of Taiwan in D.C. A former senior U.S. official who worked extensively with Beijing called this sending out "sonar pings." By the early years of the twenty-first century, those pings were reverberating throughout D.C.

Taiwan's power in D.C. was weakening for other reasons. By 2002, China's GDP was more than four times larger than Taiwan's, and growing at a much faster rate. And that year, two major Taiwan supporters, Jesse Helms (R-N.C.) and Frank Murkowski (R-Alaska), both left the Senate, marking the end of the "last great heyday" of the Taiwan lobby, Rupert Hammond-Chambers, a longtime Taiwan business advocate and the president of the US-Taiwan Business Council, told me.*[19] And Taiwan's independence-minded president Chen Shui-bian alienated some of his supporters in the White House and Congress by demanding more U.S. support than they were willing to give.

And then the dam broke. In December 2003, Bush, standing

---

* Contributing to the change was a major political scandal. In early 2002, news broke that from 1994 to 2000, Taiwan's intelligence service oversaw the distribution of $100 million to buy influence with foreign individuals and governments, including America's: a gallingly public example of influence peddling. "People will wonder about our ability to keep things secret," said the former Taiwanese presidential adviser Bi-khim Hsiao. "This has been a dark week for Taiwan."

with the Chinese premier, Wen Jiabao, at the White House, publicly rebuked Taiwan for flirting with declaring independence.[20] In October 2004 in Beijing, Secretary of State Colin Powell went further. "Taiwan is not independent," he said, pleasing Beijing by stating what had previously been ambiguous. "It does not enjoy sovereignty as a nation."[21] By December 2004, just twenty-six countries still recognized Taiwan.[22]

WITH TAIWAN SIDELINED, THE TWO COUNTRIES PARTNERING IN THE war against terror, and growing bilateral investment, relations between the United States and China peaked during the middle of Bush's second term, before the U.S. financial crisis. Several months earlier, during his November 2005 trip to Beijing, George H. W. Bush had described the mood of many by saying "that US-China relations have never been better than they are right now," adding that "the best days of the relationship are still ahead."

There were some tensions that persisted. In a case that raised worries in the business community about the U.S. government's willingness to permit the Party to purchase American corporations, in August 2005 the state-run giant China National Offshore Oil Corporation withdrew its $18.5 billion offer for the American oil and gas company Unocal, citing "unprecedented political opposition."[23]

But overall, the Bush administration, multinationals, and many in Congress believed that the Party would serve both global and American interests. In September 2005, the then deputy secretary of state, Robert Zoellick, gave an influential speech, portentously titled "Whither China?," calling for and predicting that China would become a "responsible stakeholder" in the global system the United States had built.[24] In December 2006, the United States and China launched the Strategic Economic Dialogue, a series of high-ranking meetings between the two sides. The then deputy assistant secretary of state Thomas Christensen described the purpose of the meetings in this way: "We wish China well and want to help extend your fantastic run of double-digit growth rates. Chinese growth is good for everyone. Our biggest concern is that you are not doing everything necessary to maintain it."[25]

Or as Kissinger told a group of students in Shanghai in April 2007, according to the PLA newspaper *Liberation Daily*, China's great rise will benefit everybody. He added, "If Americans were sitting here listening today, I would say the exact same thing."[26]

The government led the way, and the business community supported the charge. In a 2006 member survey from the nonprofit U.S.-China Business Council, an astonishing 97 percent of respondents expressed optimism about the prospects for their China business over the next five years.[27] "The multinationals were doing very well" in China during that period, James McGregor, a longtime China resident and business consultant, told me. "Even the stupid ones were making money." From 2003 to 2007, the country's GDP increased by more than 10 percent annually, further reshaping the world's economy. China's demand helped push the price of scrap steel from $77 in early 2001 to more than $300 in early 2004. Companies that sold scrap metal rejoiced. Buyers despaired. In 2003, California Metal-X, which purchased copper scrap to make bronze, cut its staff from seventy to thirty-eight people. Tim Strelitz, the company's co-founder, said in 2004 that "last year was a year from hell."[28] Some Americans started to feel helpless, unable to compete with the fastest-growing major economy in the world.

Indeed, this trade relationship had its discontented bystanders. The fierce November 1999 Seattle protests against the World Trade Organization, two years before China joined, was a portent of things to come. The event attracted activists from around the world, including a French sheep farmer who became a folk hero after removing the roof of a rural French McDonald's with his tractor. But for the United States, frustration with globalization was less about the power of multinationals or the homogeneity of consumer brands, which remained mostly American. Rather, it was about jobs. China's economic rise in the 2000s—the most impactful element of globalization—lowered the cost of consumer goods, increased corporate profits, and improved the economic well-being of Americans in general. It also led to concentrated job losses and the widening of the wealth gap in America.

Anxiety about jobs and outsourcing rankled voters in the 2004 campaign season. Between 2000 and 2003, the odds of losing a manufacturing job were fifty times higher than the odds of losing any job: in those years North Carolina, the hardest-hit state, lost 160,000 factory jobs, or roughly 20 percent of its total.[29] "There is no job that is America's God-given right anymore," Hewlett-Packard's CEO, Carly Fiorina, warned in a controversial speech in early 2004, while the patrician Democratic presidential nominee, John Kerry, began decrying "Benedict Arnold CEOs" who shipped jobs overseas.[30]

Meanwhile, worry about China's trade surplus started growing, years before Trump made it a centerpiece of his 2016 campaign. In November 2003, the investor Warren Buffett co-wrote an article in *Fortune* titled "America's Growing Trade Deficit Is Selling the Nation Out from Under Us. Here's a Way to Fix the Problem—and We Need to Do It Now."[31]

Mindful of sensitivities about the trade deficit, Chinese leaders would often announce purchases of products like Boeing planes and other big-ticket items during state visits; Boeing has long been America's largest exporter. But in the United States and globally, Beijing continued leveraging those imports for political gains, punishing and rewarding companies like Boeing and Airbus for the perceived political sins and virtues of their home governments. One major issue involved Tibet. The European scholars Andreas Fuchs and Nils-Hendrik Klann found that from 2002 to 2008, whenever the Tibetan spiritual leader the Dalai Lama met with a head of state, that country's exports to China declined by an average of 16.9 percent for one year after the meeting.[32] "It's an interesting phenomenon among politicians," the Dalai Lama told the German magazine *Der Spiegel* in 2007. "When they are not yet government leaders or presidents, they meet with me. Afterwards, they avoid me so as not to annoy Beijing. Then, economic relations with the People's Republic take priority."[33] For those countries' leaders brave enough to meet with Tibet's spiritual leader during that period, Fuchs and Klann coined a term for that decrease in trade: the Dalai Lama effect.

KISSINGER'S MODEL OF LIVING IN A REVOLVING DOOR BETWEEN government and China lobbying was spreading through Washington. Just forty-eight hours after leaving office in January 2001, Clinton's secretary of defense William S. Cohen founded his consulting firm, the Cohen Group.[34] "We left the Pentagon on Saturday and opened for business on Monday," he boasted.[35] An icon of democracy, Madeleine Albright was Clinton's ambassador to the United Nations before becoming the first female secretary of state. She established her own consulting firm in June 2001. A month earlier, Clinton's former national security adviser Sandy Berger founded Stonebridge International. The firms had a global remit. But—and regardless of the intentions of these former officials—they served to further link the Party with American businesses, and they raised the costs for icons like Albright criticizing China.

It worked like this: Diplomat consultants argued for better ties between the United States and China, which increased the opportunities for them to consult. And their praise for China improved their access in China, allowing them to become more effective advocates for American companies there. "I'm a consultant to government and to business, in the political and economic spheres," Berger told the state-run news agency Xinhua in 2004. "My two identities are like two hats, but they both play the role of bridge in the development of U.S.-China relations."[36]

For these former American officials, friendship was never just about the money or the power that came from access to the leaders of China. Rather, it brought the emotional rewards of feeling revered and of being at the center of things—in a way that reminded people of their time in office. Jeffrey Engel, the director of the Center for Presidential History at Southern Methodist University and the editor of George H. W. Bush's *China Diary*, traveled with Bush to China in November 2005—just days before his son's second presidential visit to China—and accompanied him on several meetings with Chinese officials.[37] Engel shared with me audio recordings of his interviews with Bush and his wife. "They weren't talking about anything substantive in my presence," he told me, "but there was a whole of 'President Bush, you're such a great Friend of China, we know you've always been there for China,'" he told me. "He was not greeted as a former President, he was greeted as President," Engel said.[38] He described driving around with Bush in the back of a limo, with the traffic in the city blocked for the ease of his transport from meeting to meeting. "He remarked at the time, nowhere else in the world did they treat him with as much reverence as when he went to China."

And inadvertently or not, the elder Bush repaid the favor. During his visit, President George W. Bush criticized China for its repression of dissidents and intellectual property rights, while the elder Bush focused on the positive, saying that ties between the two countries had "never been better."[39] George H. W. Bush expressed to Premier Wen "high praise for China's peaceful development, and that China will not become a threat to other countries," according to Xinhua.[40] "I believe China's rise will be peaceful," George H. W. Bush said. "When it comes to dealing with China, the elder Bush clearly shows he's young Bush's teacher," said an article about the trip on the Chinese internet company Sina's popular news website.[41]

George H. W. Bush's visit to the 2008 Beijing Olympics, his twenty-second since leaving office in January 1993, was one of his last trips to China. He had visited recently—the United Front's CPAFFC had invited him on trips in December 2006 and in March 2008, where he met with Hu both times.[42] But at seven days, the Olympics trip was his longest known trip since leaving his China post in December 1975. In Beijing during the Olympics, the eighty-four-year-old Bush explained his credo on China. "Give credit," Bush said, "for how far they have come; that's what I do."[43]

According to many measurements, China had indeed come far. By 2006, the country had become the world's largest holder of foreign exchange reserves and by 2008 the United States' largest creditor. U.S.-China bilateral trade grew from $7 billion in 1985 to $365 billion in 2010, the same year it overtook Japan to become the world's second-largest economy.[44] In a report just weeks after the October 2011 death of the co-founder Steve Jobs, Apple's CEO, Tim Cook, said that for his company's growth in China "the sky's the limit."[45]

For many Americans, however, the financial crisis highlighted America's worrying dependence on Beijing and the problems with outsourcing manufacturing to China. Why transition to a service economy if a crisis—whether it be financial or, later, a pandemic—can annihilate demand for services? The MIT economist David Autor called the cumulative effect of China's rise on America's economy "the China shock." He explained, "About 40 percent of the decline in manufacturing between 2000 and 2007 was due to the China shock, so roughly a million fewer manufacturing jobs."[46] One of the key findings of Autor's research on the China shock is that "the adverse impacts of trade are highly concentrated among specific worker groups and locations."[47] According to Autor, "Manufacturing is very geographically concentrated. It's not like there's a few dolls made in every county across the country—these things are made in just a few places."[48]

Meanwhile, some of Beijing's old friends recognized that the power was shifting in the relationship. In May 2007, Beijing had announced a $3 billion stake in Blackstone, the private equity firm run by the friend of China Stephen Schwarzman.[49] Amid the financial crisis, the investment lost roughly half its value. In late 2008, Schwarzman met with the former premier Zhu, who served with him on the board of the Tsinghua University School of Economics and Management.[50] To China's minister of finance, Zhu described Schwarzman as "the guy who lost your money." Long gone were the days of the Party focusing on sneaking thousands of dollars of payments to obscure political fundraisers. This new friendship was accounted in the billions, and the power balance was shifting.

The then Treasury secretary, Hank Paulson, the former CEO of Goldman Sachs, met his "old friend" vice-premier Wang Qishan for a meeting in June 2008. "You were my teacher. But now here I am in my teacher's domain, and look at your system," Wang said.[51] In his 2015 book, *Dealing with China,* Paulson wrote, "The crisis was a humbling experience, and this was one of its most humbling moments."[52]

Beijing had come far enough to start meaningfully challenging the United States. The U.S. financial crisis and the slowly dawning understanding that China could unseat American hegemony ended the superlative period of U.S.-China relations. During the 2008 campaign, Chinese hackers broke into the campaigns of both Obama and John McCain, where they stole the private correspondence between McCain and the Taiwanese president, among other classified information.[53] Amid tense negotiations during the December 2009 Copenhagen climate change summit, Beijing sent a vice foreign minister to meet with Barack Obama and Angela Merkel, a snub that helped torpedo a deal.[54]

The business climate for foreign companies grew stormier. Google, which had entered the Chinese market in 2006, left four years later, after frustrations with censorship and a series of hack attacks against the company that originated in China.[55] "I really worry about China," the GE CEO, Jeffrey Immelt, told a group of Italian executives in June 2010. "I am not sure that in the end they want any of us to win, or any of us to be successful."[56]

Immelt was right: Beijing didn't want American corporations to dominate in China, or globally, or for America to remain the most powerful country in the world.

And yet, Obama and his team took office maintaining many of the gentle and accommodating policies of his predecessors. Obama refused to meet with the Dalai Lama in 2009, while Secretary of State Hillary Clinton initially declined to push China on human rights.[57] "I certainly think we tested the limit of how far you can get with China through positive engagement," the deputy national security adviser Ben Rhodes said about the early Obama administration.[58] "We needed to toughen our line in Year 2, and we did that." In October 2011, Secretary of State Clinton wrote an influential essay in *Foreign Policy* magazine, announcing what later became known as the "pivot" to Asia: the United States, she said, would remain a Pacific power.[59] And in November, Obama announced the basing of twenty-five hundred troops in northern Australia—the first substantial U.S. military expansion in the region since the Vietnam War.[60]

The problem, however, is that the Obama administration refused to countenance challenging the Party and its rule over China. Indeed, the official policy throughout Obama's first term was to strengthen the Party, not to weaken it; as Obama liked to say, he welcomed a "strong, prosperous, and successful" China. In her essay in *Foreign Policy,* Clinton referenced America's "serious concerns" for human rights in China and the country's moves in the South China Sea. And yet, Clinton's views on China were strikingly Kissingerian. "Some in our country see China's progress as a threat to the United States; some in China worry that America seeks to constrain China's growth.

We reject both those views," she wrote in the essay. "The fact is that a thriving America is good for China and a thriving China is good for America."

Moreover, corporations refused to publicly acknowledge the reality that Beijing favored domestic companies over international or American ones. Indeed, it wasn't just a problem in America. In July 2009, amid tense negotiations between global mining companies and the Chinese steel industry over the price of iron ore, Beijing decided to detain four executives from the Anglo-Australian mining giant Rio Tinto—including Stern Hu, a Chinese-born Australian citizen and the head of the company's Shanghai office—and later convicted them for receiving bribes and stealing commercial secrets.[61] According to reporting by the Australian journalist John Garnaut, Rio Tinto hired Kissinger and paid him roughly $5 million for consulting, and reportedly to help arrange a meeting with the vice-premier Wang Qishan.[62]

Kissinger's advice for Rio Tinto? Build "trust" with its dominant partner, the Party. And so in March 2010, after the sentencing, the chief executive of Rio Tinto's iron ore group, Sam Walsh, fired all four men and condemned their "deplorable behavior that is totally at odds with our strong ethical culture."[63] That month, Rio Tinto co-sponsored the China Development Forum, a Party propaganda event, and in July it signed a major agreement with the state-owned Chinalco.[64] By 2015, China accounted for an astonishing $19 billion, or 40 percent, of Rio Tinto's global sales annually. The company's head of iron ore praised "the deep respect, the friendship and the reciprocity that has resulted from working very closely together."[65]

In a 2013 American Chamber of Commerce in China survey, 78 percent of respondents described their two-year outlook for business in China as optimistic or slightly optimistic, with only 7 percent expressing pessimism. GE quickly backpedaled from Immelt's criticism, saying that the CEO's remarks were misreported: "Mr. Immelt also discussed the attractiveness and importance of China as a market for GE during a discussion on the complexities of doing business globally."[66] Not long after Immelt's comments, his predecessor, Jack Welsh, visited Shanghai and reminisced about investing in the country in the 1990s.[67] "We all had our fingers crossed that the sky would be the limit," he said. "And we basically turned out to be right."*[68]

The business elite and the diplomat consultants both benefited from and advocated for this status quo. "The most nonpartisan foreign policy in America today is Chinese policy," Kissinger said in October 2012.[69] "Eight American administrations since 1971 have pursued essentially the same course. I am very hopeful that this will be continued." Kissinger's reputation as a realist provides cover for his China policies to seem rational and helpful for America, instead of self-serving, by benefiting Kissinger and the Party. "Friendship with China should be one of the key elements of American foreign policy, and getting to know and understand each other better is the key to the relationship," he told Xinhua in 2011.[70] "What has remained in my experience is the friendship and loyalty that Chinese people show to their friends."

Kissinger's On China—part memoir, part pop history, part plea for understanding, and part paean to Chinese strategic brilliance—came out in May 2011, just prior to celebrations in China for the fortieth anniversary of Kissinger's first trip to the country. "The Chinese people will never forget the historic achievements you have made," the then vice-chairman Xi told him in Beijing in June.[71]

In his book, Kissinger refused to consider the idea that China could threaten the United States. "The whole theme of my book is that it is essential for China and the United States to cooperate to build the new international system," he told China Daily.[72] In May 2011, Kissinger met with Bret Stephens, then a columnist at The Wall Street Journal, to promote On China.[73] For the first half hour, Kissinger parried and deflected questions about human rights, Hong Kong, Taiwan, and China's leadership. Then he paused. "I really think that what you should say is that you tried to get down this road with me," he advised. "I won't do it. I've written what I have to write on the subject. Let me take my beating as a result of that, and just stop it. That's

---

* In his 2021 book Hot Seat, Immelt wrote how the state-run firm China Railway "stole" GE's technology in the late 2000s. But even fifteen years later, the most Immelt felt he could say was, "That wasn't fair, but I viewed it as part of the learning process."

a bigger news story than anything I can possibly say in an interview. I will not now discuss a confrontational strategy with China in a formal way." How can one be a nuanced thinker and public intellectual if one refuses to countenance the great possibility of an aggressive Beijing? Or even a Beijing that, like Kissinger predicted in his 1979 memoirs, turns against the United States?

In his book, Kissinger does criticize Mao for the "brutal" 1958–1962 Great Leap Forward, which led to the deaths of tens of millions of people, but does so coyly. "But for once, Mao had set a challenge so far outside the realm of objective reality that even the Chinese people fell short of its achievement," he writes.[74]

The way Beijing manipulated Kissinger, who turned eighty-eight in 2011, exemplifies how Beijing played to the egos of ex-politicians. China was where Kissinger received, in the words of Friedberg, "the psychic rewards that come from believing that they are helping to promote peace and the gratification of being revered and well treated by Beijing."[75] Before a June 2011 trip to Beijing, a reporter asked Kissinger if he had meetings planned with Chinese leaders. "I would be amazed if there were not," he said, "because they know what I need, what I want." In October 2006, the Democratic mayor of Los Angeles, Antonio Villaraigosa, had found himself staying in the same Beijing hotel as the then eighty-three-year-old Kissinger.[76] A Los Angeles Times reporter encountered Kissinger at the hotel and asked him what he thought about the mayor's visit. "I think he's getting the Grade A treatment," said Kissinger, "and I've been here 40 times and I know what the Grade A treatment" is like. "Nobody treats ex–cabinet officials like the Chinese do," said Jorge Guajardo, a former Mexican ambassador to China. "No one does."

It wasn't just former cabinet members who were enthralled by their friendly treatment. After meeting Chairman Hu at a 2006 dinner at the White House, the Chicago mayor and Obama ally, Richard M. Daley, finally persuaded him to visit his city in January 2011—the first time in history that a Chinese leader visited Chicago. "It's a big deal," Daley told reporters before the visit. "Big, big, big. Big deal."[77] During the trip, Hu visited a Confucius Institute at a Chicago high school and told Daley that "across the entire United States, Chicago stands at the forefront in developing relations with China."[78] In March 2011, two months before he left office, Daley made his fifth mayoral trip to China, where he spent two weeks.[79] "I'm kind of envious when you come to China to see all the progress they have made," he said, and repeated his dream of making "Chicago the most China-friendly city" in America.[80] As many prominent Americans do after retiring from public service, Daley joined a series of corporate boards, universities, and law firms; he also joined the investment and advisory firm Tur Partners as its managing principal. None of this is inappropriate.

In a move that went unreported at the time, however, Tur and Daley funded the public relations and media coverage of the then vice-premier Liu Yandong's November 2013 trip to Chicago.[81] Tur Partners paid more than $50,000 to the PR firm Edelman to manage the process, including arranging speeches and events, according to a government filing.[82] During the trip, Liu told Daley to serve as a "bond" between the two countries.[83] How is it appropriate for an ex-mayor to propagandize the trip of a top Party official in that ex-mayor's home city? Tur wrote that the purpose of Liu's trip "is to encourage a people to people exchange between China and the United States."[84] Daley might not have known that "people to people exchange" is United Front code for a type of policy that links Party-approved Chinese with unsuspecting Americans. But Liu certainly knew: from 2002 to 2007, she ran the United Front Work Department.[85]

Many Chinese political institutions, while radically different from their American counterparts, can be described in American terms. China's military, the People's Liberation Army, for example, swears its loyalty to the Party, not the country. The PLA is the Party's armed wing: it both defends the nation and serves as an attack dog for the Chinese political system. By picturing if the U.S. military swore its allegiance to the Democratic Party, one can get a rough sense of the PLA. The government-owned railroad Amtrak and the American propaganda network Voice of America share some similarities to Chinese state-owned enterprises and to Chinese propaganda stations, respectively.

The United Front is radically different. Imagine if the United States had a state religion. But instead of trying to convert other governments and citizens, it tried to prevent them both from knowing the true nature of that religion and from opposing it. It tasks "foreign friends" (agents) with "telling the truth" (spreading propaganda) about China. Xi described United Front work as "drawing the largest concentric circle around the Party" and urged Chinese to show "total devotion" to it.[86]

United Front work, in other words, makes both China and the world safe for the dominance of the Party. It's hard to overstate its importance.

THE STORY OF BEIJING'S INFLUENCE ON AMERICA DURING OBAMA'S second term is a story of great naïveté. The White House still thought they could bind China to the international system and encourage it to follow the American-led world order. They still thought Americans needed to partner with and normalize the Party, to jointly tackle global challenges like climate change. Meanwhile, American friends of China encouraged Americans to overlook the Party's problems and focus on areas of collaboration. Xi, who took office in 2012, steadily increased China's power. Obama could have built a coalition of allies—both domestic groups, like unions, manufacturers, and a bipartisan group of congresspeople, and international, like Japan, the European Union, and Australia—to push back against the pernicious aspects of Beijing's growing power. Instead, Obama listened to China's friends, who counseled patience and tolerance.

Some were financially rewarded for this friendship. A profound conflict of interest came from Gary Locke, the Seattle-born politician and lawyer who served as a Democratic governor of Washington, Obama's secretary of commerce from 2009 to 2011, and then his ambassador to China from 2011 to 2014. After leaving office, Locke joined a law firm to help American companies expand in China. I have "good contacts and good relationships with high-ranking government officials throughout China, at the provincial level and the national level," he said in 2015. "I still keep in touch with many of those officials. I think I can really help use my connections and understanding to benefit Washington State and U.S. companies."

In a February 23, 2016, speech, the founder of the major Chinese multinational Wanda, Wang Jianlin, explained how he overcame U.S.

regulatory restrictions to purchase AMC Theatres, the U.S. movie theater chain.[87] "I went to the then US Ambassador of China Gary Locke and asked him to write a letter recommending us to the US government," he said. After explaining to Locke that he planned to hire American talent and not bring "a large amount" of Chinese movies to the American market, Wang said that Locke "was very pleased and wrote the letter." Soon after, in July 2012, U.S. regulators approved the deal; it closed a month later.[88] That in itself was not problematic: Locke's responsibility as ambassador included improving commercial ties between the United States and China, and that sometimes required him advocating for specific Chinese companies. But in February 2016, two years after stepping down from his ambassadorship, Wang appointed Locke to the Wanda AMC board.[89] That means Locke, while ambassador, advocated for a deal that, soon after leaving office, he benefited from. He still sits on that board. As of November 2020, he has made at least $820,000 from the appointment. This conflict of interest has not been previously reported.*

Like Kissinger, Cohen, and other former top U.S. officials, Locke now consults for U.S. companies in China while praising the transparency of the Chinese system and encouraging closer ties between the United States and China. "Chinese government officials," Locke told the newspaper *China Daily* in an interview published in November 2018, "were so open and friendly."[90]

Beijing has exploited a weakness in the American system.[91] Senators, admirals, mayors—officials at every level of the American government have stringent corruption restrictions. Ex-officials, and the family members of current and ex-officials, have perilously few requirements.

Why don't American companies hire former Chinese chairmen or premiers and bring them on fancy speaking tours of America? Why aren't former Chinese provincial Party secretaries on the boards of Chinese companies that invest in America? Why don't Americans sell the former chairman Jiang on the idea of saving America, as the evan-

---

* Wanda sold most of its AMC shares in 2021. Locke told me, "I never agreed to send such a letter and never sent such a letter." He added that he has "never shied away from criticizing China."

gelical Carter thought he was doing for China? They can't. According to interviews with several people with high-level Party connections, former Politburo members are not allowed to travel overseas without special permission from the current Politburo Standing Committee. A Chinese expert on China's leadership, who asked to remain anonymous, said that the rule is so tight that there are likely few cases of retired Politburo members traveling abroad since the death of Mao Zedong in 1976. "In China, ex-leaders basically don't leave the country," said the scholar David Lampton.

Is there a grand Party plan to corrupt American officials? I don't know. I've seen no evidence to suggest it; moreover, plans change: confidential blueprints warp as soon as reality hits them. The great lengths to which Beijing goes to prevent its ex-leaders from going overseas, however, show how aware it is of the corruptibility of former officials.

Greed is far from the only motivator of ex-officials: some did it for a misguided sense that they were actually helping. One of the saddest capitulations came from Carter, who after leaving the presidency in 1981 eschewed consulting, paid speeches, or corporate board seats. He dedicated his post-presidency years to reducing homelessness, promoting democratic elections, and stopping the spread of diseases. He won the Nobel Peace Prize in 2002, twenty-one years after leaving office, "for his decades of untiring effort to find peaceful solutions to international conflicts, to advance democracy and human rights, and to promote economic and social development."[92] For decades, the Carter Center had promoted village elections in China, to try to encourage the spread of democracy there—a worthwhile task.

But when Xi came to power, Beijing prohibited Carter from working on village elections. Instead, Xi reportedly suggested Carter take up the cause of improving the U.S.-China relationship.[93] Carter interpreted this as a call to help preserve the Party. In 2015, the Carter Center partnered on a "scholarship exchange" program and conference with the *Global Times*, a Party tabloid that is considered an embarrassingly jingoistic publication even among many liberal Chinese.[94] The Carter Center claims that its website chinaelections.org, which it launched in 2002, "became the most visited political reform

portal inside and outside China."[95] In 2008 it built chinatransparency
.org, a now defunct website which the center called "a clearinghouse
for articles related to China's transparency."[96]

That might have been true in the past, but it's certainly not anymore. When I visited the first website in December 2019, the top story
was a *People's Daily* propaganda piece about Xi; when I visited again
in August 2021, the top story was about Xi's calls to strengthen the
Party. And the second website highlights an article about heroism
among female Chinese soldiers in the Red Army during the 1930s.
Written by the brother of the longtime senior adviser to the Carter
Center's China program Liu Yawei, Major General Liu Yazhou—
who is married to the United Front's Li Xiaolin—the article debates
whether Chinese women should maintain their virginity before marriage. In a letter, Yawei expressed "firm disagreement" with the characterization of Carter and his center, and said that "for two decades,
the Center's China programming has played an instrumental role
in promoting Chinese democracy and liberalization." Today, when
Carter speaks about China, he does so in an almost uniformly positive tone. China "has not wasted a single penny on war" since 1979,
Carter said in April 2019, ignoring the hundreds of billions that the
Party spends on internal security in places like Xinjiang and Tibet
or the hundreds of billions it spends annually on its military.[97] As a
result, Carter said, the country is "ahead of us. In almost every way."

AS OFTEN HAPPENS, THE AMERICAN PUBLIC WAS MOVING IN A DIF-
ferent direction from the political elite. From 2011 to 2016, the polling
nonprofit Pew found that the percentage of Americans who viewed
China unfavorably grew from 36 percent to 55 percent.[98] Eighty-nine
percent of Americans surveyed felt that the American debt held by
China and the loss of U.S. jobs to China were serious concerns, while
86 percent worried about the growing trade deficit.[99]

During the 2016 campaign, Trump fed on this energy. "We can't
continue to allow China to rape our country, and that's what they're
doing," he said on May 1, 2016, while campaigning for the Republican
nomination.[100] And it worked: in the primaries, Trump won eighty-

nine out of the one hundred counties most affected by competition with China, according to an analysis by *The Wall Street Journal*.[101]

But the friends remained ascendant until at least 2019. Just like with Gingrich in 1995, Kissinger served as a moderating impulse for Trump's views on China once he was in office. Kissinger and Trump met on May 18, 2016, at the Kissinger Associates' office in Manhattan. "It doesn't get any more establishment than this guy," the CNN host Ashleigh Banfield said as she announced the meeting.[102] Trump complimented Kissinger's "immense talent." Trump wasn't alone in his pilgrimage. By February 2015, before the campaigning season had even begun, the Republican presidential hopefuls Scott Walker, Marco Rubio, Chris Christie, and even Rick Perry had all visited Kissinger.[103]

After Trump broke decades of precedent and took a phone call with the Taiwanese president in December 2016, Kissinger went to work. That month, on Kissinger's advice, the Trump team turned down a proposed meeting with the Dalai Lama. Trump is the first U.S. president since Ronald Reagan not to meet with the Tibetan spiritual leader and enemy of the Party. "Trump once told me, I never want to hear from you about Taiwan, Hong Kong, or the Uyghurs," his former national security adviser John Bolton said in 2019. "I didn't even want to try him on Tibet."[104]

Until the trade war accelerated in 2019, and in some areas until the coronavirus ravaged America in 2020, Trump and his administration were surprisingly moderate—even weak—when it came to Beijing. Part of it had to do with Trump stacking his team with wealthy financiers—men who both benefited greatly from China's rise and were unwilling to fully unwind their financial relationships with the country. Trump's Treasury secretary, Steve Mnuchin, his first secretary of state, Rex Tillerson, and his commerce secretary, Wilbur Ross, all had conflicts of interest with China that might have blunted their desire to push back against Beijing. In 2017, the family of Trump's son-in-law and senior adviser, Jared Kushner, even considered partnering with the Party-connected Chinese insurance company Anbang to redevelop a New York City office tower, while Kushner's sister Nicole Meyer hawked a controversial visa program to

Chinese investors.[105] Trump's ambassador to China, Terry Branstad, the longtime governor of Iowa, didn't have any meaningful financial ties to China. But he seemed to actually believe he and Xi were "old friends," because the two had met in Iowa in 1985.[106]

I obtained Chinese corporate documents that showed Ross served on the board of a Chinese joint venture until January 2019, nearly two years into his term as commerce secretary. That joint venture, now called Huaneng Invesco WLR (Beijing) Investment Fund Management Company Ltd., is an investment partnership formed in September 2008 between Huaneng Capital Services, the American management company Invesco, and a firm Ross founded, WL Ross & Co.[107] Huaneng Capital Services is an arm of China Huaneng Group, a major state-owned power producer.[108] (The Trump officials all denied any impropriety. In an October 2020 statement, Ross disputed that he had remained on the board, calling it a "false narrative.") While there is no evidence that Ross directly benefited from the joint venture while serving as commerce secretary, entanglements like this violate America's national interest and show the strength of the Party's influence in America.

It wasn't just a problem for people in the administration. Some of Trump's outside advisers and supporters blunted the impact of the trade war. The casino magnate Sheldon Adelson and his wife, Miriam, were together Trump's single largest donors; they spent more than $82 million during the 2016 election cycle and $90 million in 2020.[109] (Adelson died in January 2021.) Adelson's passion, and the cause for which he is best known, is Israel. He owned one of that country's largest newspapers and donated hundreds of millions of dollars to Jewish causes. The largest political donor in the 2012 presidential elections, the 2018 midterm elections, and the 2020 election, Adelson reliably funded candidates he viewed as supportive of the state of Israel. "I'm a one-issue person. That issue is Israel," Adelson said in 2017.[110]

But while he funded Israel, Beijing funded him: the five properties that Adelson's Las Vegas Sands owns in Macau brought in nearly two-thirds of the company's revenue.[111] Legalized gambling remains a highly regulated industry, and Beijing could easily have wiped billions of dollars from Adelson's net worth by curtailing the flood of mainland tourists to Macau—where they need a visa to enter—by legalizing gambling in the nearby Chinese province of Hainan, or by simply restricting Las Vegas Sands' ability to operate in the country. "Sheldon Adelson highly values direct engagement in Beijing," a 2009 State Department cable released by WikiLeaks says, "especially given the impact of Beijing's visa policies on the company's growing mass market operations in Macau."[112]

Moreover, Las Vegas Sands' license to operate in Macau expires in 2022. Beijing maintained a surprisingly large sway over Adelson's legacy, his fortune, and his ability to generously fund Israeli causes. And so, Adelson pushed for better relations with Beijing. In September 2019 and in August 2020, Adelson spoke to Trump and warned him that the China trade war could hurt both the U.S. economy and Trump's 2020 election prospects—a veiled threat, considering how helpful Adelson was in getting Trump elected.[113]

Even as this book goes to print in late 2021, U.S. officials often take a gentler tone on China than their predecessors did three decades ago. That partially reflects China's growing power. But it also reflects something else. "I want to be very clear about something," said Biden's secretary of state Tony Blinken in a March 2021 interview. "Our purpose is not to contain China, to hold it back, to keep it down." Until 2020, Trump himself couldn't even seem to imagine that Xi didn't want what was best for him. "Xi and I will always be friends," Trump tweeted in April 2018, "no matter what happens with our dispute on trade."[114] In January 2020, the two sides signed a provisional deal about the trade war. Xi, Trump said, is a "very, very good friend of mine."[115]

Successive generations of friends have written about the bewitching splendor of Chinese hospitality. "It was the first time I have been greeted by the entire cabinet of a government, the first time a whole city had been turned out to welcome me," Edgar Snow wrote in his unpublished diary about his 1936 arrival at Party headquarters.[116] "I was overcome at the warmth of the greeting," he added. "As a China Hand I find myself beguiled from day to day by the ethnic charm of ordinary Chinese," wrote John K. Fairbank, a Harvard professor and the father of China studies in the United States, in a 1989 letter about Snow's experiences.[117]

In November 2017, Trump visited Beijing for what Chinese offi-

cials described as a "state visit plus."[118] The Party shut down the Forbidden City, the emperor's palace in the center of Beijing, for Trump
and his wife to take a private tour, and offered a magnificent welcome ceremony near the hulking state building the Great Hall of the
People.[119] Trump later told reporters that Xi "treated me better than
anybody's ever been treated in the history of China."[120] After Trump's
trip, a former U.S. government official spoke to Kissinger about how
the spectacle, flattery, and friendship hoodwinked Trump on his trip
to Beijing. "Of course I know it worked" for Trump, Kissinger said
with a smile. "It worked for me."

PART TWO

FRIENDS IN HIGH PLACES

CHAPTER FOUR

Shangri-La

★

IN THE 1990S, RICHARD GERE WAS ONE OF THE WORLD'S BIGGEST stars: the rakish charmer in *American Gigolo* and *Pretty Woman*, whom *People* magazine called "the sexiest man alive." During the height of his fame, while introducing the Oscar for best art direction in 1993, Gere decided to make a statement. He set the scene with dramatic aplomb.

Eschewing a prepared speech about how the painters Peter Paul Rubens and Rembrandt would be art directors "if their agents could get them work"—pause for polite laughter—Gere speaks instead about his passion: freeing Tibet from Chinese rule.[1] "I had a thought about something, actually," Gere says. He glanced around nervously and then continued, with confidence, describing his vision. "I wondered if Deng Xiaoping is actually watching this right now, with his children and his grandchildren," he said about the Chinese leader, knowing "what a horrendous, horrendous human rights situation there is in China, not only towards their own people but to Tibet as well. And when it was this kind of, if something miraculous, really kind of movielike, could happen here, where we could all kind of send love and truth and a kind of sanity to Deng Xiaoping right now, in Beijing, that he will take his troops and take the Chinese away from Tibet and allow these people to live as free independent people again." Gere looks up earnestly as the audience applauds. "So, thought. We send this thought, we send this thought out. Send this out." And then, with a shy grin, he introduced the nominees for best art direction.

Gere's speech sparked a chain of events that launched a failed global movement for Tibetan independence, taught Disney how to yield to Beijing, and changed the way Hollywood made movies (more on that in chapter 5). And it helped ruin Gere's career: he hasn't starred in a studio film since 2008. "There are definitely movies that I can't be in because the Chinese will say, 'Not with him,'" he said in 2017.[2]

What happened to Gere's dream of a Hollywood-led push to free Tibet, and of Hollywood's independence from China? In a word: friendship. As it grew wealthier, Beijing learned it could trade access to the Chinese box office for acquiescence, and so it punished Hollywood studios that condemned Chinese repression in Tibet. Studios then stopped making movies critical of China in general and gradually started releasing films that promoted the Party's worldview.

It didn't all happen right away. There was a delay as the Party gathered its strength and bided its time. But the year 1997 was the beginning of the end for realistic depictions of Beijing in Hollywood. That year, Hollywood studios released three films critical of the Party: MGM's *Red Corner* starring Gere, about an American businessman imprisoned in China; Sony's *Seven Years in Tibet*, directed by Jean-Jacques Annaud, about a mountaineer in that Himalayan kingdom before the Party invaded; and Disney's *Kundun*, directed by Martin Scorsese, a coming-of-age story about the current Dalai Lama.

Back then, China felt persuadable. By the mid-1990s, the Soviet Union had collapsed and Communism seemed defeated, representing the "end" of history, as a popular book title claimed. China, the lone major exception, was desperately poor and still ostracized for slaughtering unarmed students in Tiananmen Square. Many Americans felt they could change China and persuade it to grant Tibet its independence—including Congress, which described Tibet as "an occupied sovereign country."[3] In 1994, young Tibetans and Americans founded Students for a Free Tibet, an organization that mobilized college students to advocate for the independence of the plateau.

In 1997, China's GDP was a measly $864 billion—roughly 6 percent the size of 2020—and Beijing offered Hollywood and other American institutions almost no financial or cultural capital. China's box office was minuscule. Like building schools in Africa or improving access to clean drinking water, advocating for the independence of the Chinese region of Tibet seemed safe. Indeed, in the mid-1990s, Tibet felt outside global politics. Unlike the atrocities occurring in places like Rwanda, Burma, Bosnia, and East Timor, Tibet seemed both more remote and more potent, a holy land sullied by Communist invaders.

Free Tibet T-shirts and bumper stickers proliferated. Celebrities embraced the movement. Americans embraced Tibet. In 1995 the J. Peterman catalog, parodied on *Seinfeld* for its obsession with exotic items, sold a $175 Tibetan shaman's jacket. "It's official," the catalog said.[4] "Crystals are out, Tibetan Buddhism is in."

BUDDHISM AND TIBET HAVE A LINK THAT GOES BACK TO THE EIGHTH century, when the Tibetan king decreed the religion to be the faith of his people. Starting from the sixteenth century, some of the monks found to be the reincarnation of Avalokitesvara, the god of compassion, held political power over Tibet. Tibetans called these monks the Dalai Lama, which means "ocean of wisdom."

The thirteenth Dalai Lama, who lived from 1878 to 1933, became the political and spiritual ruler of a unified Tibet, independent from foreign rule. He was a skillful judge of people—the ninth, tenth, eleventh, and twelfth Dalai Lamas all died under suspicious circumstances before the age of twenty-two—and lucky. In the 1920s and 1930s China was a failed state, riven by warlords and the Japanese invasion. But he was complacent. When he died in 1933, he bequeathed a troublingly anachronistic society, with a hidebound education system and a minuscule army.

When the Chinese announced the "liberation" of Tibet in 1951—two years after Mao announced the founding of the People's Republic of China—most of the Tibetan government supported the arrangement as a reasonable return to past relationships between an empire and a tributary. They had little choice. Besides, "they knew that when a great power had risen on Tibet's borders in the past, the Buddhist leaders had usually come to an arrangement with it," writes the historian Sam van Schaik. "In each case these foreign leaders had left Tibetans to run the country and allowed the monasteries to thrive. Why then should Mao be any different?"[5]

But Mao was different from the rulers of the past. Thousands of

Tibetans starved to death from 1958 to 1962, joining tens of millions of other Chinese who died during the Great Leap Forward, a mobilization campaign that created the worst famine in history. In the 1960s, the Party created what it disingenuously calls the Tibet Autonomous Region and what some Americans call "Tibet proper," a mountainous nearly 500,000-square-mile territory that encompasses the capital city, Lhasa, the Chinese side of Mount Everest, and Mount Kailash, a major pilgrimage site. Four other Chinese provinces engulfed the rest of Tibet. In 1966, Mao launched the Great Cultural Revolution, a violent, anarchic period where Chinese worshipped Mao as a god. Photographs of Tibet during the Cultural Revolution show Tibetans marching with posters of Mao, burning holy Buddhist scriptures, and attacking monks and spiritual leaders.[6] Thousands more died.

In his will, the thirteenth Dalai Lama had predicted the terror of the Mao years. "Barbaric red communists" will force us "to wander the land as the servants of our enemies," he wrote in 1932.[7] "Both day and night will be an unending round of fear and suffering."[8]

WHILE TIBETANS MOSTLY IGNORED THE WEST UNTIL THE 1980S, Westerners had long been fascinated with the mythical idea of a magical and untouched Himalayan kingdom, the plateau's altitude implying spiritual elevation. "Here are to be found the most skillful enchanters and the best astrologers," Marco Polo wrote in his thirteenth-century *Travels*. While the Tibetans are the world's "greatest rogues," he wrote, they possess the power to "bring on tempests and thunder-storms when they wish and stop them at any time."[9]

The 1933 novel *Lost Horizon* by the British writer James Hilton and the 1937 film version by Frank Capra sparked a worldwide craze for an exoticized Tibet. "In these days of wars and rumors of wars," reads the text on the screen in the beginning of the film, "haven't you ever dreamed of a place where there was peace and security, where living was not a struggle but a lasting delight?" *Lost Horizon,* which originated the term "Shangri-La," told of a Himalayan utopia governed by a wise monk whose people remained ageless and unravaged. When President Franklin Delano Roosevelt converted a government camp in the woods of Maryland into a presidential retreat in 1942, he dubbed it Shangri-La. (In 1953, President Dwight D. Eisenhower renamed it Camp David, in honor of his father and grandson.)[10]

The current Dalai Lama is a mythical figure, enthralling most of the people who meet him, bridging the ancient and the modern with his saffron robes and infectious smile. "I have never seen any body assume more complete and natural control of great assemblies," wrote a British political officer in 1940, after observing the Dalai Lama's enthronement in Lhasa, when the Dalai Lama was only five years old.[11]

After fleeing China in 1959, the Dalai Lama established a government in exile in Dharamshala, a city in the Indian Himalayas. In the 1960s and 1970s, the Beats adopted Tibet; *The Tibetan Book of the Dead* entered, in the words of one scholar, "the LSD canon."*[12] The U.S. government didn't allow the Dalai Lama to visit until 1979, and even then only as a religious figure and not as a leader in exile.[13] But gradually, the Himalayan kingdom and its spiritual leader worked their way back into the American cultural imagination. In the 1980 comedy *Caddyshack*, Bill Murray's character grumbles about how the Dalai Lama, with his "flowing robes, the grace, bald, striking," refused to tip him after a round of golf. The 1983 Star Wars film *Return of the Jedi* had the mammalian Ewoks speaking high-speed Tibetan, and 1986's schlocky *Golden Child* featured Eddie Murphy as a social worker who saves a mystical Tibetan boy (a film that even Murphy later called "a piece of shit").[14]

Tibet really resurfaced in public consciousness in the United States in late 1987 after the Dalai Lama, addressing the Congressional Human Rights Caucus, called for greater autonomy for Tibet and urged Beijing to stop its "great destruction" of the region.[15] In the riots that erupted after the Dalai Lama's remarks—some Tibetans believed the Dalai Lama addressing Congress meant the U.S. government would save Tibet—Chinese police detained John Ackerly and Dr. Blake Kerr, two Americans who happened to be in Lhasa at the time. When the two men returned to the States, they spoke at dozens of television

---

* Led Zeppelin sang about a "yellow desert stream, like Shangri-La beneath the summer moon," while the Kinks, in a 1969 concept album about the fall of the British Empire, titled a song "Shangri-La," which had the lyrics "You've reached your top and you just can't get any higher."

networks, universities, and think tanks across America. "We were credible witnesses" to Chinese brutality, Kerr told me, "not as a bunch of tourists, but as a doctor and a lawyer." And what they witnessed sickened them. "I saw Chinese police shooting Tibetan men, women, and children from the rooftops and while hiding behind poles, walls, and windows," Kerr said.[16] "I watched in horror as a Chinese soldier shot a ten-year-old boy through the heart, soon dying in his father's arms while I tried unsuccessfully to save him." In December 1989, nine months after Beijing ordered martial law in Tibet, and six months after Chinese soldiers massacred protesters in Tiananmen Square, the Dalai Lama won the Nobel Peace Prize for his "nonviolent opposition to China's occupation of Tibet."[17]

By the mid-1990s, the idea of mystical Tibet, a land of spiritual wisdom whose people yearned to break free from the yoke of evil, became an easy cultural reference point. The Dalai Lama called himself "a simple Buddhist monk," but he also led a "sunrise meditation for world peace" in Central Park for Manhattan's 1991 "Year of Tibet," guest edited the Christmas 1992 issue of French *Vogue,* and lent his face to a famous Apple advertisement exhorting consumers to "think different."[18] When Bernardo Bertolucci attended the Paris premiere of his 1993 film, *Little Buddha*—starring Keanu Reeves as the Buddha—the Dalai Lama sat next to the Italian director, holding his hand.[19] "When His Holiness won the Nobel Peace Prize, there was a quantum leap," Gere said. "He is not seen as solely a Tibetan anymore; he belongs to the world."[20]

Gere has said that meeting the Dalai Lama in 1982 changed his life and set him on a Buddhist path.[21] "Once you come in contact with these people, you're in the family and you never want to leave," Gere said in 1996. "You feel like you're onto something true and right."[22]

In 1997's *Red Corner,* Gere played an American TV executive framed for murdering the daughter of a Chinese general in Beijing. Possibly the last major American feature film to show Tiananmen Square, *Red Corner* features an imprisoned Gere tortured by Chinese guards, until a beautiful Chinese lawyer manages to win his freedom. Beijing detested the film. Critics did too: Roger Ebert called it a "contrived and cumbersome thriller designed to showcase Richard Gere's unhappiness with Red China."[23] Ebert was right about the last part:

Jon Avnet, the film's director, described it as a "pretty good shot at the Chinese judicial system," while Gere said it highlighted the country's human rights abuses.[24] "If you talk about the judicial system in China you're clearly talking about the judicial system in their colonies," he said. "And if it's that bad in China, imagine how bad it is in Tibet."

Gere wasn't alone in his sensibility toward the Tibet situation: Ethical and spiritual reasons inspired the directors of *Seven Years in Tibet* and *Kundun* to make their movies. "In the early stages of my life I was a director of commercials," the *Seven Years* director, Jean-Jacques Annaud, said in 1996. "I was like a whore! And I had a nervous breakdown before I was twenty-eight. When I went into movies, I resolved that henceforth I would only go upstairs for love, not money." And that was how *Seven Years* spoke to him. "For Westerners, Tibet taps into this unconscious reservoir of yearning," he said. "And Tibet represents one of the most extreme alternative ways of structuring a society. If that disappears, then our own lives become something like a highway with no exits."

The film follows the Austrian mountain climber and Olympic skier Heinrich Harrer, played by Brad Pitt, as he escapes a British prisoner-of-war camp and takes refuge in Tibet, a delightfully foreign society where he finds purpose and meaning as the tutor to the young Dalai Lama. "It's not hard to understand why Hollywood likes this subject," the film's screenwriter, Becky Johnston, said. "After all, it's epic and huge in scope but kinder and gentler in message." She added, "I was drawn to the subject because I hoped to find paradise."[25]

A meeting with the Dalai Lama himself convinced Martin Scorsese. "Something happened," he said of his meeting with the spiritual leader. "I became totally aware of existing in the moment. It was like you could feel your heart beat; and as I left, he looked at me. I don't know, but there was something about the look, something sweet. . . . I just knew I had to make the movie."[26]

Named for an honorific of the Dalai Lama meaning "the presence," *Kundun* featured an entirely Asian cast of mostly amateur actors, with an enchanting score by the Buddhist Tibet supporter Philip Glass. The film tells of the Dalai Lama's youth, enthronement, education, meeting with Mao—who charms the young leader, until he tells him that "religion is poison"—and escape to India. In the last lines of the film, an Indian soldier asks him if he is "the Lord Buddha." The Dalai Lama replies, "I think that I am a reflection, like the moon on water. When you see me, and I try to be a good man, you see yourself."

Scorsese's films had long depicted violent retribution, and often in a sympathetic light, but in *Kundun* pacifism reigns. It opens with the claim that "in a war-torn Asia, Tibetans have practiced nonviolence for over a thousand years," and an early scene shows the child who would become the current Dalai Lama separating two insects from fighting. In a scene from *Seven Years,* a Tibetan monk chides Harrer for killing earthworms, saying, "Those earthworms could have been your mother." (The Tibetan writer Jamyang Norbu said that "every Tibetan I know shudders over that scene" for its absurd caricature of Tibetan pieties.)[27] While Scorsese might have been naive—the writer Ian Buruma compared him to a "gushing schoolgirl" in the presence of the Dalai Lama—he seemed to be involved for the right reasons.[28]

In the mid-1990s, studios had several more films about Tibet under development. The production company Merchant Ivory purchased the film rights from the climber Kerr's book *Sky Burial,* about witnessing the 1987 uprising in Lhasa; while Ismail Merchant, one half of that production company, was producing a film based on the mystic explorer Alexandra David-Néel's 1929 book, *Magic and Mystery in Tibet.* And the martial artist Steven Seagal's production company optioned the 1992 climbing novel *The Ascent,* written by the mountaineer and writer Jeff Long.

While in a Nepali prison in 1977, Long had befriended leaders of the CIA-sponsored Tibetan guerilla movement: In the 1950s and 1960s, the CIA had secretly flown dozens of Tibetans to Colorado, to train them as guerilla fighters to fight against the Chinese Communists. But the then secretary of state Kissinger ended the program, to lay the groundwork for his meeting with Mao, and the CIA quietly paid off the Tibetan fighters. Seagal had planned to turn *The Ascent* into a CIA adventure story. He would star as a CIA agent in the film, provisionally titled *Dixie Cups,* after a slang term for the dispensability of native allies for the CIA: use them and toss them.

Tibet-minded activists in Hollywood and elsewhere didn't know it at the time, but the mid-1990s "were really the high point" for the movement, said Ackerly, the then head of the International Campaign for Tibet, an organization fighting for democracy and human rights on the plateau. In June 1996, the rap trio the Beastie Boys and the band the Smashing Pumpkins headlined the Tibet Freedom Concert in San Francisco, the largest benefit concert of the 1990s.[29] Acts like the Red Hot Chili Peppers, Yoko Ono, and Rage Against the Machine performed for a crowd of more than 100,000 people. Several months later, Harrison Ford introduced the Dalai Lama at a fundraiser for Tibetan causes. He addressed an audience that included Gere, Sharon Stone, Leonard Nimoy, and R.E.M.'s Michael Stipe. The longtime China journalist Orville Schell, who attended the event, wrote that the Hollywood elites "exhibit a respect bordering on veneration that few besides Nelson Mandela or Mother Teresa could have elicited."

Meanwhile, the Party watched this happen from across the world. There were indications that Hollywood's Tibet fascination upset Beijing. It denied *Kundun* and *Seven Years* permission to film in Tibet and pressured the Indian government, which hosts the Dalai Lama and the Tibetan government in exile in the northern city of Dharamshala, to reject them as well. *Seven Years* ended up filming in the Argentinian Andes, and the otherworldly Atlas Mountains in Morocco served as the backdrop for *Kundun*.

In 1996, Schell visited the set of *Seven Years* in Argentina. He spoke with Lama Kyab, a Tibetan extra, then in his early twenties, who had fled Tibet by foot when he was fifteen. "Oh, it's great!" he said, when asked what he thought about the film. "This will be a big punch in the face for the Chinese government."[30]

TO UNDERSTAND HOW BEIJING IMPROVED ITS FORTUNES IN HOLLY-wood, we must look at China's long relationship with film and its negotiation with its own image abroad.

Long before China came to dominate Hollywood, Hollywood dominated China's film industry. In the 1930s and 1940s, as the Communists, the Nationalists, and the Japanese fought for control of the country, Chinese citizens flocked to Hollywood movies: American films represented more than 75 percent of the box office.[31] Disney's Mickey Mouse appeared in China as early as 1931, and *Snow White and the Seven Dwarfs* later screened in Beijing and Shanghai, helping to spur the creation of China's animation industry.[32]

After the outbreak of the Korean War in the summer of 1950, the newly triumphant Communist government banned American films. China has almost "swept out American movies that poison the Chinese people," the Party newspaper the *People's Daily* proclaimed in January 1951. Indeed, until five years after Mao's 1976 death the only American movie Beijing permitted to screen in China was 1954's *Salt of the Earth*, a film about striking miners made by a team blacklisted during Hollywood's McCarthy paranoia, which Beijing deemed sufficiently leftist and anti-imperialist.

In the late 1970s, as the Party slowly began to engage with the outside world, American media executives once again saw the possibility of a massive Chinese market for their content. Bob Iger, who ran Disney as CEO from 2005 to 2020, first visited Beijing in 1979 while working for ABC Sports. "I stayed in a hotel—I swear, this is the complete truth—my mattress was filled with straw," he said. "No one spoke English. I spoke no Chinese. It was almost a joke, but a great adventure."[33]

China's media market steadily grew more open in the 1980s. In 1986, Beijing allowed Disney to sign a licensing agreement to supply cartoons for Sunday evening broadcast: Disney's then president, Frank Wells, told *The New York Times* that the allure of hundreds of millions of potential customers drew the company to China.[34] Meanwhile, Chinese intellectuals started to debate whether to import Hollywood movies, even though, as one critic wrote, the films "are fraught with pornography, violence and crimes."*[35] While Beijing closed the country after the 1989 Tiananmen massacre, several years later the Party felt secure enough to permit the entry of some major American movies. Nineteen ninety-three's *Fugitive* ("Fleeing to the Ends of the Earth" in Chinese), the first Hollywood blockbuster screened contemporaneously in China since the 1940s, attracted huge crowds

---

* The critic Zhou Mingrong: "After providing sensational stimulations, what these films leave for us is only restlessness, fear and lost hearts."

in China during the brief window the Party allowed it in theaters.*[36] "More than 50,000 people saw the film here," the manager of a cinema in Shanghai told the *Los Angeles Times*.[37] "Most people said they hadn't seen a film like this for a long, long time."

Meanwhile, China's homegrown box office was struggling. In 1953, Beijing nationalized its film industry and created sixteen state-owned studios, to produce between 120 and 150 feature films annually.[38] For four decades, most movies these studios made faced two problems: they were awful, and no one wanted to watch them. A 1999 journal article titled "The Embarrassment Caused by Importing Major Films" cites a survey interviewing fifteen hundred residents in five Chinese cities. While 46.9 percent said going to the cinema was their favorite pastime, less than 10 percent said they regularly watched Chinese movies. And while some of China's best films were made in this period—the understated love story *Farewell My Concubine*, which Miramax distributed in the United States, won the top award in the 1993 Cannes Film Festival—the industry suffered: as China grew considerably wealthier from 1979 to 1992, annual cinema attendance actually decreased, from 27 billion to 10.55 billion.

To improve its film industry, Beijing decided to use Hollywood expertise and channels to improve and market Chinese films, a strategy it called "going to sea by borrowing a boat." Chinese leaders revered the power of Hollywood movies to change minds and sway beliefs: to propagandize, in other words. In March 1998, Chairman Jiang encouraged top Chinese leaders to watch *The Titanic*, "not to propagate capitalist things," but because "we absolutely cannot think we are the only ones who do 'ideological work'"—a Party concept about persuading people to follow the Party's thoughts to ensure that they adhere to the "correct" ideology.†[39] The Party, in other words, respected and feared the power of Hollywood films and needed Holly-

---

* Beijing allowed the release of 1978's *Superman* in 1986, only to withdraw it one month later.

† Public Security Bureau officials gave the fifty-four-year-old dissident Xu Wenli, who had spent twelve years in solitary confinement for advocating democracy in China, a free ticket to see *Titanic*. "I told them I've seen the movie," Xu said. "But they said it doesn't matter, I can go and see it one more time."

wood as an ideological ally. And so when *Red Corner, Seven Years,* and *Kundun* appeared, it acted. Starting roughly a year before the three films' 1997 releases, Beijing began publicly and privately excoriating the films, the actors who starred in them, the studios that made them, and the Hollywood that nurtured them.

Beijing employed a two-pronged strategy to counter Hollywood's support for Tibet and the three films. First, it tried to advance its own myth—its "ideological work"—to persuade Americans to see the plateau as a place of ethnic harmony where Tibetans lionized Han Chinese and the Party. That strategy failed. A senior Disney executive told me that the Chinese pushed for Disney to distribute their "truly terrible low-budget propaganda films," including one that featured "noble peasants explaining Communist slogans. There was just no way we could put our corporate name on those dreadful films," he said. In April 1997, Beijing released a $1.7 million propaganda film, *Red River Valley,* about Chinese and Tibetans working together to oppose a 1904 British incursion into Tibet. The minister of radio, film, and television, Sun Jiazheng, called the film "the best I have seen in my post"; a *Variety* reviewer, one of the few Americans to actually see the film, called it "spectacularly lensed but deficient in most other aspects" and added that it had "enough political baggage to overload an army of Sherpas."[40]

The far more effective strategy attacked the companies themselves, and evoked the resonant myth of the Chinese market—the fabled market that American businesses and their diplomat consultants strove to conquer. In September 1997, Beijing announced it was banning the three studios that made the films for "viciously attacking China and hurting Chinese people's feelings."*[41]

Disney was the prime target of Beijing's ire. The company "has indicated a lack of respect for Chinese sovereignty," said a vice-director of the Ministry of Radio, Film, and Television in December 1996.

---

* In May of that year, news broke that the mountaineer Harrer, played by Brad Pitt in *Seven Years in Tibet,* was a member of the SS, Hitler's feared secret police. Even with the gift of Harrer's secret Nazi past—"The Tibet craze set off by Hollywood is being used by a Nazi to advertise himself," trumpeted the *People's Daily*—Beijing still focused on Disney.

"Because of this, we are thinking over our business with Disney." Beijing canceled the visit of a high-level Chinese delegation to Disney's headquarters in California and pulled Disney's popular program *Dragon Club* from Chinese networks.[42] Rumors circulated that Beijing would exclude Disney from future deals.[43] "Has Disney become the forbidden studio?" Bloomberg News asked in 1997. "All of our business in China stopped overnight," Disney's CEO, Michael Eisner, said later.[44]

The controversy came at a pivotal time for Disney. Founded in 1923, the studio began flourishing in the 1930s and 1940s, with fantastical and uplifting films like *Snow White and the Seven Dwarfs* and *Dumbo*.[*][45] As the company opened Disneyland in California in 1955 and Disney World in Florida in 1971, it continued to expand, from a corporation to an institution to a state of mind; a place where, as Jiminy Cricket croons in *Pinocchio*, "anything your heart desires will come to you."

But in 1993, Disney purchased a studio known for controversial films—the Weinstein brothers' Miramax. That year, Miramax had received twelve Oscar nominations. (The much larger Disney received only five, and all for *Aladdin*.) Disney thought that it could manage the Weinsteins and their contentious films while benefiting from their films' prestige. But the partnership was complicated from the beginning. "It would be hard to imagine two companies more ill-suited than the white-bread, wholesome Burbank home of Mickey and Donald, and the two slobs from Queens with their ragtag, anything-goes company," writes the journalist Peter Biskind.[46] Indeed, the Weinsteins' irascibility—more than two decades before more than eighty women accused the co-founder Harvey of

---

* "People sought deliverance from their black and white lives, filled with unemployment, hunger, and despair, hoping for escape into a colorful utopia," writes the researcher Tracey Mollet in an article about the popularity of 1937's *Snow White and the Seven Dwarfs*. Snow White's "patient, self-reliant, and sincere character," she writes, "keeps the hope alive within Americans that if they remain positive and hardworking, good will triumph over evil and they will be released from the suffering of their everyday lives." Adjusted for inflation, the film grossed nearly $1 billion domestically in 2019's dollars, more than *Jurassic Park* and *Avatar*.

sexual assault, sparking the #MeToo movement—and their films worried Disney executives. Nineteen ninety-four's *Priest*, about a gay reverend—which the Weinsteins tried, and failed, to release on Good Friday—and 1995's *Kids*, about the sex lives of New York City teenagers, seemed about as distant from Disney values as could be imagined.

In April 1994, the company's president, Wells, died in a helicopter crash. In a power struggle that shook the company for a decade, two of Hollywood's most powerful men—the super-agent Michael Ovitz and the Disney executive Jeffrey Katzenberg—fought to succeed Wells. Ovitz won, in part on the strength of his connections. Tasked with managing international operations in the mid-1990s, Ovitz expressed confidence about his understanding of China and his friendship with Chinese officials. "I had the mayor of Shanghai to my home for dinner," he later boasted about that period, "because I have the most definitive collection of Ming Chinese furniture in the United States of America."*[47]

Disney in the Eisner-Ovitz era emphasized international expansion. While *Aladdin* (1992) and *The Lion King* (1994) were huge commercial and critical successes in the United States, Disney also planned for them to appeal to the Middle East and Africa markets, respectively, in what one film scholar called an "exotic offensive."[48] *The Lion King* and *Toy Story* (1995) had both performed well in China, and Disney wanted to sell Chinese consumers toys and books tied to the movies, and to build theme parks that would further build support for its brands. By the time of the *Kundun* controversy, they had big plans to sell their library of animated films into the Chinese market, and for *Mulan* (1998), an animated story about the eponymous ancient Chinese heroine who dresses as a boy to become a war hero and to honor her father. Disney executives thought *Mulan* would please Chinese moviegoers and government officials alike by promoting Chinese culture globally. A senior executive at Disney in the 1990s, who asked to remain anonymous, told me that back then the company was investing in the future of its relationship with

---

* Eisner fired Katzenberg in 1994. Ovitz lasted two tumultuous years as Eisner's second-in-command, until getting fired in 1997.

China. "Make or lose a little bit and get our characters known to the public, use that leverage and popularity to get permission for a dedicated Disney channel, which we knew was a long shot, and then maybe one day, far off, open a theme park," he told me. "Bunt now, home runs later."

At first, Disney and the other studios reacted admirably to the *Kundun* controversy. "We have an agreement to distribute 'Kundun' domestically, and we intend to honor it," said a Disney spokesman in November 1996.[49] The press praised Disney for its resolve. This "was a welcome stand at a moment when the American government and American companies seem increasingly prepared to put aside important democratic principles in hopes of expanding commerce with China," *The New York Times* wrote.[50] *Newsweek* published a cartoon showing Mickey Mouse staring down a Chinese tank in Tiananmen Square. Beijing's threats "won't change anything that's happening here at all," Frank Price, the former CEO of Columbia Pictures, told *The New York Times* in December 1996. "If anything, it will stiffen the resolve of the creative community to do what they think is right."[51] Hollywood had moral and financial right on its side. Who cared if Beijing retaliated? And what could it even do if it tried?

BUT THE LURE OF THE FABLED CHINESE MARKET BECKONED. BEHIND the scenes, Disney decided to hire the man who could move between the American and the Chinese governments with more ease than anyone else: Kissinger, by this time known as the top fixer for China. "I, unfortunately, have not been trained in the political environment and I'm learning," Eisner told Charlie Rose in October 1997. "Kissinger is telling me what to do."[52]

The hiring of a consultant like Kissinger reflected another reality of the studios and their relationship with China: they did not just represent themselves. Beijing understood the studios belonged to major corporations that produced far more than films. Sony, which released *Seven Years,* dominated in sales of electronics, music, and video games. Besides its list of other brands, like ABC and ESPN, Disney sold a fantasy, purchasable not only via a theater but through theme parks, action figures, clothes, books, and cruises.

In 1995, the head of the Seagram's conglomerate, Edgar Bronfman Jr., purchased an 80 percent stake in Universal Studios. Bronfman, who had worked with Scorsese on his previous film *Casino,*
heard that his next film featured the Dalai Lama. "With Seagram's, we
had a huge spirits and wine business in China, so I was like, 'I'm not
doing this. I don't need to have my spirits and wine business thrown
out of China,'" Bronfman said.[53]

The cold reality of influence took a while to dawn on the star actors and directors whom the studios relied on for content. "This idea
of suddenly a filmmaker in foreign policy," a PBS interviewer said
in an October 1997 interview. "This is a new territory," Scorsese responded.[54] Meanwhile, Pitt upset many in the Tibet community by
refusing to take a stand. "You shouldn't speak until you know what
you're talking about," Pitt told *Time* for an October 1997 article.
"That's why I get uncomfortable with interviews. Reporters ask me
what I feel China should do about Tibet. Who cares what I think
China should do? I'm a fucking actor! They hand me a script. I act.
I'm here for entertainment, basically, when you whittle everything
away. I'm a grown man who puts on makeup."

While many in the Tibet community cheered the attention brought
by the films, Disney prepared to bury *Kundun.* "We're distributing
it, and hopefully the Chinese'll understand," Disney's CEO, Eisner,
told Charlie Rose in October 1997, several weeks before the release
date, hinting at his company's strategy. "In this country you put out
a movie, it gets a lot of momentum for six seconds and is gone three
weeks later."[55] *Kundun* grossed only about $6 million domestically,
on a production budget of $28 million.[56] Disney "didn't push the
picture," Scorsese said. He added, "The market China represents is
enormous, not just for Disney but many other corporations around
the world."[57]

WITH HIS ROARING AMBITION AND EGO, EISNER WAS A PRIME TAR-
get for Party friendship. This is nowhere better recorded than in the
transcript for a secret meeting Eisner had with the Chinese premier
Zhu Rongji in 1998, but only released thirteen years later.

The conversation is so striking that it's worth quoting at length. Zhu brilliantly opened the conversation by claiming not to recognize Eisner. "I've met the head of the Disney Company twice. Was it you I met with last time?" Zhu asked.

"It was Frank Wells," Eisner responded, referring to Disney's former president, who reported to Eisner. "I welcome you, your wife, and your colleagues to China," Zhu responded.

The "purpose of my trip is to put an end to the problems caused by *Kundun*," Eisner said. "We made a stupid mistake in releasing *Kundun*," Eisner told Zhu. "I don't want to go into the details of that film release here. I didn't know anything about the release of that movie, though of course I realize that is no excuse. I learned about it from the *New York Times* and was shocked." (Eisner, of course, didn't learn about a Disney film from *The New York Times*.)

He continues, "Afterward, we released the film in the most passive way, but something unfortunate still happened. This film was a form of insult to our friends and it cost a lot of money, but other than journalists, very few people in the world saw it. The bad news is that the film was made; the good news is that nobody watched it. Here I want to apologize, and in the future we should prevent this sort of thing, which insults our friends, from happening. In short, we're a family entertainment company, a company that uses silly ways to amuse people."[58]

In Disney's defense, it is a corporation with shareholders, and Beijing had warned it. "I remember hearing frequent admonitions" from China Film Group, the senior Disney executive told me, about the disaster that would ensue if Disney released *Kundun*. Though Disney would never say so baldly, it was beholden to its shareholders, not to ethical guidelines. "Disney's potential business in China is infinite," the entertainment lawyer and media adviser Peter Dekom said in 1996. "But Disney had to decide whether it wants to facilitate business or stand for free speech."[59]

Disney decided. It admitted its mistakes and apologized. For its tagline, the Gere film *Red Corner* used the Party expression "leniency for those who confess, severity for those who resist," a concept that, according to the Chinese legal scholar Jerry Cohen, "has been the fundamental maxim of criminal justice" in China—regardless of whether the accused is guilty or innocent.[60]

After Eisner apologized, Zhu replied, "I very much admire your courage in correcting mistakes and the efforts you've made to promote Sino-American friendship. This also proves that you're a very far-sighted businessman, and it's also an important factor in ensuring the success of the Disney Company." As part of Disney's forgiveness gesture, it bought two Chinese films to distribute in the United States, including one of those "dreadful" propaganda films. Disney released it as *A Time to Remember;* the film's Chinese title is *Red Lover.*

Disney's financial performance in 1998 was poor, and the company slashed Eisner's annual bonus. On Eisner's October trip to meet Zhu, he noticed the proliferation of McDonald's golden arches throughout Beijing. In Disney's unusually pessimistic shareholders' letter later that year, China represented a rare ray of hope. "I am completely confident that the Chinese people love Mickey no less than Big Mac," Eisner wrote.[61]

Beijing didn't overturn the Disney ban until February 1999: too late to save *Mulan,* which Beijing ensured performed worse in China than almost any other American film of that era. And when NATO forces accidentally bombed the Chinese embassy in Belgrade in May, it sparked an anti-American backlash that prompted Chinese officials to remove Hollywood movies, including *Mulan,* from Chinese screens.[62]

But Disney had repented. In November 1999, Disney could announce Hong Kong Disneyland, its fifth theme park. Amid the Asian financial crisis and the uncertainty following Hong Kong's 1997 return to the Chinese government, Disney negotiated a financially favorable deal. But it marked the first time it built a theme park majority owned by a political institution—in this case, the Party.[63]

In February 2000, Eisner joined several other media tycoons in the China Trade Relations Committee, a body that lobbied Congress to permanently normalize trading relations with China, facilitating China's entry into the World Trade Organization in December 2001. When it joined the WTO, Beijing increased the quota of foreign films allowed from ten to twenty annually. "Not only does it take patience,"

Iger said in 2001, in reference to expanding in China, "but a level of cooperation with the government that is obviously unique."[64]

TIBET AS A SOCIAL JUSTICE ISSUE FOR THE AMERICAN ENTERTAIN-ment elite always had an air of theater to it. Like any polity that has ever existed in the history of Earth, the independent kingdom of Tibet was no utopia. Violence, sexism, and destitution disfigured it. The Chinese, who claimed they "liberated" Tibet, were right that for many people, both rich and poor, the plateau was a dismal place—a "hell on earth ravaged by feudal exploitation," writes the Tibetan scholar Tsering Shakya in *The Dragon in the Land of Snows: A History of Modern Tibet Since 1947*. In 1934, a committee of Tibetan hard-liners arrested the liberalizing politician Tsipön Lungshar and planned to execute him. But they "feared that the spirit of someone as willful of Lungshar might become a vengeful ghost," the scholar Melvyn C. Goldstein writes in his history of modern Tibet. So instead, they removed his eyeballs: one with a knife, and one by squeezing his scalp until the eyeball popped out. In 1947, three years before the Chinese invasion, the former regent of the fourteenth Dalai Lama died in mysterious circumstances: possibly from poisoning, or choked by a silk scarf, or from the pain caused by torture to his testicles.

Nevertheless, the legend persists. Growing up in bleak Syracuse—"Snow City" in Chinese—I dreamed of escaping a painful adolescence for someplace otherworldly and strange: a sort of Dungeons and Dragons with mountains. After my senior year of high school in 2002 and six months after China entered the WTO, I spent a month in Tibet. I joined a student adventure program called Where There Be Dragons, so named because early cartographers placed dragons on unknown spaces on maps. Our Tibetan guide, a mountain of a man, bragged about killing Han Chinese. The Tibetans working at our hostel in Lhasa drank barley beer out of tin mugs and played Bob Marley's "Redemption Song" on repeat:

> *Won't you help to sing,*
> *These songs of freedom?*

My idealistic companions and I had thought Tibetan independence would be only a matter of time—a common view in the Clinton and early George W. Bush years. "I will not stop working until I meet the Panchen Lama in a free Tibet," said the Republican congressman from New Jersey Chris Smith in 1998, referring to the spiritual leader second in importance only to the Dalai Lama in Tibet.[65] "I believe the Dalai Lama will return to Tibet, having saved His country, having completed the task set before Him in childhood," the screenwriter of *Kundun* (and *E.T.*), Melissa Mathison, wrote in May 1997, in the foreword to the Dalai Lama's autobiography *My Land and My People.* "If He does not, we will all share in the blame. But if He does, we all share in the glory."[66] At the August 1996 Tibetan Freedom Concert, the Beastie Boys co-founder and practicing Buddhist, Adam Yauch, said, "If everyone focuses simultaneously on this one issue, then Tibet will quickly become free."[67] We didn't just assume Tibet would be independent; we knew it, like the faithful waiting for the Second Coming. We were all wrong.

In 1998, China produced only $18 million in revenue for major Hollywood studios—roughly the same as Peru.[68] And yet Disney still capitulated. It knew which way the winds were blowing.

CHAPTER FIVE

Hollywood Learns to Please Beijing

★

IN THE EIGHTEENTH MOVIE IN THE JAMES BOND FRANCHISE, 1997'S *Tomorrow Never Dies,* a mad press baron attempts to start a war between China and Britain to improve his ratings. As he prepares to unsuccessfully murder Bond, Carver, as Bond villains are obligated to do, describes his master plan: a Chinese general will "take over the government, negotiate a truce, and emerge as a world leader, with a Nobel Peace Prize." Carver himself fights for a bigger prize: "exclusive broadcasting rights in China for the next hundred years."*

Tomorrow Never Dies originally had a radically different plot. They had to "junk" the script shortly before shooting, the film's director, Roger Spottiswoode, told the film critic John Brosnan. "The first version involved the hand-over of Hong Kong to the Chinese and, of course, there was a nuclear reactor under the island that was about to explode," Brosnan wrote. Spottiswood steered the film in a different direction after the production company hired Kissinger as the film's "diplomatic adviser."[1]

Tomorrow Never Dies is the first known example of a major Hollywood movie rewritten to please Beijing. Starting in the late 1990s, moviemakers began to alter their movies to fit Beijing's whims. It didn't happen overnight. But by late in the first decade of the twenty-first century, Hollywood was allowing Beijing to dictate how China was portrayed. In the same way that friends of the Party no longer

---

* The idea is nonsensical: A media market will remain static enough that one entity—especially a foreign one—can hold exclusive rights for a century?

need explicit directives (or direct cash payments), the image makers of Hollywood no longer even attempt to create movies that will portray China in a way the Party might deem negative.

It goes well beyond just the representation of China in film. Hollywood now routinely releases censored versions of its films in China and complete versions in the United States. Beijing's influence on Hollywood has increased the stereotyping of Muslims in films and guided the output of movies toward the crude blockbuster, the kind of movie that relies on familiar characters (and explosions) rather than nuanced storytelling. Today, Hollywood often advocates and lobbies for the Party's interests in America.

Most problematically for American national security, the Party's influence on Hollywood gives it a monopoly on the portrayal of China in film. Remember that unlike Moscow's, Beijing's influence on America is not about sowing chaos. Rather, it's about controlling the way Americans think about China. Beijing wants Americans to believe that China's continued rise, and eventual global dominance, will be both peaceful and inevitable. Over the last fifteen years, Hollywood movies have taught Americans that China is a force for good. "Leave it to the Chinese," said the White House chief of staff in the disaster film *2012* (2009), played by Oliver Platt, after Beijing partners with America to save the world. "I didn't think it was possible, not in the time we had."[2]

In a sense, the Party's influence on Hollywood has enabled it to practice its technique of friend recruitment on a global scale. It will never be able to invite every American voter into a closed-door meeting for tea and blandishments; so it propagandizes its view of China via the most powerful mass media the world has ever seen.

It could have happened differently. (American television, for example, is far more honest in its portrayal of China, a dynamic I discuss in chapter 7.) On the Chinese side, partnering with Hollywood was risky; Chinese officials, worried about entangling with the wolfish Americans, sometimes referenced the relationship as the 1990 Kevin Costner film *Dances with Wolves*.[3] How much Western "spiritual pollution" should the Party import? Some believed Hollywood's mastery of ideological work could spread anti-Party thoughts disguised as "universal values," and even encourage Chinese citizens to overthrow the Party. As the Wanda founder Wang Jianlin put it in 2007, "Always eating McDonald's and watching US films will eventually cause problems for our national culture and beliefs."[4]

But partnering with Hollywood allowed Chinese leaders to improve the technical and soft skills of their film studios so they could make movies Chinese citizens want to watch. It also taught them about the levers of power in Hollywood and how to ensure that American studios toed the correct ideological line. Or, as China's then leader Jiang said as he recommended his colleagues watch *Titanic,* only by "knowing one's enemy and knowing one's self can we win a hundred battles."

Party officials often condemned Hollywood executives and other Americans for "politicizing" the U.S.-China relationship, by including in films or commentary anything that could be construed as critical. But speaking in Chinese, Party officials often make clear three things: that everything is political; that film is one of the best methods for convincing people of the benign strength of the Party; and that film should advance the Party's politics. As China's then chairman, Hu Jintao, said in a December 2005 speech, "All those working with China's film industry should stick to the correct political direction all the time."[5]

IT MAKES SENSE THAT BEIJING WOULD WANT TO PARTNER WITH Hollywood, but why the reciprocation?

In the early years of the twenty-first century, Hollywood still made movies featuring Beijing as the nemesis. *Spy Game* (2001) starred Robert Redford as a grizzled CIA agent and Brad Pitt as his protégé. The film features the latter jailed in a horrific Chinese prison after failing to rescue his paramour, who had killed the Chinese premier's nephew. But the relationship was shifting, and not just because of Party influence. The Taiwanese American director Ang Lee's *Crouching Tiger, Hidden Dragon* (2000), a subtle martial arts tale of love and loyalty, earned ten Academy Award nominations, broke the record for highest-grossing international film in America, and convinced some studio executives that films with Chinese elements could be profitable.

China was still a tiny film market: in 2000, Hollywood films earned less than $20 million in the Chinese box office.[6] The country's piracy rate was the world's highest, with illegal DVDs eating up roughly 90 percent of potential revenue.[7] And studios received only 13 percent of a film's profits in China, much lower than in other foreign markets.

But like executives at other American consumer products companies, film executives salivated over the size of the potential market. Back in 1997, MGM's president of worldwide marketing, Gerry Rich, had praised his studio's *Red Corner,* calling the film "the first time that the communist Chinese legal system has been portrayed as painfully accurate as it is."* Just three years later, MGM's chief financial officer, Daniel Taylor, focused on a different aspect of China. "No matter how you measure it," he said in 2000, "you're looking at about more than one billion sets of eyeballs."[8]

And so, during the turn of the century, Hollywood quietly canceled the films it had planned about Tibet. "It petered out," Blake Kerr said, when I asked him about Merchant Ivory's plans for the film based on *Sky Burial,* his book about his experiences in Lhasa during the 1987 protests. Merchant Ivory found itself swept up in the Tibet craze, and when that faded, Kerr said, the film "just wasn't going to happen."

What about *Dixie Cups,* Steven Seagal's rollicking CIA adventure story set in Tibet? "Warner Bros. was on the verge of greenlighting it, when we got the word that China shut it down," Jeff Long told me. "The word I got was that Warner Bros., and Hollywood, were not going to have any sort of audience in general for any products if they continued on this path of criticizing China and its human rights. I was told that China had expressed extreme displeasure." Long sighed. "*Dixie Cups* would have been smack in the middle of it all. But after that, Hollywood drifted away."

Amid the improvement of ties that coincided with China's entry to the WTO in 2001, Beijing increased the number of foreign films per-

---

* In 1997, Beijing allowed only ten foreign films to screen annually in China. In the understatement of the century, Rich said, "My guess is *Red Corner* will not be one of them."

mitted under its quota system from ten to twenty.[9] To increase their access to the Chinese market in the early years of the twenty-first century, American studios starting co-producing films with China, a method that allowed them to skirt the twenty-film quota by localizing production.

Co-productions also started acclimatizing studios to how and why the Party censored. Universal Studios' first joint production in the country was *Pavilion of Women* (2001), a love story set in chaotic World War II–era China and starring Willem Dafoe and the Chinese American actress Luo Yan.[10] The producers submitted their script to the Chinese Film Bureau, which offered "comments and advice," Luo said, like requiring them to rewrite a character to make him seem less "depressing."[11]

Teaching Hollywood how to censor for Beijing was a subtle process. As China's box office grew in the first decade of the twenty-first century, countless meetings between studio executives and Chinese directors, producers, and Party officials gradually convinced Hollywood decision makers that it was easier to yield to the small changes Beijing demanded.

Indeed, most of the changes Hollywood studios had to make for Beijing seemed insignificant. In 2006's *Casino Royale*, the first Bond film permitted to screen in China, Judi Dench as M, the head of the British Secret Intelligence Service, had to replace the single line "Christ, I miss the Cold War" with "God, I miss the old times." Subtle, but, as Dench told an interviewer, "not quite the same thing."[12]

Beijing was training Hollywood to develop the awareness required to pass Chinese censorship. And so Hollywood studios experimented, studied, and tinkered with what would allow them to please the Party and thrive in the Chinese market. In 2005, Sony released *Memoirs of a Geisha,* based on a popular American historical novel about a mid-twentieth-century Japanese entertainer. Sony expected its casting of three Chinese stars—Zhang Ziyi, Gong Li, and the Malaysian-born Michelle Yeoh—would appeal to mainland audiences. But in November censors accepted the film, only to block it several months later, claiming that Chinese playing Japanese would offend Chinese audiences.[13]

In 2005, less than a decade after it dropped its plans to adapt *Sky*

Burial, Merchant Ivory released *The White Countess,* the first Western film shot entirely in mainland China.[14] Starring Ralph Fiennes and Vanessa Redgrave, the film tells of a love between an American diplomat and a Russian refugee in 1930s Shanghai. The film's screenwriter, the novelist Kazuo Ishiguro, complained about the film's censorship and the impact it had on the American version of the film. "I didn't go to China with them, but there would be messages sent back saying that because of government censorship, I'd have to change lines, or words, throughout the script," he said in 2006. Ishiguro had to remove every mention of the word "revolution" from the screenplay.[15]

In 2007, Disney released its third movie in the franchise it created from its hugely popular theme park ride. *Pirates of the Caribbean: At World's End* starred Johnny Depp and Keira Knightley from the first two films and the Hong Kong actor Chow Yun-fat, who played the pirate lord of the South China Sea. With a budget of more than $300 million, it was at the time the most expensive movie ever made.

The series' first film succeeded in China in 2003, but Chinese censors banned *Pirates of the Caribbean: Dead Man's Chest* (2006), possibly because of the sequel's portrayal of ghosts and cannibalism.[16] Disney expected the casting of Chow to appeal to Chinese audiences. In early May, several weeks before the film's premiere, Disney even sent Chow on a promotional trip to Hong Kong Disneyland, an event covered widely in Chinese media.[17] But censors "weren't ecstatic with how the Chinese pirate was portrayed," said Anthony Marcoly, distribution chief at Walt Disney Studios Motion Picture Distribution International.[18] Censors halved his screen time in a Chinese version, from twenty minutes to ten minutes, and the film earned a disappointing $17 million in China.

Sometimes the censorship justifications seemed logical, or at least consistent. Sexuality, especially between two men, flummoxed censors. Beijing almost certainly banned Ang Lee's *Brokeback Mountain* (2005) for its depiction of a love affair between two male cowboys, and it cut nude scenes in the version of the Brad Pitt and Cate Blanchett global drama *Babel* (2006) permitted to screen on the mainland.[19]

But just as often, the censors decisions baffled their counterparts in Hollywood. Chinese censors approved *The Da Vinci Code,* and its May 2006 release to nearly four hundred screens was the largest in Chinese history.[20] Just twenty-two days later, Beijing pulled the film. Some officials from the Chinese government claimed that the film jeopardized social stability among Chinese Christians with its depiction of Jesus fathering children, while others bemoaned that it stole box office from domestic movies.[21] A spokesman for China Film Group blamed *Da Vinci Code*'s declining ticket sales, even though the film was on track to become the second most popular foreign movie in Chinese history, behind *Titanic*. And in December 2007, Hollywood executives said Beijing prohibited the release of all American movies for three months, with no readily identifiable reason.[22] Days later, Chinese officials denied that there ever was a ban. It was all very confusing. The low-ranking Chinese officials speaking to American media probably didn't even know the reasons themselves.

Consistent with Party techniques for exercising power, this capriciousness is a feature, not a bug. Some randomness in the system means that Hollywood moviemakers must constantly be on edge and ready to heed the call from Beijing to change—or else. Too much clarification is a sign of weakness, almost an apology.

This unpredictability, piracy, and unprofitability of the Chinese market frustrated Hollywood executives. And yet, many of them committed to making it work. "We're going to hit bumps in the road, we may even crash the car once in a while, but there is no choice," the entertainment lawyer Peter Dekom said in 2006. "You have to be there."[23]

There are echoes of a toxic relationship in the dynamic between the Party and Hollywood—the latter constantly trying to prod the former for cues to where it stands and how it can curry more favor. And Beijing understands the strength of ambiguity. In 2007, representatives of China Film Group asked Annaud, the director of *Seven Years in Tibet,* to direct a film version of the best-selling Chinese novel *Wolf Totem*. His career faltering, Annaud agreed. He then engaged in what the Party calls a "self-criticism": he admitted his ideological mistakes in making *Seven Years* and asked for forgiveness. "Because I lacked a thorough understanding of China's history and culture, I was unable to predict that after this film came out it would have a negative impact in China; for this, I deeply apologize," he wrote in a 2009 open letter. "Actually, my original intention with the film was always to spread a desire for 'peace.' But things turned out the opposite of what I wanted. That this desire wasn't fully comprehended by some of my audience, I express a deep regret." He "solemnly declared" that he "never participated in any Tibet-related organization or association . . . never supported Tibetan independence, and never had any private contact with the Dalai Lama, and moreover, becoming friends with him is out of the question." In an email, Annaud said he couldn't recall writing those words—and denied that his career was faltering—but said that it "is absolutely correct that I never supported Tibet independence."[24]

It's unlikely that anyone told Annaud what to write. Instead, Annaud, like many others in Hollywood, was internalizing Beijing's demands and speaking in the language of the Party. (Annaud's reply? "To convey identical ideas, I don't use the same wording with my colleagues at the Academie Française and with my grandson.")

He ended the letter with a plea that *Wolf Totem* would "make more people more ardently love China, more ardently love the profound spirit of the people of China."*

PERHAPS IF NOT FOR THE FINANCIAL CRISIS THAT SWEPT THE WORLD in 2008, Hollywood would have continued making movies that contained content deemed offensive by the Party. The Batman film *The Dark Knight* (2008) is one of the last major Hollywood film with a Chinese villain. One of the supporting characters is a corrupt and wealthy Hong Kong accountant—a casting choice which implied that corruption existed in China.†[25]

In March 2007, the actress Mia Farrow and her son Ronan wrote an op-ed in *The Wall Street Journal* criticizing Beijing's support for the

---

* After first denying that he apologized to Beijing, Annaud admitted to writing the open letter "to stop this silly thing."

† *Dark Knight* reigned as the highest-grossing film not to play in China—until 2019's anarchic *The Joker,* which didn't mention China once, but perhaps incited uncomfortable parallels with the unrest and dissatisfaction in Hong Kong. The anti-hero in the 2021 Marvel film *Shang-Chi* is the famous Hong Kong actor Tony Leung, and a smaller villain, a gang leader, is played by the Hong Kong–born American actor Raymond Ma. Besides Hong Kongers, there are no Chinese enemies in modern American cinema.

Sudanese government and its genocide in Darfur, "where more than 400,000 people have been killed and more than two-and-a-half million driven from flaming villages." Beijing, they noted, had appointed Steven Spielberg an artistic adviser to the 2008 Summer Olympics. Did he "really want to go down in history as the Leni Riefenstahl of the Beijing Games"? Spielberg did not. In April, he wrote a letter to Chairman Hu, asking for him to change China's policy toward Sudan.[26] "I believe there is no greater crime against humanity than genocide," Spielberg wrote. In February 2008, he resigned from his position with the Olympics, stating that his "conscience will not allow me to continue with business as usual."[27]

In February 2008, the chairman of the Hollywood lobbying group the Motion Picture Association of America (MPAA), Dan Glickman, told *BusinessWeek* that he "respected" Spielberg's decision on Darfur. Why, the interviewer asked, was Spielberg willing to take a political stance that might offend Beijing and jeopardize opportunities to access the Chinese market? "They are just potential opportunities," Glickman said.

But during the financial crisis, as Hollywood's hiring rates dropped 16 percent and entertainment stocks plummeted, the foreign market began to guide Hollywood decision making. The year 2010 saw no revenue growth in the United States and Canada, while the international film market grew to $31.8 billion, reaching a record 67 percent of Hollywood's total revenue.

China was a rare bright spot for the industry.[28] From 2008 to 2012, while Hollywood was slowly climbing out of the Great Recession, the Chinese film market grew from roughly $630 million to $2.7 billion.[29] Each Hollywood blockbuster that screened in China seemed to mint more money than the last as those potential opportunities turned into actual ones. In July 2009, *Transformers: Revenge of the Fallen* became China's biggest movie ever; several months later, the disaster film *2012* broke that record. *Avatar,* which debuted in January 2010, grossed $204 million, more than triple the take of the film *2012.*[30] And in May 2011, when Walt Disney's *Pirates of the Caribbean 4: On Stranger Tides* opened in China, it beat *Avatar's* opening weekend figures. That month, Katzenberg's DreamWorks released *Kung Fu Panda 2,* which eventually grossed $665 million worldwide. In

China, it grossed $93.19 million, breaking both China's opening-day record and the record for highest-grossing animated film, which was set in 2008 by *Kung Fu Panda*.[31]

The year 2012, which saw Xi become the head of the Party and the military, was pivotal for the Chinese film industry. In May, the real estate conglomerate Dalian Wanda purchased American Multi-Cinema (AMC), at the time the world's largest operator of IMAX screens and now the world's largest movie theater chain.* And a year after China's economy leapfrogged Japan's in 2011, China overtook Japan as the world's second-largest film market.

In February, Xi, then China's vice-chairman and the Party's heir apparent, visited the United States. At a State Department luncheon, he was joined by Katzenberg and Iger (and Kissinger, among others) at the head table.[32] While in Washington, Xi renegotiated the film quota with Vice President Joe Biden. Xi agreed to import up to thirty-four foreign films, provided fourteen were IMAX or 3-D. More important, Xi permitted foreign studios a distribution fee of 25 percent, up from 13 percent and near the roughly 30 percent studios earned in many other foreign markets.[33] This was an exciting change for many in Hollywood, and they were willing to make the sacrifices necessary to maintain their friendship with the Party. "We have a huge market, and we want to share it with you," Zhang Xun, the president of a state-run film body, told Hollywood executives around that time.[34] How? "We want films that are heavily invested in Chinese culture, not one or two shots," she said. "We want to see positive Chinese images." By 2013, the MPAA was publishing a very different message.[35] We recognize, the organization said, "China's right to determine what content enters their country."

WHY DOES IT MATTER IF THE PARTY HAS VETO POWER OVER HOL-lywood films? The question is more clearly answered by plainly describing the situation: for the last two decades, Hollywood has

---

* In 2021, amid both a Chinese crackdown on conglomerates with overseas assets and a Reddit-driven campaign to push up the value of AMC's stocks, Wanda sold the vast majority of its shares in the company.

produced Party propaganda. If this description sounds alarmist or irresponsible, it is because the nature of propaganda has been forgotten in this country.

Propaganda can be far more subtle and common than people think.[36] "There is no means of human communication which may not also be a means of deliberate propaganda," wrote the father of public relations, Edward Bernays, in a 1928 book, "because propaganda is simply the establishing of reciprocal understanding between an individual and a group."[37] *Merriam-Webster* defines propaganda as "the spreading of ideas, information, or rumor for the purpose of helping or injuring an institution, a cause, or a person"—a description broad enough to encompass many Hollywood films, Abraham Lincoln's Gettysburg Address, and most of Trump's tweets.[38] The problem with propaganda, in other words, is often less the content of the message and more the intent of the messenger.

The term "propaganda" only became pejorative in the United States in the 1920s and 1930s, amid the overlapping dawnings of the eras of film and totalitarianism. The power of film alarmed some intellectuals but thrilled the fascists and Communists taking power in Europe and Asia. It especially delighted Lenin and the German minister of propaganda, Joseph Goebbels, who saw its engrossing totality as the supreme method to convince the wavering. The brilliant 1935 documentary *Triumph of the Will*, which opens with Hitler's plane flying through the heavenly clouds and descending to his ecstatic supporters, established in the minds of many Germans the righteousness, purity, and inevitability of the Nazi leaders and their cause.

But most Nazi films were far more subtle than *Triumph of the Will*; they barely seemed to propagandize at all. For every *Triumph of the Will*, there were dozens of saccharine love stories, character studies, and historical dramas. The thirteen years of the Third Reich saw the production of roughly 1,150 feature films. The philosopher Gary Jason, in a 2013 essay on film and propaganda, estimates that less than 20 percent of those films were "outright propaganda pieces."[39] What is wrong, Jason asks provocatively, with those other Nazi feature films?

How, for example, does one explain why the subtle propaganda in the Nazi war romance *The Great Love* (1942) is worse than the subtle propaganda in, say, *Joker* (2019), a coming-of-age film about Batman's nemesis? Both films emotionally manipulate the audience—all feature films with any power do—and both lack transparency of intention. Did the *Joker* director, Todd Phillips, want viewers to understand and condemn murderous psychosis, or to rebel against the unfairness of society? Or did Warner Bros. just think this was the most effective mechanism to impel audiences to consume more media about Batman?

The differences between the two films are their inevitability and integrity. *The Great Love* features a charming German pilot who prioritizes his duty to his squadron above his love for a singer. *The Great Love* had to spread ideas beneficial to the Nazis—loyalty to the war effort and stoicism in the face of personal restrictions. The director, Rolf Hansen, had only a narrow band to express dissenting opinions, while Phillips could have made a movie with a different ideological bent, or make a sequel exposing a different philosophy. In other words, it's inevitable that Hansen's film reached the same conclusions, while Phillips had a wide range of ideological options. He chose; therefore, the movie has more integrity.

How does this relate to Beijing's influence on Hollywood? The issue is not that the Party has corrupted Hollywood over the last two decades. Film has always been a business where commercial considerations often trump art and integrity. Even low-budget films require at least hundreds of thousands of dollars but can provide fantastic returns for investors, who often demand cuts that violate the artists' ideals, to reach a wider audience. "I always thought the real violence in Hollywood isn't what's on the screen," the writer and director David Mamet said in 1997, before China really mattered in Hollywood.[40] "It's what we have to do to raise the money."

Rather, it's that American films allow for a worryingly narrow band of viewpoints about China. Like the distinction between the Nazi film *The Great Love* and *Joker,* the issue is films' inevitability and integrity. Chinese propaganda directed internationally seeks to convince Americans of two things: that China does not threaten the world, and that China's dominance is inexorable. And so that's what American films do.

Like Goebbels, Chinese officials prioritized film as the method for indoctrination, a "transformative emotional mass experience," wrote one Chinese scholar of early Communist history.[41] And like Goebbels, Chinese officials eventually learned that the best propaganda films are the ones that the audiences in China, the United States, and globally don't know are propaganda. The *Seven Years in Tibet* imbroglio had overlapped with the Party's growing acceptance of harnessing capitalist forces. "The film sector must win the market in order to prosper," the Party's propaganda chief, Ding Guan'gen, said in 1998.[42] Or, as the Chinese writer Zeng Yuli put it, make the films "look good, and then use them to transmit the party's preferred values to audiences without them even noticing."[43]

IN HOLLYWOOD, 2012 SAW THE RELEASE OF TWO MOVIES THAT EXEMplified the two types of Chinese censorship and propaganda geared toward Americans. That year's version of *Red Dawn* was MGM's remake of a 1984 cult classic about a Soviet invasion of the United States, with Patrick Swayze, Charlie Sheen, and Jennifer Grey in a small Colorado town fighting off the invaders. The screenplay of the new version featured Chinese invading America. Promotional posters for the film featured the emblem of the PLA on the American flag, with the words "Your freedom has been a lie. Liberation is here."[44]

Beijing responded to the film deal by punishing MGM and the original distributor, Sony. It issued unfavorable release dates for some of their other films in China. And after the screenplay leaked, drawing criticism from Party newspapers, MGM caved. It spent roughly $1 million digitally remaking the film so that North Koreans, rather than Chinese, invade America. The censorship was clear: MGM decided to pull its punches rather than risk jeopardizing its relationship with Beijing.

Red Dawn's capitulation received far more attention than the film *Looper,* which featured a type of censorship that is both more common and more pernicious. "I'm from the future," a mob boss played by Jeff Daniels tells an assassin played by Joseph Gordon-Levitt in *Looper* as he offers him career advice: "You should go to China." The film is set amid a dystopian Kansas City overrun by tent cities, where the only legal tender is silver or gold bars and Chinese money, and in a happy and prosperous Shanghai. Bruce Willis, who plays an older assassin, gets the Chinese character for tiger tattooed on his neck and marries a Chinese woman—the only character in the film not besmirched by poverty, greed, or insanity. "Learn Mandarin," Daniels's character exhorts: in a world where China leads, that's excellent advice. And *Looper* is an excellent film. The China elements aren't jarring. They work.

The problem lies in the making of the film.[45] The screenplay originally envisioned France as the future and cast Willis's character without a Chinese wife. But the director had a difficult time securing funding.[46]

The Los Angeles–based media company Dynamic Marketing Group (DMG) agreed to fund the picture, but only if the director introduced elements pleasing to the Party.*[47] And so the studio replaced the French elements with Chinese ones. DMG partnered with the Shanghai municipal government to design how the city would look in the future.[48] The issue is not the believability of *Looper*'s portrayal of a futuristic Shanghai, but the inevitability—the same problem with the Nazi film *The Great Love*. "They showcased a future China powerfully in the film," DMG's then president, Chris Fenton, wrote. "It was music to the ears of the Politburo and a delight to the Communist Party municipal officials in Shanghai."

Red Dawn represents what you might call a kind of negative censorship: the removing of information harmful to the Party. *Looper,* on the other hand, is a kind of positive censorship: the introduction of information pleasing to the Party. *Looper* represents both an anxiety about a future where China dominated and America declined and a capitulation to that anxiety. And *Red Dawn* reflects the suppression of that anxiety.

The *Red Dawn* scandal embarrassed Sony in both China and the United States: the studios were learning the value of making films inoffensive enough to the Party that they could screen unedited in both China and the United States. While Hollywood movies in the second decade of the twenty-first century occasionally still had Chinese and American versions, studios increasingly preemptively self-

---

* "In the States, we're always focused on what the fans want, what the consumers want," said the co-founder Dan Mintz, "whereas in China, there are two groups of people we need to be aware of: the government and the consumer."

censored, to avoid both public criticism of kowtowing by releasing two versions of the same film and the risk that the American version of the film would upset Chinese censors.

The 2014 hack of Sony Pictures was a milestone in the unfolding story of Hollywood's acquiescence to Beijing. In the Sony film *Pixels* (2015), starring Adam Sandler, aliens attack Manhattan, the Taj Mahal, and the Washington Monument. An earlier script for the film had the aliens breaking a hole in the Great Wall of China as well. But in a December 2013 email released during the hack, the company's chief representative in China called hitting the Great Wall "unnecessary because it will not benefit the Chinese release at all," she wrote. "I would then, recommend not to do it."

Conversations in dozens of emails show how deeply and carefully studio executives discussed censorship. "The film has commercial potential in China and has a very good chance of being accepted by CFG [China Film Group] and passed through the censorship process," wrote Steve Bruno, a senior vice president for international distribution at Sony, in a September 2013 email about a remake of the sci-fi film *RoboCop*. "If we adopt the most conservative and safest approach, that would entail striking any reference to China in the feature," he wrote.[49] Sony's president, Steven O'Dell, agreed. "Changing the China elements to another country should be a relatively easy fix," he wrote. "There is only downside to leaving the film as it is."

Sony's competitors reached the same conclusion: better to placate Beijing in the American version. Studios learned from films like *Skyfall* (2012), where Beijing cut dialogue between the protagonist James Bond and a hostess in Macau, and *Men in Black 3* (2012), where Beijing cut a scene when the heroes wipe the memory of Chinatown residents who have witnessed an attack—in other words, censoring a scene about censorship.[50] "If we only change the China version, we set ourselves up for the press to call us out for this when bloggers invariably compare the versions and realize we changed the China setting just to pacify that market," O'Dell wrote.*

---

* Even before the hack, Sony struggled. "Our world has changed," Sony Pictures' studio head Amy Pascal wrote in an August 2014 email to a colleague. "With disney buying pixar marvel and starwars they left the rest of us in the dust [*sic*]."

Since the *Red Dawn* fiasco, the major studios have not made a film that contains Chinese elements that may offend Beijing. In 2015, the screenplay *Star One,* based on the same Cold War CIA missions to Tibet that so enthralled Seagal in the mid-1990s, appeared on the Black List.[51] Founded in 2005 by a young studio executive aiming to increase diversity in Hollywood, the Black List is a survey of the best unproduced screenplays, many of which eventually got made.[52] *Spotlight, Argo, Slumdog Millionaire,* and *There Will Be Blood* all had appeared on the list, and the *Star One* screenwriter, David Cogge-shall, was thrilled at his inclusion. "It's a public stamp of approval from the town, and gets you on the radar of studio executives and producers who might not have considered you before," he told me by email.

But his film remains unmade. Coggeshall, who described the film as a "road movie through a foreign country with no love story," recognizes it as a difficult sell. Still, he believes perceptions about China play a role. "I do sense a skittishness toward projects that China's government might not approve of or actively ban because that's a significant market taken off the table," he said. "Studios only make a handful of movies each year, so for any (studio) movie to get made, a large number of people have to say yes and continue saying yes over a long period of time, so one reason to say no is usually enough to keep any project from gaining momentum."

Hollywood's growing reliance on China overlapped with an increasingly repressive Beijing. "The present government seems more conservative in all aspects," the then chief representative of Sony Pictures in China, Li Chow, wrote in a February 2014 email. "Lately, members of the censorship board seem uncertain, fearful and overly careful."[53]

In February 2018, Beijing removed the term limits for Xi's chairmanship, a move widely interpreted as signaling that Xi would break the precedent set by his two immediate predecessors and not step down in late 2022 after ten years in power.[54] Amid other changes intended to increase the Party's control over China and the government, in March 2018 Beijing also announced that the Propaganda Department would now oversee the relationship between China and Hollywood.

This was a monumental step for the film world. Previously, a government body called the State Administration of Press, Publication, Radio, Film, and Television (SAPPRFT) managed the relationship. While government officials are often Party members—and SAPPRFT serves the Party's interests—government and Party institutions differ. Party institutions tend to be more obsessed with how China is portrayed and more sensitive to slights against the country. And because they are more powerful, their decisions tend to matter more, and they have more sway. The reorganization, according to a description of the plan released on China's official news wire Xinhua, reflects the "especially important role of cinema in propagating ideas and in cultural entertainment."[55]

Beijing was moving to ensure that the Chinese film industry served the Party. In November 2017, the Party had convened dozens of top actors, directors, and musicians (including the jingoistic *Wolf Warrior 2*'s star and director, Wu Jing; the official Chinese ambassador of the Star Wars franchise and singer, Luhan; and the auteur Jia Zhangke) to study Party directives.[56]

The U.S. government blamed the North Koreans for hacking Sony Pictures: the studio had just released *The Interview* (2014), a screwball comedy about a plot to assassinate the North Korean dictator Kim Jong Un. MGM had replaced the Chinese in *Red Dawn* with North Koreans. But after the 2014 Sony hack, studios feared offending Pyongyang as well. After Moscow's meddling in the 2016 elections, U.S. producers recognized both the demand for stories about Russia and the risks of angering Putin. Films need enemies. What could they do about casting antagonists?

There was no known secret meeting, no cabal that banned producers from casting Chinese or North Koreans as villains. Rather, over the last decade, studios organically reached four solutions. The first and the saddest seemed to be an increase in Muslim antagonists.

The Bond film *Skyfall* features lovingly shot scenes of an intensely wealthy Shanghai: a city of skyscrapers and futuristic technology. The film opens in Istanbul, portrayed as a dirty, dusty city filled with pushcart vendors selling fruits and spices. Neither portrayal is inaccurate, but both are misleading: parts of Istanbul have a modern, cosmopolitan vibe, while parts of Shanghai are impoverished, claustrophobic, and dirty. Moreover, Istanbul at the time was a wealthier city: in 2012, Shanghai's per capita income was $20,436, while Istanbul's was $24,771. "People from the Middle East seem to be taking the brunt and will probably continue to do so until it has its own rising film market," the Chinese film producer Peter Shiao said.[57]

The second involved accelerating the trend toward comic book movies. Placating Hollywood is expensive, but many countries are willing to spend the money to protect their national brand. The Mexican government had offered up to $20 million for the Bond film *Spectre* (2015) to cast a Mexican Bond girl and to ensure a non-Mexican actor played the villain.[58] In the summer of 2020, Norway provided a several-million-dollar subsidy to the production team of *Mission: Impossible 7* so that they would film scenes in the country—and even waived some of its coronavirus requirements for the star Tom Cruise and his team.[59] In 2020, as the pandemic decimated the film business across the world, the global box office grew to 81 percent of the total market, leaving the United States and Canada with just 19 percent.[60] Comic book supervillains, those beasts of no nations, avoid angering foreign governments while sidestepping the racism of constantly featuring a protagonist who stops a terrorist in some dusty Arab city.

Third, studios increasingly emphasized the valor and bravery of Chinese characters and of the Chinese state. "Any time if you make the Chinese out to be a bad guy, it would be a problem," said Wayne Wang, the Chinese American director, in 2011.[61] "There was more and more focus on not making a stupid mistake" with China, he said. "Not casting China in the role of the villain, or casting China as a hero, could be a small but clever maneuver."

In *Gravity* (2013), a Chinese space station saves an American astronaut. But even casting Chinese as heroes could require onerous government approval. Because *Arrival* featured a Chinese general, Beijing wouldn't permit its screening in China until it received special approval from the People's Liberation Army.[62] "I think China will be happy with the portrayal," said the Chinese American actor Tzi Ma, who played the general.[63]

The fourth, and most bizarre, is a return to the whitewashing of an earlier era, where Hollywood cast white actors to play minority roles. The firm Dragon Horse Films compiled a list of the declining

Chinese villains in Hollywood movies—and, in some cases, the white actors who replaced them. *The Dark Knight Rises* (2012) features Liam Neeson as the criminal mastermind Ra's al Ghul, born of a Chinese tribe in the Arabian Peninsula.[64] In the sci-fi monster movie *Pacific Rim* (2013), Ron Perlman plays a Hong Kong organ smuggler who calls himself Hannibal Chau. ("I took my first name from a historical figure I respect, and my last name from my favorite Chinese restaurant in Brooklyn," he quipped.[65])

It wasn't just white actors. *The Hangover* (2009) and its popular 2011 and 2013 sequels all feature the comically villainous Chinese drug dealer Leslie Chow—played by the Korean American actor Ken Jeong.[66] In the comic books, *Iron Man*'s nemesis is the Mandarin. Born in prerevolutionary China to a Chinese father and an English mother, the Mandarin discovers ten rings that give him fearsome power. *Iron Man 3*'s director, Shane Black, called the character a "racist stereotype," and so cast Ben Kingsley (Indian father, English mother) in the role.[67]

What effect has the rise of China had on Hollywood's on-screen treatment of blacks, gays, Muslims, and Japanese? Disney's *Star Wars: The Force Awakens* (2015) starred the black actor John Boyega.[68] The American film poster prominently featured Boyega and his white co-star Daisy Ridley; the Chinese film poster, however, downplayed Boyega.

The poster controversy went viral on Twitter, and it sparked the curiosity of the Johns Hopkins University marketing professor Manuel Hermosilla. "I mostly study innovation, but I wondered about this," he told me. And so along with two colleagues teaching at Spanish universities, Hermosilla studied the casting decisions in roughly thirty-four hundred American films made between 2009 and 2015, the years framing the 2012 quota increase in Hollywood films Beijing permitted to screen in the Chinese market, and codified the skin color of actors in the more than ten thousand starring roles in those films. Hermosilla and his colleagues found what they called a "light-skin shift": the rise of the Chinese market caused the increase in "the participation of pale-skinned actors" by roughly 8 percent. Animation, where the movie and its marketing materials often obscure the skin colors of the stars, saw no such shift.

In July 2019, the online platform Sina Movie polled viewers on what they felt about the casting of the black singer Halle Bailey as the star in an upcoming live-action remake of Disney's *Little Mermaid*.[69] The casting of a black actor to star as Ariel, portrayed as white in the 1989 original, incited controversy in the United States and, among the small group of fans who knew about it, a more vociferous response on the Chinese internet.[70] The Sina Movie poll found that while roughly five thousand respondents supported the decision, more than sixty thousand disapproved. In an English-language tweet, the Party newspaper the *Global Times* called it "a rare occasion when a colored actress will be cast as a Disney princess." Even 2018's *Black Panther,* the highest-grossing film ever made by a black director, did worse in China than expected. One film blogger with more than nine million followers on Weibo wrote, "Most of the cast is black, but the film surprisingly has many scenes shot at night, and so watching this with 3D glasses is unbearable."

"History has said that African American movies don't translate," Casey Silver, the then chairman of Universal Pictures, said in 1998. "They have on occasion, but it's the exception rather than the rule." That's still true in China today. "Black-themed films can succeed in China," the Chinese online magazine *Sixth Tone* wrote in March 2021, "as long as their Blackness remains in the background."[71] Dozens of Hollywood studio executives, filmmakers, and actors have spoken on the record about making films that appeal to the Chinese market. Why wouldn't the darker skin color of certain actors be a factor that weighs against them when studio executives consider the Chinese market?

TO IMPROVE ITS RELATIONSHIP WITH THE PARTY, WANDA HAS invested heavily in propaganda. In December 2018, Wanda signed a $1.74 billion deal to build a theme park in the city of Yan'an, the base of the Communists from 1935 to 1947 and today a living shrine to the Party.[72] Xi likes to praise the "red baptism of the spirit" that happens when tourists visit places like Yan'an.[73] "Wanda Group, in line with historical mission and social responsibility, promote the Yan'an spirit and make the Yan'an Wanda City a new national red tourism trademark," Wang Jianlin said in a statement announcing the Yan'an park.[74] He opened it in June 2021, "as a gift to the 100th anniversary of the founding of the Chinese Communist Party."[75]

Sadly, some Americans have been doing the same thing, though many of them don't know it. In the years since Disney distributed the 1998 propaganda film *Red Lover* in the United States as an apology for *Kundun,* hundreds of Westerners have abetted Chinese propaganda films. They've starred in, produced, distributed, and written the music for Chinese films that glorify the Party.

The films don't only idolize the Party's rule over China; they facilitate China's global dominance. And they mock Americans, denigrate Japanese, and infantilize Africans. "An hour ago, these people didn't know if they'd live to see tomorrow. Why are they so happy?" one Chinese former soldier asks another after a tense day in an unnamed African country in the film *Wolf Warrior 2* (2017)—tagline: "Anyone who offends China, no matter how remote, must be exterminated"— made with the help of several prominent Americans.[76] "Our African friends," he replied, "it doesn't matter if it's war, disease, or poverty. Once they're around the bonfire, all their cares go away." *Wolf Warrior 2* was one of the biggest Chinese box office hits in history, grossing more than $850 million.[*77] Joe and Anthony Russo, the directors of four Marvel movies for Disney, consulted for the film, in which a fictional Chinese military unit fights evil Westerners in an unnamed African country. The character actor and Disney Marvel villain Frank Grillo played the film's antagonist. Ninety percent of the film's actors had reportedly served in the Party's military, including the film's star Wu Jing.[78]

It is appropriate for Westerners to appear in some Chinese films, as the British facial acrobat Rowan Atkinson did in *Top Funny Comedian* (2017), about hijinks in the gambling city of Macau.[79] The line grows blurrier with films like 2016's co-production *The Great Wall,* a monster movie set in eleventh-century China starring Matt Damon, at the time the most expensive Chinese movie ever made.[80] American

---

* Wolf Warrior is also the namesake of China's recent aggressive brand of diplomacy: The Chinese ambassador to Sweden was being a Wolf Warrior in 2019, when he offered "good liquor to our friends, and a shotgun to our enemies."

reviewers criticized the film for portraying a white actor helping to save China. But Damon's real misstep was appearing in a fascist film that glorified the need of a strong army to protect against foreign threats. "Dwarfed by the gigantic Great Wall," the scholar Ying Zhu wrote, the crazed Europeans "appear captivated literally and figuratively by the enormity of China and Chinese culture."[81]

In 2017, the former Tibet supporter Seagal appeared with Mike Tyson in the Wanda film *China Salesman,* which follows a Chinese IT rep who prevents a civil war in Uganda. Tyson, who plays the henchman of a corrupt French spy and fakes an African accent, commits suicide at the end of the movie. Seagal plays a mercenary and a bar owner. Besides the content of this film—sample line from the protagonist: when Chinese reached the shores of Africa, "they only left friendship and peace"—there is an easy way to tell that it is propaganda. The film had seven co-producers: the central committee of the Communist Youth League, an important party organization formerly run by Chairman Hu, and six (six!) different propaganda departments.

It was also inappropriate for Westerners to help with *Sky Hunter* (2017). One of the film's co-producers was the PLA Air Force's Political Work Department, a Party body tasked with using "psychological warfare" to "disintegrate enemy armies."[82] The film features Chinese air force pilots defending the fictional Republic of Mahbu and has the famous Chinese actress Fan Bingbing as the love interest. The pilots and air force generals often repeat Party talking points about noninterference in a country's sovereignty and respect for a country's citizens. China is a "powerful and peaceful country," even the film's villain, a terrorist played by the Israeli actor Tomer Oz, must admit, "spreading compassion to people suffering in the world." The Academy Award–winning Hans Zimmer, who composed the music for Disney's *Lion King* and the *Pirates of the Caribbean* series, produced *Sky Hunter's* score.[83]

In 2019, DreamWorks finally released a Tibet film—the first Hollywood film about Tibet since 1997's *Kundun.* Set in present-day China, *Abominable* follows a hardworking sixteen-year-old named Yi who discovers an escaped yeti on her roof. She names him Everest and vows to return him to his home in the Himalayas. The film begins in a city based on Shanghai and follows the characters as they travel across China.

But *Abominable* is a propaganda film that portrays a China divorced from reality in ways suspiciously similar to how the Party wants foreigners to see the country. Although the film takes place entirely in China, its villains are two white Americans, who seek to capture the yeti, for reasons of greed and arrogance. I counted six different shots of Chinese money: when someone paid Yi for walking her dogs, for example, or when one of the evil American's henchmen bribes a bystander. But in each case, the money is shown facedown. We don't see the side of Chinese money that features a portrait of Mao, the People's Republic of China's founding dictator. Ubiquitous in China today—including on the 1-, 2-, 5-, 10-, 20-, 50-, and 100-renminbi notes—but no glimpse of him appears in the film. Ignoring Mao modernizes and normalizes China's repressive political system: Mao still plays a major role in Chinese politics today, and yet the film refuses to acknowledge that reality.

Similarly, the film shows a landscape divorced from the intensely political nature of Chinese cities—parroting the claims of Chinese officials, who in English often pretend their country is "apolitical." Yi's city features Chinese advertisements and restaurant signs, but not even one of the common propaganda signs exhorting citizens to "build a prosperous socialist motherland" or even more neutral slogans like "respect the old and love the young."

The film ends when Yi, joined by a cousin and a neighbor, returns Everest to Tibet, where his family of yetis envelops him, and peacefully waves goodbye.[84] The Tibetan writer Tsering Woeser told me that the scholar Edward Said's *Orientalism,* about the often infantilizing way some Western intellectuals and travelers described Asia, baffled her. "But then," she said, "I put the West as China, and the East as Tibet, and it made perfect sense." In *Abominable,* Tibet is a land devoid of people; the only humans are the protagonists of the film: the Han Chinese from the east. No one in the film even mentions the word "Tibet."

Abominable is not the exception; it's the rule. In September 2018, a judge sentenced the formerly beloved actor Bill Cosby to prison for sexual assault. In the months following that upheaval, I met a Hollywood insider worried about China's influence, and he marveled at how thoroughly Cosby had been removed from the Hollywood firmament. "Today in Hollywood," he told me, "the Dalai Lama is as popular as Bill Cosby."

Beijing has successfully persuaded Hollywood to erase the idea of Tibet. The QuoDB movie database returns not a single mention of Tibet, Tibetan, Lhasa, or the Dalai Lama in any Hollywood film released after 2015. The most high-profile absence came from Disney's *Doctor Strange* (2016), which cast Tilda Swinton as the Tibetan character the Ancient One.[85] "If you acknowledge that Tibet is a place and that he's Tibetan," the film's screenwriter C. Robert Cargill explained, "you risk alienating one billion people."[86]

Twenty-two years after *Kundun* and *Seven Years in Tibet,* Hollywood finally made *Abominable,* another Tibet film. But this time, it didn't show a single Tibetan.

CHAPTER SIX

Universities and Self-Censorship

★

BESIDES THE MEETING ROOMS IN WASHINGTON AND THE MOVIE lots in Hollywood, the other major American breeding grounds for ideas are the public and private universities distributed across the country.

Despite recent funding woes and challenges posed by the coronavirus, the American university system remains the envy of the world. Austerity budgets and exploding expenses have created new realities for some of these universities, especially those that do not have the enormous endowments accrued by elite schools. As in Hollywood, that reality has been an opportunity for the Party to access and influence these hot spots of American ideology.

IN SEPTEMBER 2017, A UNIVERSITY OF MICHIGAN PHD STUDENT opened Facebook and learned that Chinese customs agents had banned the import of certain soft European cheeses, like Brie and Gorgonzola.[1] The customs agents blamed "too much bacteria," but because Chinese companies could legally make the same cheese, European trade councils criticized the bizarre move as protectionist.

The news frustrated the student, who asked to remain anonymous and had spent years living and researching in China. "I thought, 'Oh no, where would I get my cheese from now on!'" she told me, and she considered posting about it. But even though the Chinese system would ignore an American graduate student complaining about an event as absurd and insignificant as a Brie ban, she feared criticizing

Beijing's trade policies. "I have no fantasies that my social media presence isn't being monitored to some extent," she said. So she closed her browser. Several years prior, she attended an event commemorating the twenty-fifth anniversary of the Tiananmen Square massacre. Even though the violence disgusted her, she worried that if she criticized Chinese soldiers gunning down unarmed protesters, students could report her to the Chinese authorities. And she worried if that happened, it could jeopardize her research, her access to interview subjects, and even her entire academic career. Even though it bothered her to do so, she kept quiet. This self-censorship "that I cultivate, it comes through in many creepy and insidious ways," she told me.

Party influence has permeated American society so much that many Americans already engage in self-censorship about China without even knowing it. The type and severity of yielding vary. Some censor themselves on current events involving China, as the NBA did in a major October 2019 scandal. The academic Perry Link told me about an American actor working on a China project in the summer of 2019 who was "tied up into knots" about his "frustrations on the situation in Hong Kong," where protesters had been fighting for more freedom and democracy. The actor told Link, "Obviously, with the industry I'm in, I cannot express these opinions openly." Some, like Kissinger and Neil Bush, knowingly or unknowingly parrot Party propaganda and advocate for policies beneficial to Beijing and detrimental to America. Few have the intellectual courage to discuss it on the record.

Academic compromises pose a special problem. People expect companies to compromise for financial gains, and the political and entertainment worlds already bear a deserving reputation for selfishness. But universities, think tanks, and publishing houses appear ethical and trustworthy. Moreover, these institutions are among the best sources of information about China. Excessive censorship and self-censorship have reduced the utility of Chinese journalists and academics working in China. The March 2020 expulsion of most American journalists based in China who worked for *The Washington Post, The New York Times,* and *The Wall Street Journal,* as well as the June 2020 passing of Hong Kong's National Security Law criminalizing dissent in and about the city, further chilled the reporting environment.[2] And COVID travel restrictions are making it much more difficult for journalists—as well as academics, businesspeople, and tourists—to bear witness and circulate information on what is happening on the ground in China.

Compromises and censorship within American universities restrict the ability of U.S. policy makers, businesspeople, human rights advocates, and the general public to make smart decisions about how to interact with China. They also limit debate, funnel students and scholars away from topics that may upset the Party, and amplify Chinese propaganda.

The problem comes less from the billions of dollars Chinese individuals and the Party spend in U.S. universities, or the influx of students from mainland China. Rather, it is that some people in American academia, too eager to please Beijing or too fearful of offending the Party, have submitted to a sophisticated global censorship regime. This weakens not only their scholarship and integrity but also their negotiating power with Beijing over issues such as access for research, conferences and other academic collaborations, and joint programs between American and Chinese institutions.

In what ways are Americans advancing Chinese propaganda, and why does it matter? Those issues Beijing wants Americans to perceive as the most sensitive are known as the three *T*s: Taiwan, the self-governing island of twenty-four million people that Beijing views as a province pretending it is independent; Tibet; and Tiananmen, the massive public square in the center of Beijing, the site of student protests and the notorious 1989 massacre. (Over the last three years, that short list has grown to include the protests in Hong Kong and the situation in Xinjiang, a region in northwest China where authorities have imprisoned more than a million Muslims in concentration camps.)

I first learned about the three *T*s while studying Chinese literature as an undergraduate at Columbia University. Learning Chinese was delightful and unmooring. In his 1982 book, *China: Alive in the Bitter Sea*, the journalist Fox Butterfield recalls asking a Harvard librarian for Chinese-language tapes in the 1950s. She "peered at me over the top of her glasses as if I had stumbled into the wrong church," he wrote.[3] " 'Chinese? Chinese?' she repeated. 'Isn't Chinese a dead language?'" The field had exploded over that half century. But when I arrived at Columbia in 2002, Chinese still felt like a secluded garden of a language, guarded by pictographs.

I can't remember my first conversation about the three Ts, but I remember thinking that their avoidance was crucial for surviving in an alien world, and that they were a fixed concept, like a grammar rule baked into the language. The editor Anne Henochowicz, who now often translates essays relating to human rights in China, recounts visiting the country as a high school student in 2001. Her teachers told her to avoid the three Ts. "And I was a good girl, and I didn't talk about them," she told me.

I had thought self-censoring meant deferring to China's cultural norms, not its political ones. It wasn't until years later, when I had reflected on the political structures I internalized in my six years in the country, that I realized my mistake. Much of what the Party calls "Chinese culture" actually shares more with the Soviet Union of the 1970s than Taiwan, a country today ruled by politicians whose parents and grandparents fled from mainland China and where the political discourse is raucously open.

There is no good polling in China on sensitive issues. Yet it's safe to assume that Chinese people hold a wide range of views when it comes to the three Ts and other sensitive issues, and why wouldn't they? It's an incredibly diverse country with a multiplicity of viewpoints. In October 2019, the owner of the Brooklyn Nets, Joseph Tsai, posted an open letter on Facebook postulating why Beijing reacted so strongly to an NBA general manager tweeting about Hong Kong. "The one thing that is terribly misunderstood, and often ignored, by the western press and those critical of China," he wrote, "is that 1.4 billion Chinese citizens stand united when it comes to the territorial integrity of China and the country's sovereignty over her homeland." But Tsai is describing the political system of a country that marshals many individual views into one political cudgel, not the views of Chinese people themselves. That month, a Chinese Houston Rockets fan named Wang Haoda living in the northeastern city of Liaoning posted a photo of himself holding up a Chinese flag and a lighter.[4] "I live and die with my team," he wrote. "Come and catch me." Several hours later, police came and caught him.

In the thousands of conversations I've had with Chinese people over the past two decades, only a small minority expressed offense at perceived American positions on those issues, and only a slightly larger minority shared views on these issues that accorded with Beijing's. On the topic of Taiwan, for example, while some Chinese people expressed anger that Beijing hadn't reclaimed the island, others saw it as a democratic model Beijing should emulate. In April 2018, I guest-taught a Chinese professor's class on international affairs at a Shanghai university. When I asked the several dozen students how many would join the army to fight against Taiwan, not a single person raised their hand. It's not that the three Ts aren't sensitive; they're just not as sensitive as the Chinese government would have its critics believe.

The Party wants Americans to think that not only the three Ts but also a wide range of issues are too controversial, and that they should leave the discussions of them to representatives of the Party. These include women's rights, China's often contentious relationship with its neighbor Japan, and even seemingly obscure subjects like territorial expansion during the Qing, the last Chinese dynasty.

After years in an environment where such sensitivities about China abound, some Americans learn to be timider about Beijing, more supportive of the Party's worldview and ambitions, and unwilling to share potentially sensitive viewpoints with a wider audience. "You rarely get them to soften their views overnight, but through a patient process of explanation, incentivization, and rationalization you gradually bring about an evolution in their views so that they begin to avoid certain topics and phrasing that might offend Beijing," said Joshua Eisenman, an associate professor at the University of Notre Dame who studies China's foreign policy. "Moving the mountain one stone at a time. That's where China excels."

The first part of Beijing's strategy is convincing Americans of the need to tiptoe around the three Ts, as well as Hong Kong and Xinjiang. The second, more complicated, and more pernicious part of Beijing's strategy is that fixating on the three Ts or issues like the protests in Hong Kong makes Americans more likely to overlook what actually *are* the most sensitive issues: exposing wrongdoing by or criticizing specific policies of top Chinese leaders; encouraging political organizing in China; calling for regime change or suggesting the Party should not rule China; and actively campaigning for the independence of Taiwan, Tibet, Xinjiang, and, more recently, Hong Kong. Even some of Beijing's most strident foreign critics gingerly avoid suggesting the possibility of regime change.

Of these, the most sensitive issue involves suggestions that because of incompetence, corruption, or iniquity the Party and the men—and they're all men—who run it do not deserve to rule China. Should the Party rule China? And if not, what should Chinese and the rest of the world do about it? Those are the existential questions. Outside these issues, academics, politicians, journalists, businesspeople, and institutions can often stand up to the Chinese government and emerge with their access and integrity intact. And yet many—including myself, for most of my career—don't.

Sometimes the compromises have been flagrant, such as when North Carolina State University canceled a visit from the Dalai Lama in 2009. "I don't want to say we didn't think about whether there were implications," said the university's provost, Warwick Arden. "Of course you do. China is a major trading partner for North Carolina." Or in January 2015, when the publishing arm of the legal nonprofit the American Bar Association canceled a book by the Chinese intellectual Teng Biao, living in exile in New Jersey, for fear of "upsetting the Chinese government."[5] Or a month later, when Harvard Law School's vice-dean for International Legal Studies William P. Alford asked Teng to cancel a talk at Harvard that would overlap with the Harvard president visiting Beijing. Alford admitted he did it because he thought the timing might "harm Harvard activity" in China.[6] Or in October 2017, when the think tank the Brookings Institution published a report praising the telecommunications giant Huawei— a report that Huawei funded.[7] Or in August 2017, when the world's oldest publishing house, Cambridge University Press, removed more than three hundred journal articles from its Chinese website.[8] Or in October 2017, when news broke that the world's largest academic publisher, Springer Nature, removed more than a thousand articles from its websites in China.[9] After an outcry from scholars, Cambridge reversed its decision, saying it would "uphold the principle of academic freedom on which the university's work is founded."

Springer did not; instead, it claimed that only "a small percentage of our content" is censored. Or when the journalist Bethany Allen-Ebrahimian gave a keynote at Savannah State University in May 2018 and found that the director of the local Confucius Institute had insisted the school delete the word "Taiwan" from her bio.[10] The school complied.*

Institutions in other countries face similar problems. In October 2017, administrators at the University of Salamanca in Spain canceled a series of Taiwan events because they feared jeopardizing their relationship with Beijing. "They were really scared," a University of Salamanca professor said, "the 'Oh my God, we have angered China, Beijing's going to retaliate' kind of scared." In the summer of 2018, the University of Nottingham Ningbo China, a joint venture between the British university and a Chinese one, removed an academic from its management board after he wrote an article criticizing the Party. In May 2019, a university in Hungary barred Taiwanese students from presenting their cuisine at an international food day under a banner reading "Taiwan."† For a June 2021 report, Human Rights Watch interviewed twenty-two academics in Australia. More than half admitted to practicing "regular self-censorship" about China.[11]

Indeed, it tends to be worse at less prestigious schools and institutions, worse when academics or administrators with just a passing familiarity with China make the decision, and certainly worse for American satellites in China, which claim to offer the same level of academic freedom as their campuses in the United States. Kean, a public university in New Jersey, opened a branch in the eastern Chinese city of Wenzhou in 2012: a 2015 job post for the university's specialist for residence life and specialist for student conduct said that "membership in the Chinese Communist Party is preferred."

---

* The ABA had responded in a statement that they canceled the book because they believed it wouldn't sell well, and the "reasons resulting in the decision were miscommunicated" to Teng. Brookings had responded: "Brookings will not accept gifts from donors who seek to undermine the independence of its scholars' research or otherwise to predetermine or influence recommendations."

† In a statement, Nottingham had said it makes changes to its management board yearly, "when contracts expire or we recruit new talent."

An August 2016 study by the U.S. Government Accountability Office surveyed twelve American universities with branches in China and found that less than half offered uncensored internet access to students and faculty.*[12]

In 2015, the university vice chancellor Jeffrey S. Lehman told a congressional committee that NYU "would have absolute control over the school's curriculum, faculty, teaching style and operations, and that it would receive an ironclad guarantee that it could operate the school according to the fundamental principles of academic freedom." Chinese students at New York University's Shanghai branch must take a "civic education" class that glorifies the Party's contributions to China, and starting from 2017, Beijing required all American joint venture universities in China to appoint a Party secretary, who must have a seat on the board of trustees, and for them to establish internal Party committees. NYU Shanghai has far more limited freedom of speech than NYU. In a 2020 legal filing at a U.S. court, NYU Shanghai claimed that it is, in fact, not controlled by NYU—and that it can't be, because Chinese law "prohibits a foreign entity from having control of a Chinese academic institution." That statement, which directly contradicts Lehman's, is the sad truth."[13]

More often, the compromises remain hidden, or more nuanced and subtle, or sins of omission rather than commission. It's different from Hollywood, where viewers watch China saving the world. "You're not going to get a lot of China specialists openly confessing that self-censorship is a big problem," Minxin Pei, a professor of government at Claremont McKenna College in California known for his critical stance toward the Party, told me in 2018. And yet Pei believes that the academics who communicate to general audiences, thus increasing the likelihood that the Party will see their work, and those who work on sensitive issues like Tibet must watch what they say. "You don't want to go out on a limb," he said. "You want to come across as very measured." Sounding "too strident" about China, he said, not only risks "the ire of the Chinese government but could

---

* While there hasn't been an updated study since then, the fact that circumvention tools like virtual private networks are mostly illegal in China today means the number is likely higher.

also lose the respect of your peers, who value evidence above opinion." (The framing is disingenuous. Having an opinion about Trump, say, or Putin, is considered more appropriate than an opinion about Xi.) Robert Barnett, who ran Columbia University's Modern Tibetan Studies Program from its founding in 1999 until stepping down in 2017, said that Columbia never actively restricted his work; there exists "a very strong tendency within the university, and with many prestigious institutions in the U.S., not to include people who study the kind of subject I work on in any kind of academic collaborations in China or in dialogues with Chinese delegates."

The Georgetown University professor Jim Millward, who struggled with getting a Chinese visa for more than a decade after publishing a book chapter on the controversial Chinese region Xinjiang in 2004, faced a similar situation.[14] Georgetown had partnered with the Chinese Communist Party School, an important training center for Chinese officials. And yet the university decided mentioning Millward's case to the Party School was a "nonstarter," he told me. "They thought that if they breathed a word that I exist, it would sour the relationship."*[15] He continued, "What is the point of a university having high-level contacts with China or other authoritarian states if they don't use them when necessary to support access for their faculty and students?"

In March 2018, at the annual conference of the Association for Asian Studies, I spoke with Henochowicz, who studied Chinese literature and folklore at Ohio State University. Part of her research involved the oral tradition and folk music in Inner Mongolia, and she struggled with how forthright to be in her writing and research about a potentially politically controversial topic, in part because she feared Beijing might deny her a visa in the future. "I frequently hear graduate students and younger scholars, people with academic jobs but pre-tenure, being advised not to explore sensitive subjects in their research, so they can preserve visa access," said an American historian of China. As Dartmouth art historian Allen Hockley said

---

* Around the same time, in 2008, the student newspaper published an op-ed warning that "in exchange for the right to collaborate with Chinese researchers, Georgetown must self-censor its institutional voice."

in September 2020, "China scholars need to be careful what they say if they want a career."[16]

THE CAMBRIDGE ENGLISH DICTIONARY DEFINES SELF-CENSORSHIP as "control of what you say or do in order to avoid annoying or offending others, but without being told officially that such control is necessary."[17] The definition's mention of "offense" is key: roughly a dozen people I spoke with told me that they don't self-censor, but sometimes word things differently to avoid offending their Chinese hosts, partners, or students. And some analysts and researchers who claim they don't self-censor explain that criticizing Beijing would make them sound "shrill" and "sensationalize" their research.[18]

"The art is learning to judge when you're censoring yourself out of fear," wrote the economist Dominic Meagher in April 2018 on Chinapol, a members-only email listserv for academics, journalists, lawyers, and activists who specialize in China, which he permitted me to quote publicly. "If you're doing it out of fear, you have to then ask if your fear is warranted and outweighs the import of what you're saying and the damage to a culture of saying what we believe or know to be true. If you put any worth on your own values, sometimes you have to be willing to accept the cost of upholding them."

According to dozens of conversations I had over the last five years, students from China, Chinese professors, and Chinese Americans face more pressure to self-censor in U.S. universities than do white Americans, who rarely have family in China, are far less likely to be living in China and taking remote classes, and never hold Chinese citizenship. (The field in the United States is, problematically, almost entirely white and Asian.) This undermines an especially useful source of knowledge, because ethnically Chinese professors and students often benefit from more advanced linguistic skills and a deeper or more nuanced understanding of the country than their American counterparts.

Chinese students who don't self-censor can face real consequences. Consider what happened at the University of Maryland in May 2017. The graduating Chinese student Yang Shuping gave a commencement speech praising the "fresh air" of the American system and said democracy and freedom were "worth fighting for." A video of the speech went viral, garnering millions of views and hundreds of thousands of comments—many of them negative—on various social media platforms and publications in China, including the vitriolic Party tabloid *Global Times*. A day later, after the home address of her family had been widely shared online, Yang apologized for her speech. "I had no intentions of belittling my country," she wrote. "I am deeply sorry and hope for forgiveness." Or to the University of Minnesota student Luo Daiqing, sentenced to six months in prison in November 2019 after mocking Xi on Twitter, in the United States.[19]

Some Chinese students, American faculty members, and human rights activists say that Chinese students and faculty sometimes spy on other Chinese students and, to a lesser extent, American professors. A Chinese PhD graduate of a U.S. university told me a classmate approached her when she was a graduate student at a Chinese university in 2008 and asked if she wanted to work for him in China's Ministry of State Security. "He knew that I had an offer to an American university and asked if I'd like to 'acquire a second stipend.'" She politely declined.

In Cambridge in March 2018, I spoke with a Chinese doctoral student. She told me of a "creepy" experience in D.C. in 2016 to 2017 featuring a Chinese visiting scholar from Shanghai. A colleague of hers sent the scholar a paper she had written, and he responded with what he called "friendly advice": the term "coercion," which she had used to describe Beijing's behavior, "is not a nice word." He chastised her for calling the June 1989 slaughter in Tiananmen Square a "massacre," as opposed to an "incident," the Party's preferred term. The visiting professor started following her to "every seminar, workshop, and [public] dinner," she attended, she said. "I can't prove he had orders from the security apparatus," she said, "but he was overly concerned with my project, which made me suspicious." So she started to publicly self-censor. When he attended her events, she said, "I decided to moderate what to say," she said.

In February 2018, after Beijing announced the removal of term limits restricting Xi to two terms as the country's chairman, a group of Chinese students papered some American campuses with posters featuring the phrase "#Not My President."[20] In a pseudonymous essay about the dangers of his protest in America, one of the students wrote, "We know that our career prospects back in China are likely to suffer if we are publicly known to have criticized the party; it will be more difficult for us to make connections, snag interviews, and receive job offers and promotions." After protests erupted again in Hong Kong in April 2019, the impassioned debate among students in America has sometimes grown threatening. Frances Hui, a student from Hong Kong at Emerson College in Boston, said that a Chinese classmate responded to an article she wrote by posting on Facebook, "Whomever opposes my greatest China, no matter how far they are, must be executed."[21]

BEFORE 2020, SOME CHINESE STUDENTS, AND AMERICAN AND CHInese professors, feared that classmates could report them for criticizing the Party or its policies, and they might have worried about a classmate recording the class. For those students who during the pandemic took classes at American universities remotely from their laptops in cities across China, the problem is much more real: Beijing can access the sessions Zoomed across China. "If our students' participation in our classes is known to Chinese authorities, and it seems clear that it easily could be, their academic freedom is at least chilled and they or their families' safety potentially endangered," wrote Millward in June 2020. "Unfortunately, this is not an alarmist threat."[22]

Some academics, like the Princeton political science professor Rory Truex, have offered blind grading, where students use codes instead of their names, to help prevent linking the students to their potentially controversial arguments. Not only are some political science class discussions—like whether China should be a true democracy, or if Hong Kong should govern itself—illegal under broad interpretation of Chinese laws, but so is the unauthorized use of virtual private networks to access banned websites, like columbia.edu and mit.edu.[23]

Western universities struggle with the impossibility of following Chinese laws and respecting academic freedom at the same time. SOAS University of London warned students and staff that they may be arrested if they carried class notes into China or Hong Kong, because those could violate the country's draconian security laws. "If we, as a Chinese teaching community, out of fear stop teaching things like Tiananmen or Xinjiang or whatever sensitive topic the Chinese government doesn't want us talking about, if we cave, then we've lost," Truex said.[24]

A new threat arose in 2021: that of actual sanctions. During Joe Biden's inauguration, the Foreign Ministry announced it was sanctioning twenty-eight Trump administration officials, including the former secretary of state Mike Pompeo and the former deputy national security adviser Matt Pottinger, for "violating China's sovereignty." The sanctions not only ban the individuals from entering China but restrict the companies and institutions "associated with them" from doing business with China. Pottinger later joined the Stanford University think tank the Hoover Institution. It's unclear yet if Beijing will enforce its own laws and close off Stanford's broad academic or economic ties with China, but it complicates things both for academics and for university lawyers, who work to ensure that Stanford complies with the laws of the countries in which it operates.

Several months later, Beijing went further and sanctioned several European scholars who had produced research critical of the Party, as well as the German think tank MERICS. And in July 2021, Beijing also sanctioned the China director for Human Rights Watch, Sophie Richardson. "Repression tactics against China scholars used to be 'rare but real,'" said the academic Sheena Greitens, who has studied self-censorship and China, in March 2021. "They are increasingly not rare."[25]

These incidents can chill the environment in college classrooms across the United States for both Chinese and Americans, especially among junior faculty who don't have the job security that tenure brings. "I always worry that there are folks in the room who are reporting back on what they're hearing," an assistant professor of political science at an American university told me. "And there almost certainly are. Reporting back on each other, too." A white American graduate student, who asked that I identify her race because she believes there is even less freedom for people of color and Chinese Americans to speak openly about China, told me she worried about Chinese students monitoring her speech and behavior. "If I said something in the classroom, and a student reported me, then maybe

I would be under scrutiny for something," she said—something that also might jeopardize her ability to get a visa to conduct research in China in the future. "That's part of the minefield of teaching in the United States." It extends to lectures too. "People routinely say no pictures, no recording" from paranoia that Chinese spies will jeopardize someone's access to China for attending a sensitive event, a professor at an American university told me in November 2018. She spoke of attending an event on Xinjiang and Tibet featuring Chinese panelists. "There was a Party operative in the back of the room, and he harangued panelists for their disloyalty," she told me.

There are some Chinese people who are more comfortable than their white American counterparts navigating issues the Party deems sensitive. "I feel that I am more okay to criticize China in front of Chinese students, because I am Chinese," Yuhua Wang, an assistant professor in the department of government at Harvard University, told me in 2018. "I feel there is more trouble for other colleagues who teach Chinese politics. The students might be thinking, 'Okay, this is a white guy criticizing China who doesn't know anything about China.'" Generally speaking, however, those with a more direct link to China have more to lose. A recent graduate of a PhD program at a top-tier university told me how having relatives in China meant that he and others "face a starker choice about whether they will phrase things in a way that will cause them problems."

This leverage also extends to universities with campuses in China or joint ventures with Chinese universities. Many top American universities maintain a presence in China, through summer language programs like the Harvard Beijing Academy; institutes such as the Stanford Center at Peking University that serve as platforms to attract students, fundraise, allow faculty to conduct research, and host events; or even as full campuses, like New York University Shanghai and the Hopkins-Nanjing Center. But as repression increases, so does the vulnerability of those American universities. Jason Lane, co-director of the Cross-Border Education Research Team at the State University of New York at Albany, compared it to "boiling a frog," where "the heat is slowly turned up and you don't realize what's happening until it's too late."[26]

Those institutions in China are "hostages," said Pei, the Claremont

McKenna professor, because the universities don't want to jeopardize the status of their satellite institutions. Beijing "could make their life miserable in many ways," he said—for instance, by restricting visas, ramping up health and safety inspections, and even issuing threats of closure. "If you're Stanford or Harvard and you have operations in China, are you going to host a famous dissident to speak?" he asked. (Lisa Lapin, Stanford's vice president for university communications, said in June 2018 that the suggestion of self-censorship at its campus in Beijing is "not accurate." Jennifer Li-Chia Liu, the director of the summer language program at the Harvard Beijing Academy, did not respond to multiple requests for comment.)

The last five years have seen academic freedom in China shrink drastically. In 2016, Xi said China must "build colleges into strongholds that adhere to Party leadership" and that higher education "must adhere to correct political orientation." In March 2018, Shaanxi Normal University published a description of the responsibilities of student spies, whom it called "information officers."[27] They must keep an eye on the ideologies of the students and teachers and report on their opinions of "major social events." In December 2019, the prestigious Fudan University in Shanghai removed the phrase "freedom of thought" from its charter and added clauses such as the school should "serve the Party's governance of China."[28] And in August 2021, the Ministry of Education officially added Xi Jinping Thought—the leader's governing philosophy—to the curriculum, starting in primary school. Those sort of changes "have been disorienting," said Jeffrey Wasserstrom, a historian of modern China at the University of California Irvine. "We felt that things were moving in the direction where there would be less and less need to watch what you said in China, because in the 1990s until the early 2000s there was less reason to be careful."

Complicating the issue is the potential virality of a controversial, misspoken, or provocative claim and shifting norms about free speech and political correctness. "There is more careful choosing of words—not just about China—but in general," said Wasserstrom, "because of the ease with which things you say can be captured on a cell phone and get you in trouble." This was especially true in the Zoom pandemic landscape of 2020 and 2021, with many classes recorded.

Because of technology, "censorship affects our research in real time more than it ever has before," said the University of Michigan PhD student. "It's not that you write a book in five years, and publish it, and then you're out of the game. It can be as simple as a tweet about Taylor Swift in a *1989* T-shirt," she said—a reference to the singer's popular album named after her birth year, which happens to be when the Tiananmen massacre occurred.

In early 2017, the University of California San Diego (UCSD) invited the Dalai Lama to deliver a commencement speech. In response, the local branch of the Beijing-supported Chinese Students and Scholars Association issued a note condemning the decision as contravening the spirit of "respect, tolerance, and equality"—buzzwords borrowed from protest movements like #MeToo and Black Lives Matter.[29] "So you guys protest against Trump because he disrespects Muslims, blacks, Hispanics, LGBT," one Chinese student wrote on Facebook, but invite "this oppressor to make a public speech?? The hypocrisy is appalling!" Another student wrote, "#ChineseStudentsMatter." In an era of safe spaces, universities struggle with Chinese students who argue that inviting the Dalai Lama or discussing Taiwanese independence is "triggering." The Chinese Johns Hopkins University undergraduate Tie Shizheng used similar language in a petition seeking to cancel a February 2020 event with the Hong Kong democracy activists Nathan Law and Joshua Wong.[30] "We believe," she wrote, "that the appearance of the leaders of this racist movement on our campus is extremely inappropriate."

While the coronavirus has caused the number of Chinese students physically studying in the United States to plummet, the number of Chinese students enrolled in American universities hasn't dropped all that much. The most worrying role those more than 300,000 Chinese studying at American universities play in the self-censorship regime is not as individuals contributing to censorship but as a financial punishment or reward to universities.[31] The Commerce Department estimated that Chinese students contributed more than $14.9 billion annually to the U.S. economy in 2018.[32] Beijing's ability to direct Chinese students to cash-strapped universities—or threaten to take them away—incentivizes universities to act carefully.

An example of this occurred at UCSD, which has a student body made up of roughly 14 percent Chinese foreign students: the school's overall enrollment grew by 12,113 students since 2008, with more than 40 percent of them from China.[33] After the Dalai Lama spoke at the 2017 commencement, Beijing froze funding to Chinese scholars wishing to attend the school. "We're taking the quiet route," a UCSD professor told me, when I asked how the school was trying to return to China's good graces. Undergraduates from China at UCSD pay more than twice what students from California pay, and the university could face severe financial pressure if Beijing limited students' abilities to study there. And while there is no public evidence anyone from UCSD has self-censored to return to Beijing's good graces, it reminds other universities of the financial consequences of opposing Beijing.

The universities need the money. "We are in this austerity period," Michael Gibbs Hill, a professor of Chinese studies at William & Mary in Williamsburg, Virginia, told me. In October 2019, researchers from the progressive think tank the Center on Budget and Policy Priorities analyzed state spending on higher education.[34] Adjusted for inflation, they found that state funding for public two- and four-year colleges was more than $6.6 billion *lower* than it was in 2008.

And so some universities have turned to China's Confucius Institutes for funding and programming. Overseen by the Chinese Ministry of Education, Confucius Institutes are a global phenomenon, enrolling more than nine million students at 541 institutes in 162 countries and regions around the world, according to the program's website. Since the organization's founding in 2004, it has opened more than 100 Confucius Institutes in the United States, the most in the world, though many of those have since closed.

The institutes offer instruction in Chinese language and culture and encourage faculty and administrators to step gingerly around issues considered taboo, to prevent risking the loss of their funding. "We avoid sensitive things like Taiwan and Falun Gong," said Yin Xiuli, the director of the Confucius Institute at New Jersey City University, referring to the outspoken spiritual group banned in China. "We don't touch it."[35]

Confucius Institutes are far from the only examples of political interference on U.S. campuses. In April 2018, a scandal roiled George

Mason University in Virginia after faculty members learned that the Charles Koch Foundation, which had donated large sums to the school, had a say in the hiring and firing of professors. "When Koch buys influence over the hiring of professors who can achieve tenure, he can steer the direction of how economics, a foundational discipline, is taught for decades," Hill tweeted.*36 "These guys make Confucius Institutes look like they're doing it wrong." And Saudi businessmen and royals donate handsomely to top American institutions, including Harvard, Yale, and Georgetown.

Confucius Institutes are different. They are arms of the Party, a much more powerful force than Riyadh and a far wealthier one than the Koch brothers' foundations and, indeed, than all of the right- or left-wing funders in the United States. In 2009, Li Changchun, then a member of the Politburo Standing Committee, China's top decision-making body, called Confucius Institutes "an important part of China's overseas propaganda apparatus" and in a 2011 speech at the Beijing headquarters of the Confucius Institute called them an "appealing brand," adding that "using the excuse of teaching Chinese language, everything looks reasonable and logical."

Trump administration officials targeted Confucius Institutes. In August 2020, the State Department designated them foreign missions, not nonprofits, accurately reflecting their state ties. "Our State Department," Pompeo said in December 2020, "has made very clear these Confucius Institutes are literally up to no good." By July 2021, only thirty-five Confucius Institutes remained open at U.S. universities.

In a world of severed ties, COVID travel restrictions, and reduced funding for foreign-language learning, however, how should the United States train the next generation of China scholars?

Taiwan is helping to bridge some of the gap: The number of U.S. applicants to Fulbright Taiwan programs doubled from 2018 to 2021—albeit from a low base. More funding is necessary: a reality faced by countries around the world. In the summer of 2021, the German government announced it will invest $24.8 million over the next

---

* In a statement, the Charles Koch Foundation said, "We are committed to the independence of the professors and programs we support."

four years, for "independent China competence" at its research institutes and universities. That is a good step.

Another key need is recognizing that Confucius Institutes are just a small piece of the pernicious elements of Beijing's influence on U.S. universities. Take Tufts, for example. In March 2021, after a thirteen-week protest from local Tibetans, Chinese, and Uyghurs, Tufts closed its Confucius Institute. Why? In a statement, a Tufts dean explained that it was so the university could "focus more on our strong and growing direct relationship" with China's Beijing Normal University. That's not a solution for independent critical thinking on China.[37]

Unfortunately, instead of rushing to study America's biggest rival and most important trading partner, American students have been forsaking Chinese studies. Anecdotal and statistical evidence abounds. Data released in November 2020 showed that the number of American students in China has dropped by more than 20 percent since it peaked in the 2011–2012 school year. The University of Pennsylvania used to enroll more than 1,000 students in its Chinese classes. Now it's around 700. It's not just an American problem; in 2019, a mere 1,434 people studied China at universities in Britain. "As China's power waxes," *The Economist* wrote in November 2020, "the West's study of it is waning."[38] Whether one sees China as an adversary or a partner, maintaining ignorance about the country and its people is a losing strategy.

I spoke with Lawrence C. Reardon, a political science professor at the University of New Hampshire, before and after the closure of his school's Confucius Institute. The university struggled for years to find quality Chinese instruction. "We pulled a retired person from the community to teach the language, which was a complete disaster," he told me. The university had opened a Confucius Institute in 2010. The teachers provided decent lessons, and Reardon said he saw no attempt to "influence American thought or students." More important, in 2015 he used the popularity of Chinese studies on campus to persuade the provost to fund a tenure-track position in Chinese literature and languages. Yet in November 2019, the university canceled its Japanese-language program, and he worries that without outside funding, like from a Confucius Institute, the school would do the same thing with Chinese.[39] Senators Marco Rubio (R-Fla.) and Ted

Cruz (R-Tex.) supported legislation that prohibited universities with Confucius Institutes from receiving Defense Department funding for Chinese-language training. And indeed, in April 2021 the university announced it would close its Confucius Institute, because of concerns from Washington. "The federal government has made it increasingly difficult for us to operate the Institute, including the real possibility of losing significant federal research funding if we do not close the institute," a university spokesperson said. But the Defense Department spends only several million dollars annually funding these programs and, as of September 2021, at only thirteen universities—not including the University of New Hampshire.

"The trainings I got at Columbia were far superior to what is provided here. But this isn't Columbia," Reardon told me. His Confucius Institute–sponsored program, he said, "was a decent, introductory-type program that will spur people to try to study Chinese." He added, "Is this the best of situations? No." There is now less opportunity to study Chinese at the University of New Hampshire than there was a year ago.

When I started studying Chinese in 2002, my textbook taught me the words for "comrade" and "production brigade" before "sleep" or "school." Some Taiwanese and Chinese scoff at the way the Party—with its clunky talk of "win-win cooperation," "harmonious society," and "Politburo Standing Committee"—has cheapened the Chinese language. To understand China today, however, one must comprehend Party-speak. Confucius Institutes are not ideal, nor are partnerships with Chinese universities. But unless the U.S. government spends tens of millions of dollars more supporting the study of Chinese, they are necessary. Studying Chinese offers key insights into China. An imperfect and politically tinged understanding of Chinese is better than no understanding at all.

IN A SHANGHAI AIRPORT IN SEPTEMBER 2019, I SAW A CHINESE EDItion of *Bloomberg Businessweek*. I wondered to myself if they eliminated sensitive words in their translation of stories—in other words, if they censored their Chinese edition. I debated buying it and comparing it with the original, but then I stopped myself. My mind turned to Bloomberg TV: I don't have a financial relationship with the studio, but I regularly appear as a commentator on their shows, and I would be delighted if they paid me. Bloomberg producers never once told me to change the way I spoke or to tone down my criticism of Beijing: the closest they came was when they booked me to discuss a Chinese company's ownership of Grindr and asked me not to use the phrase "dick pics."

I consoled myself by thinking that my workload was too heavy and that the story was unimportant. But it's hard not to call it a moment of intellectual cowardice.

I self-censor. Sometimes I temper my criticisms to avoid offending people more supportive of the Party. I've also taken money from organizations linked to the Party and consulted for corporations that strive to maintain access to China. As is true with many of the targets of this book, my worst crimes were sins of omission rather than commission. What key stories did I shy away from because I wanted to preserve my access? What truths did I not uncover out of fear or greed? What crucial questions didn't I ask powerful people because I feared offending them?

Many people I interviewed about censorship mentioned a 2002 *New York Review of Books* article by Perry Link, a noted China scholar at the University of California Riverside who hasn't been able to enter mainland China since 1995.[40] Link said he doesn't know exactly why he was blacklisted, but that his work on the Tiananmen massacre cemented his status as unwelcome. In the article, Link compared China's censorship to an anaconda in a chandelier. "Normally the great snake doesn't move," he wrote. "It doesn't have to. It feels no need to be clear about its prohibitions. Its constant silent message is 'You yourself decide,' after which, more often than not, everyone in its shadow makes his or her large and small adjustments—all quite 'naturally.'"

Perhaps my biggest conflict of interest comes from the World Economic Forum, the much derided and envied convener of an annual conference in Davos, Switzerland. For the last several years, I've written reports for it, attending sessions at Davos and taking notes for the forum to publish. It pays well and allows me both a free trip to Davos and access to prominent global officials. Do I hold my tongue about the sycophancy with which the forum addresses the Party leadership, allowing them to appear as a paragon of globalization and development while overlooking their crimes against humanity in Xinjiang? Yes. In January 2020, I attended a session with Rao Yi, a brilliant neurobiologist who spoke eloquently about renouncing his American citizenship after hearing of the horrors in Iraq and in Guantánamo Bay. But the idea that Party officials are committing atrocities in Xinjiang never emerged. When the moderator asked for questions, I wanted to break the quiet in the room and artfully ask about the hypocrisy. Or just say, "But what about the camps in Xinjiang?" But I was working for the forum, and so I maintained silence. It felt lousy.

Or perhaps my largest conflict of interest comes from the company I now run. In the summer of 2020, I grew frustrated with how environmental, social, and governance (ESG) rankings—a popular way for investors to measure the societal impact and sustainability of businesses—addressed China. A Chinese company like Hikvision could receive a high ESG score because of its climate policies, even though it makes surveillance cameras for concentration camps. I then realized that there were no good ways of measuring corporate exposure to China, and so I launched a firm, Strategy Risks, that ranks companies on their exposure to the Party. My company doesn't work with the companies it ranks, closing off one avenue for conflicts of interest. But we do consult, for nonprofits as well as companies. And like Kissinger's and Albright's firms, we don't disclose our client list.

Does this change the way I speak publicly? Undoubtedly. How much do my clients' interests influence me? I don't know. Keeping one's intellectual independence is a tricky proposition. "Most lobbyists are not born with a position on catalytic converters," said Harry McPherson, a top aide to President Lyndon B. Johnson and a longtime lobbyist. "In developing the argument for the client's position, they often convince themselves of its truth."[41]

And on a much smaller level, I treasure my relationship with *The Washington Post*, a newspaper where several friends work and where I'm a contributing columnist, and so I don't criticize it for the money it has received from the Propaganda Department of the Communist Party to publish excerpts from the newspaper *China Daily*.

When is it appropriate to self-censor? The definition, remember, is "control of what you say or do in order to avoid annoying or offending others, but without being told officially that such control is necessary." Bloomberg is a rare journalism organization that strictly prohibits its staff from commenting on the company without permission; in most others, it's considered bad form—intuitively unattractive and ungrateful—to call out one's own supporters, funders, and employers.

But Bloomberg the company, and Bloomberg the failed presidential candidate, showed major weakness on China. They started strong; in 2012, the company ran an impressive series of stories on the wealth of the families of the senior politician Bo Xilai, and Xi.[42] While they uncovered no evidence of illegal behavior, the influential articles showed how the families of both leaders traded on their connections to earn tens of millions of dollars. Before the Xi story ran, the Chinese ambassador to the United States had warned Bloomberg's then editor in chief, Matt Winkler, that "bad things" would happen if they published the story and "good things" if they spiked it.[43] After the Xi story, Beijing blocked Bloomberg's website, limited its ability to sell its lucrative terminals in China, and restricted some Bloomberg journalists from getting China visas.

And so Bloomberg hired Kissinger to help the company solve the crisis, and improve relations with Beijing.[44] It's unknown what advice Kissinger gave or if he raised the Bloomberg case to Chinese leaders. But soon after the hiring, Bloomberg editors killed a story Bloomberg journalists had been reporting on the government backing enjoyed by Wang Jianlin, the founder of the Chinese conglomerate Wanda. On an October 2013 call with colleagues, Winkler compared China to Nazi Germany in the 1930s and made the unlikely claim that running the story would get them kicked out of China: though Beijing has restricted individual journalists, it has not banned a major foreign news outlet in decades.[45] Bloomberg himself repeated that claim. "If a country gives you the license to do something with certain restrictions, you have two choices: You either accept the license and do it that way, or you don't do business there," he said during a January 2014 company town hall meeting. He added, "Some people tried to make this into something that we should be ashamed of, and we have nothing to be ashamed of."[46] In March 2014, Bloomberg's chairman,

Peter Grauer, reportedly told his staff in Hong Kong that the journalists forced his sales team to do a "heroic job" repairing the company's relationship with Beijing, and that the company would be "straight back in the shit-box" if they ever did anything like that again.

In February 2015, Bloomberg finally ran a profile of Wang. Titled "Chinese Billionaire Is Ready for His Hollywood Close-Up," it contains nothing critical of Wang, instead portraying him as an exemplar of "discipline" and "simplicity."[47] Bloomberg journalists who worked on the story reportedly tried to include information connecting Wang to the families of Party elite, but senior editors removed it.[48]

Bloomberg isn't the only American publication to yield to China. In 2014, a Hong Kong–based investment group called Integrated Whale Media purchased a majority stake in Forbes Media, one of the United States' best-known media companies. It's hard to demonstrate causality in these cases. But since that purchase, there have been several instances of editorial meddling on stories involving China that raise questions about *Forbes* magazine's commitment to editorial independence[49]—including the deletion of the articles written for *Forbes* by a well-known China critic. The magazine later partnered with Bank of China, to launch a list of the top Chinese international schools, which they published in May 2021. It's not uncommon for American media companies to work with financial institutions. It is rare, however, for them to partner with an arm of the Chinese state. In an email, a *Forbes* spokesperson said that "Forbes' investors don't interfere with Forbes' editorial independence, and they are not involved in Forbes' editorial decisions . . . Forbes works with financial institutions around the world, and China is no exception."[50]

The situation with Starbucks' Howard Schultz, who flirted with a presidential run in 2019, illustrates the conflicts inherent in many billionaires' presidential ambitions. Schultz has long wagered that Starbucks would succeed in China. Speaking in July 2018 at the world's then largest Starbucks—in Shanghai, of course—Schultz said, "I will say, unequivocally, that anyone who is betting against Starbucks in China is dead wrong."[51] But how could Americans expect a businessman like Schultz to enact policies that contravene both his interests and his legacy? When Apple—a company that's less exposed to the

Chinese market than Starbucks—announced in January 2019 that iPhone sales were down in China, its stock price dropped nearly 10 percent.[52] (If that happened to Starbucks, Schultz's net worth would lose tens of millions of dollars in a day.) In April 2017, Schultz spoke at Tsinghua University, Xi's alma mater and one of China's top universities. "We are operating Starbucks in China, not as an American company; we are actually operating here as a Chinese company," he said.[53] That's an excellent strategy for building a successful foreign business in China but a disqualifying one for a U.S. presidential candidate and a worrying strategy for an American business.

And so for Bloomberg, who owns 88 percent of Bloomberg LP and is the twentieth richest person in the world, with a net worth *Forbes* estimates at $59 billion.[54] Bloomberg is the news service China "respects the most because they think we're straight up," Bloomberg said in 2019. Hong Kong accounts for 4 percent of Bloomberg's $10 billion annual revenues, and the mainland 1 percent, but, as Bloomberg said in 2019, their terminal business in China is "growing very rapidly."[55]

SELF-CENSORSHIP DOESN'T JUST MEAN TEMPERING CRITICISM OF the Party; it also means restricting praise. After several years of debate, many academics have grown more aware of Beijing's influence on the academy. But roughly a dozen scholars and activists have told me privately that because of growing worries in the United States, they've felt impelled to criticize China, or withhold praise for the country and its policies, in ways they felt to be intellectually dishonest. "Any time I praise China, I add 'although,' afraid of being seen as a CCP propagandist," the Stanford University professor Xu Yiqing tweeted in May 2020.

Victor Shih, an associate professor of political economy at the University of California San Diego, told me he fears the U.S. government, in its attempts to protect American institutions from Beijing-backed spying or industrial espionage, may "cause some degree of self-censorship among Chinese Americans" as they start to fear the consequences of being seen as insufficiently loyal to America. The deplorable rise of violence in the United States against Asian Americans since the start of the coronavirus pandemic has exacerbated these fears.

This self-censorship occasionally enters into the D.C. policy debate. In April 2020, a foreign policy analyst at a D.C. think tank was editing a white paper on arms control and wanted to include contributions from Chinese military experts. Someone on the Hill told him that if he invited Chinese experts, he risked Congress ignoring the project, because they wouldn't trust what the Chinese said. Think tanks and educational institutions have to balance their vigilance against the Party's influence with the need for excellent primary and secondary source material about and instruction on China and the Party itself.

Perhaps nothing exemplifies the complexities of speaking about China in an American academic setting more than the experience of David Shambaugh, a political science professor at George Washington University and one of America's best-known China experts. A frequent speaker about Sino-U.S. relations at organizations like the prominent nonprofit the National Committee on United States–China Relations (NCUSCR), Shambaugh described himself to me as "one of the most candid and outspoken China scholars in the field."

In March 2015, Shambaugh published a widely circulated article in *The Wall Street Journal* arguing that "the endgame of Chinese communist rule has now begun." Shambaugh's piece forthrightly addressed his views on the most sensitive issue in China. "Communist rule in China is unlikely to end quietly," he wrote. "Its demise is likely to be protracted, messy and violent. I wouldn't rule out the possibility that Mr. Xi will be deposed in a power struggle or coup d'état."[56]

After the article came out, Shambaugh faced reprisals from Beijing. "I have been punished by the Chinese government," he said in March 2018 at an event at the Brookings Institution.[57] "I have paid a personal and professional price." He added that "Chinese state retribution is real, and that's a price that everybody has to consider when they say something." Though he didn't elaborate, several people I spoke to said that after the article was published, the Chinese government treated Shambaugh with less respect than he was accustomed to receiving as a top China scholar: his Chinese counterparts seemed less interested in his thoughts and advice, and he got less important meetings, a bruising insult in status-conscious D.C.

In August 2021, Shambaugh told me, "The fact of the matter was not necessarily one of *respect*—but one of *invitations*. Following the publication of the *Wall Street Journal* article I was completely cut off (to this day) from invitations from Beijing-based institutions that previously regularly invited me. I was told, informally, that there was a ban on inviting me," he said, adding that "I have *never* had a visa application denied." (Italics in the original.)

Writing about the three *T*s didn't hurt Shambaugh's relationship with Beijing; predicting the collapse of the Party did. "He clearly spoke his mind back in 2015, when he predicted the collapse of the Party," said a China academic, who asked to speak anonymously. "And it seems clear that he has paid a price for it in terms of access to China and top Chinese scholars, analysts, and officials."

Pei, who shares some of Shambaugh's views about the Party's weaknesses, told me he has tried to avoid some of the difficulties Shambaugh has faced, adding that "in my own writing, I don't use words that will provoke, such as 'collapse,' because that is such a sensitive word." He prefers the word "unraveling." "It's a lot safer to describe the process," he said, "than predict the event."

Yet Shambaugh has encouraged other academics to self-censor. Several years before the *Wall Street Journal* article, in late 2012, Shambaugh offered a very different view on how, or whether, to speak publicly about China to a group of young academics at the NCUSCR. "At some point, you'll receive a call from a journalist, who will ask you about Taiwan, or Tibet, or Tiananmen," Shambaugh said, according to three of the young academics. "And when that happens, you should put down the phone and run as far away as possible." When I asked Shambaugh about this anecdote, he responded, by email, "I said no such thing, would never say such a thing, and do not believe such a thing." But as Pei, the Claremont McKenna professor, put it, American academics "have to be very careful" about what they say or do about China publicly. "We sort of know where the red lines are. But of course, the lines keep moving." When I emailed with Shambaugh in August 2021, he reiterated that the headline of the article—"The Coming Chinese Crackup"—misrepresented his views in 2015 and today. Moreover, he said his views have shifted. Xi has "recognized the fragilities and serious challenges facing the Party," he said, and today, the CCP is "stronger, more disciplined, and less corrupt."

Until about 2019, being an American scholar or journalist in China was akin to walking around with a ring of fire: you're mostly protected—especially as a white male—but it's easy to burn those you encounter. The Columbia University professor Andrew Nathan is the co-editor, with Link, of *The Tiananmen Papers,* a controversial book on Tiananmen featuring Party documents smuggled out of China. Both Nathan and Link have been systematically denied visas to China. Nathan also chairs one of Columbia's Institutional Review Boards, which oversees research ethics. He told me the board would likely reject the application of a student who planned to interview and visit with dissidents in China, because "you're going to get those people in danger, and those are human subjects, and you're not allowed to create risk."

With the crackdown in Xinjiang, worsening tensions between the United States and Beijing, and Xi's centralization of power, the calculus has shifted: more and more subjects bring danger to those who wish to research them. The arbitrary December 2018 detention and the March 2021 trials of the former Canadian diplomat Michael Kovrig, who was conducting research for the nonprofit International Crisis Group, and the Canadian tour guide Michael Spavor personalized the issue for many Westerners. "A lot of the new advice we are getting, as graduate students, is to do a project that does not require you to necessarily do fieldwork in China," said Lev Nachman, a PhD student at UC Irvine.[58]

This matter of practicality intersects with Beijing's growing opacity. "When I'm advising a PhD dissertation, I'm always thinking about access to data," Nathan said, adding that he discourages students from pursuing theses about power struggles in Beijing, or on the relationship between civilians and the Party's People's Liberation Army, not because they're sensitive topics, but because their inaccessibility makes them incredibly difficult to study. "Feasibility is always a reasonable criterion," he told me. Some students consider this when they choose their subjects. "I wanted to stick with research that could be safely and effectively conducted from outside of China," said Peter

Marino, a PhD student at the New School studying how Chinese political elite use philosophical traditions in their public discourse, "because I did not want to be concerned about the Party restricting my access to China, let alone researching there."

Self-censorship is certainly not omnipresent. I have yet to meet an American academic who claims that his or her career has been ruined because he or she offended Beijing. Nor do I know of any cases where a Confucius Institute ended its relationship with an American university or where Beijing forced an American university to close its campus or institution in China because the school declined to self-censor. And being blacklisted has "actually been pretty liberating," Millward said. It "cuts you off from worry," he told me. "Before, I worried about" self-censorship, Link said, "and cut corners. Not anymore."

The debate over self-censorship is a proxy for the larger and more important debate over how to react to the rise of China. Should the United States protest it? Accede to it? Try to stop it? Should U.S. policy be to live with the Party, strengthen it, weaken it, or overthrow it? It's a conversation begging for a national debate. (Those academics who support the Party should have the platforms—and the intellectual courage—to argue their side of the debate.) Regardless of the reservations many U.S. academics have about American global dominance, many China studies professors have spent enough time in China to conclude they don't want to live in Beijing's world. It's heartening that amid the genocide in Xinjiang, overwhelming digital surveillance in China, and the growing difficulties of conducting fieldwork there, some academics are methodically challenging various aspects of the Party and its control of information. More Americans should think critically about how to respond to China's growing influence, and not act as Xi's willing censors.

PART THREE

WITH FRIENDS LIKE THESE . . .

CHAPTER SEVEN

Friendship and Its Discontents

★

HOW MANY LIVES WOULD IT HAVE SAVED IF AMERICANS COULD HAVE imagined a pandemic emerging from China and spreading throughout the world? Max Brooks did just that, in his 2006 novel, *World War Z*. In the book, a zombie apocalypse precipitates a Chinese civil war, which ends when a Chinese nuclear submarine destroys the Politburo's bunker with a warhead.[1] Patient zero is a boy living near the Chinese metropolis of Chongqing. After the zombie attack, Tibet declares independence and its capital, Lhasa, thrives, becoming the world's most populous city. "The Social Democrats have smashed the Llamist Party in a landslide victory," Brooks imagines, in a free and fair Tibet election, "and the streets are still roaring with revelers."[2]

If it had been faithful to the novel, the film *World War Z* would have had a similar plot. But the 2013 film makes no mention of Tibet. An early version of the film features a scene where characters say the outbreak originated in China, but Paramount, the studio releasing the film, censored it.[3] "A zombie plague in China implies the fallibility of the government," Brooks told me, explaining the decision. And a disaster plague "implies the system is flawed." In the film version of *World War Z*, China doesn't appear at all.

Contrast *World War Z* with the television show *The Last Ship* (2014–2018), about another global pandemic, which decimates 80 percent of the world's population. While the pandemic doesn't originate in China, it does cause a coup there and a leader intensely antagonistic to American interests. "Rumor is he killed all of the top leadership and waited out the plague next to their rotting bodies," says a former navy intelligence officer about China's president and former minister of state security Peng Wu.[4] "Listen," another American official says in *The Last Ship*, "Peng is a thug, plain and simple."[5] *The Last Ship* presented the uncensored vision of a fantastical reality. The film version of *World War Z* did not. Indeed, other successful American industries show that Hollywood's way of dealing with China is not the only way.

Why is it so important that Hollywood refuses to imagine China as the source of a virus? Because Hollywood's fantasies inform both our reality and our imagination. From *Guess Who's Coming to Dinner*, the landmark 1967 Sidney Poitier film about an interracial couple, to 2005's beautiful cowboy love story *Brokeback Mountain*, Hollywood can spur a more equitable reality. But just as Hollywood can marginalize communities—in 2015 and 2016, all twenty of the acting Oscar nominations went to white actors, sparking a diversity push encapsulated in the viral hashtag #OscarsSoWhite—it can also marginalize ideas. The best way to understand just how beholden Hollywood is to the Party is to compare it with similar cultural industries: industries that manage to flourish and maintain their freedom of speech when it comes to China. In other words, powerful American institutions and individuals do not need to be friends with China. Many choose not to and, more often than not, emerge with both their integrity and their bottom line intact.

For someone who rarely watches television, bingeing on shows that portrayed China was a hidden oasis. Not because I craved watching portrayals of Chinese as enemies or victims, but because after watching dozens of films that bloodlessly portray Chinese people, I wanted to see them portrayed as humans, with the faults and complexities that characterize our species.

And I wanted to see Americans grapple with the changes wrought by the looming potential loss of exceptionalism. Will China replace America as the world's most powerful country? Should it? If so, what is a way to gracefully yield? And if not, what should Americans do to stop it? The culture industry helps Americans process and debate existential questions like these.

Indeed, the television and music industries' behavior rebuts Hollywood's cowardly insistence that this is the way the system must work. These industries have a freedom of speech that Hollywood refuses to even dream about: dramas, talk shows, satires, sitcoms, and songs, and the celebrities themselves comfortably analyze, mock, and occasionally skewer the Party for its foibles and failings. "It is different in TV than it is in movies," the producer of *The Last Ship* Brad Fuller said in 2016. "We never heard, 'No, you don't want China to be the bad guy in the TV show.'"[6] Television shows have been surprisingly forthright when they talk about China, across a wide range of issues—from politics, to trade, to racial issues, to pandemics. *Contagion* (2011), the other major disease film of the last decade, portrayed a virus that spread from Hong Kong and Macau, but not mainland China—a subtle but important distinction. A 2014 episode of the TV thriller *The Blacklist,* however, features a Chinese scientist with knowledge of her country's secret germ warfare program who escapes a Chinese prison to tell the American government.[7]

The self-censorship that hobbles Americans' understanding of their most important foreign relationship is nowhere in TV land. And that is a great thing.

This partially arises from the divergent histories of the industries' relationship with China. Television executives never obsessed over the Chinese market with the same fervor that their Hollywood brethren did, nor was there a *Kundun* incident to chasten them. China, in other words, never loomed over television studios as it did over Hollywood.

In November 1998, the month after Disney's CEO, Eisner, apologized to China's premier, Zhu, for *Kundun,* American television aired its first-ever episode shot in China: an episode of *The Drew Carey Show,* where Drew gets stranded in a Chinese village.[8] "In America we think of China as the other end of the Earth," said the series director, "and the joke we wanted to do here was that Drew got sent as far away as possible, and China seemed like the natural place."[9]

In the first decade of the twenty-first century, China remained distant for television producers. Rupert Murdoch's well-publicized failure to stream foreign television channels in China—we hit a "brick wall," he said in 2005—dissuaded other television studios from obsessing over the market.[10] (The music industry might have been even more pirated in China than film and TV DVDs: in 2007, a trade group estimated that 85 percent of CDs sold in China were counterfeit.[11])

And television is just more difficult to export than film. Humor, a larger slice of the television business than the film business, is more culturally specific. Foreign markets tend to prefer licensing and remaking reality TV or game shows, rather than importing the American version.[12] "Chinese audiences love the film spectaculars," said Lindsay Conner, a lawyer who has structured entertainment deals between the United States and China. "They're not especially in need of our TV comedy and dramas." And forget about American news shows, which are far too uncensored and America focused for China.

As a result, twenty-first-century television has much more closely mirrored the American national conversation about China. In 2003 the crime series *Law & Order: Special Victims Unit* ran an episode about the murder of a young Tibetan dissident who was tortured before fleeing China for New York City. "In prison, she was stripped naked, held in a small cage without food, and beaten around the clock," an activist explains to the investigators. "As if the taser to the genitals wasn't enough."[13]

In an October 2008 episode of *South Park*, the totalitarian synchronization of the drummers in Beijing's Summer Olympics opening ceremony gives the nine-year-old Eric Cartman nightmares. "The Chinese are taking over the world and nobody's doing anything!" he says to his classmate Butters. "We have to stop the Chinese now." ("Aw, I can't stop the Chinese tonight!" Butters replies. "I'm supposed to make a model car with my dad.")[14]

In December 2008, in the depths of the financial crisis, the law dramedy *Boston Legal* finds the protagonists' firm under siege from a Chinese law firm that wants to acquire them. "The good news is they intend to keep on most of the attorneys here, so as transitions go, this will—" one senior partner explains, before the firm's name partner, played by William Shatner, interrupts him. "Yeah, I saw their transition in Tibet, I'm not a fan. We're not selling out to a bunch of Communists," he says. He pulls out two paintball pistols and starts shooting the Chinese, who scatter. "I don't want to fall into their hands," says another senior partner, played by Candice Bergen. "As Hillary Clinton said, 'How do you get tough on your banker?' The United States may very well work for China one day, I get that, it's a new world order."[15]

As Hollywood grew more beholden to China in the second decade of the twenty-first century, the gap between film's and television's portrayal of the country grew starker. The film *Blackhat* (2015) and the TV show *Mr. Robot* (2015–2019) both feature brilliant misanthropic American hackers untangling a mystery related to China. But that's where the similarities end. In *Blackhat*, about a shadowy group of terrorists who hack into a nuclear reactor with the goal of earning money by disrupting global commodity prices, the hacker partners with both the FBI and a captain in the People's Liberation Army. "We go head-to-head with the Chinese" constantly, says an FBI special agent. "Not a bad idea to be face-to-face working with them, for once."[16] The film portrays the PLA as a reasonable and orderly force attempting to reduce hacking in America. Released by the American film production company Legendary Pictures, a year before Wanda bought the studio, *Blackhat* censored to please Beijing. During the making of *Blackhat*, U.S. studio executives communicated a list of things related to China that could not happen in the film, a source familiar with the matter told me. "We were told that any scenes in [mainland] China couldn't have any guns, or gunfights in them, because 'there are no guns in China,'" the source said. (Legendary didn't respond to multiple requests for comment.)

Mr. Robot—which is literally a delusion in the mind of the hacker protagonist—feels more realistic than *Blackhat*. In the show, China annexes the Congo.[17] The time-obsessed Zhang Zhi, when dressed as a man, runs the Ministry of State Security; as a transgender woman, she leads a Chinese hacker group, the Dark Army. An FBI agent visits Beijing and wears a face mask; pre-COVID, many Chinese and foreigners would occasionally wear masks on polluted days. I can't remember seeing a Hollywood film made after 2008 where an American wears a mask in Beijing.

In the 1996 *Independence Day*, the president displays a large framed photograph of himself with the Dalai Lama, between a photograph with his wife and a photograph with the pope. In the 2016 sequel, however, the Dalai Lama was nowhere to be seen. The film critic Donald Clarke called the sequel, with its Chinese product placements and casting of a wooden Chinese actress, a "cynical love song to China."[18] Meanwhile, in a March 2017 episode of *Madam Secretary* (2014–2019), the secretary of state calls the Chinese foreign minister a "toddler" for his views on Tibet.[19] Airing three months after Kissinger persuaded the Trump team to reject a meeting with the Dalai Lama, the episode features a soulful meeting between the secretary of state and the ailing Dalai Lama, who passes away at the end of the episode.

Hollywood is of course not a monolith. Over the last decade, several American directors have publicly—albeit gently—challenged Beijing. Even after Quentin Tarantino complied with censors' requests to tone down the violence in *Django Unchained* (2012), Beijing yanked the movie from screens; it eventually allowed the release of a more censored version.[20] "I have a lot of Chinese fans who buy my movies on the street and watch them and I'm OK with it. I'm not OK with it in other places, but if the government's going to censor me then I want the people to see it any way they can," said Tarantino, in a rare example of a Hollywood director sanctioning bootlegs.[21] "It sucks really," Lana Wachowski, the co-director of *Cloud Atlas* (2012), which lost thirty-eight minutes to the censors before they permitted the screening in China, told a Chinese publication. "But I believe you can watch the full version online."[22] Voices like Tarantino's and Wachowski's were rare: even *Cloud Atlas*'s co-director Tom Tykwer disagreed. "Although the mainland version is a bit constrained, [we] fully believe in the regulator's editing standards," he said.[23]

Indeed, comments like Tykwer's are far more common. Hollywood filmmakers in the second decade of the twenty-first century employed striking verbal contortions to describe the cutting, banning, and sometimes desecration of their films. "I'm not morally offended or outraged," the director Steven Soderbergh told *The New York Times* about his film *Contagion* (2011), shot partially in Hong Kong and censored by Beijing. "It's fascinating to listen to people's interpretations of your story."[24] While allowing that American censorship is "not as draconian" as Chinese censorship, James Cameron said in May 2012 that he "can't be judgmental about another culture's process," after Beijing screened a censored 3-D version of *Titanic*, the first major Hollywood film to gross more in China than in the United States.[25] In 2011, the American director Wayne Wang compared Chinese censorship to getting called on the set of his Jennifer Lopez romance *Maid in Manhattan* to complain about "so and so's hair. It's the same thing."[26]

Besides the Tibet supporters Gere and Sharon Stone, there are only two major exceptions to Hollywood's acquiescence. While shooting a movie in China in 2011, the actor Christian Bale read about Chen Guangcheng, a blind dissident held under house arrest in a village in the province of Shandong. "It literally made me want to vomit," Bale later said, "hearing about this man who should have been celebrated." In December, the actor joined CNN on a journey to visit Chen; several months later, Chen fled into the U.S. embassy, sparking an international incident. In October 2012, a free Chen finally met Bale in New York.[27] When I interviewed Chen in D.C. in 2013, the biggest smile I saw was when he described his January 2013 trip to Disneyland with Bale.[28] Bale "dared to lose the Chinese market," Chen told me. "That's not something just anyone would do." Some protest quietly. "At least on the creative side, partnering with China has become more distasteful, and rightly so," one prominent Hollywood screenwriter who has written about China, and who asked to remain anonymous, told me in August 2020. "It's fucking concentration camps." But Hollywood's content remains fettered, and most people remain silent. "I think it happened very slowly and insidiously," said the filmmaker Judd Apatow, the other major exception. And now "there are a million or more Muslims in reëducation camps in China, and you don't really hear much about it."[29]

Until recently, Hong Kong was a thriving source for films which offered realistic portrayals of both mainland China and Hong Kong. But Beijing's crackdown ended that. As this book is going to press, Hong Kong filmmakers are panicking about the planned amendments to a film censorship law, which would ban screenings of films that hurt national security. Like many of the recent legal changes in Hong Kong, this one also extends retroactively: older films can have their approvals revoked under the new rules. Those who violate the law may face up to three years of jail, and fines of up to $128,000.[30]

Some Hollywood producers say no market exists for content that portrays China more critically—realistically, in other words.* But American television belies that notion. It shows that there is a demand for these issues to be on-screen in the United States—and in China, as well. Hundreds of Chinese films and television shows feature Chinese antagonists; for most Chinese media, which doesn't feature foreigners, when a show or a film needs an enemy, it has to be Chinese. Even the Party occasionally approves of American media with Chinese antagonists. The second season of *House of Cards*, the Machiavellian political drama that skewered political corruption in both China and the United States, streamed freely in China: possibly because the high-ranking politician Wang Qishan reportedly approved of the show.

In the satirical show *Veep*, the narcissistic vice president Selina Meyer, played by Julia Louis-Dreyfus, frees Tibet from Chinese rule, calling her accomplishment "some man on the moon legacy shit." And then, in exchange for the Chinese government interfering in the 2020 U.S. election to support her candidacy, she promises to return Tibet to China. When she dies, her former press secretary says Meyer "is fondly remembered for briefly freeing what was once known as the nation of Tibet."[31]

The disruptive power of American television comes from its critical and realistic portrayal of China. For the music industry, it's less the music itself than the celebrity power of musicians that can prompt American individuals and institutions to push back against pernicious aspects of the Party and also remind Americans that free speech extends to American conversations about China too.

The most meaningful role that musicians have played involves their support of Tibet. In the heyday of the Tibet movement in the 1990s, musicians shared the vanguard with Hollywood royalty. Second only to Richard Gere in the firmament of stars supporting the Tibet movement was the Beastie Boys co-founder Adam Yauch.[32] A Tibet activist until his death in 2012, Yauch started the Milarepa Fund, which produced the Tibetan Freedom Concerts, in 1994. (The

---

* Imagine how flat—and problematic—American films would be if they refused to critically address America's myriad problems?

following year he met his future wife, the Tibetan activist Dechen Wangdu, when the Dalai Lama lectured at Harvard.[33])

In the years since Disney helped destroy the Tibet movement in Hollywood, American musicians have become the Dalai Lama's most famous supporters and the most voluble critics of Beijing's human rights abuses in the entertainment world. More than twenty years after Guns N' Roses' first album, *Appetite for Destruction,* debuted at number one, the band released a record titled *Chinese Democracy* (2008). Inspired, the band's front man Axl Rose said, by Scorsese's *Kundun,* the title song claims "you're keeping your own kind in hell / when your Great Wall rocks, blame yourself."[34] Several months before the Beijing Olympics, the Icelandic pop star Björk performed in Shanghai and earned herself a ban from performing in China by adding the word "Tibet" to her song "Declare Independence." The pop stars Lorde and Sting joined on a 2015 album celebrating the Dalai Lama's eightieth birthday, while Lady Gaga, one of the world's most popular performers, interviewed the Dalai Lama in June 2016 about self-esteem, happiness, and eating disorders.[35] "They won't let us" into China, the Red Hot Chili Peppers' drummer, Chad Smith, said in December 2018. "We've got Dalai Lama connections, they don't like that."[36]

In February 2019, I attended the thirty-second annual benefit concert for Tibet House, a nonprofit founded in 1987 by the Columbia University professor and Buddhist monk Robert Thurman—father of the actress Uma Thurman, who serves on the board.[37] Often held at Carnegie Hall, the show has long been the premier Tibet event in the entertainment industry. I thought its 2019 incarnation would feature musical has-beens or never-beens. And while one designer I spoke with at the after-party said the decor evoked a "Tibetan bar mitzvah of the 1980s," the event shone with the talent and star power often conspicuously lacking in events that brush against Chinese human rights issues.

"It's hard to imagine living here without Tibetans," said Laurie Anderson, the composer and wife of the late Lou Reed, before leading the audience in a therapeutic ten-second scream. After chanting a Neil Young song, the seventy-two-year-old punk goddess Patti Smith thrillingly spit on the stage at Carnegie Hall, while her bandmate Lenny Kaye shouted "we want a free Tibet" to cheers. "All hail Mother Nature," she boomed before strutting into the wings. Debbie Harry sang a "Heart of Glass" mash-up while wearing a cape that read, "Stop Fucking the Planet." Stephen Colbert joked, "I'm not here just because I'm trying to book the Dalai Lama on the show. But if he's got a rep here or anything like that."

Do the entertainers worry this hurts their opportunity to play or sell in China? "I thought about it," Bernard Sumner, a founding member of New Order and Joy Division, told me, after he performed at the 2019 Tibet House benefit. But in the end, he said, it didn't seem worth sacrificing his beliefs. It's an easier decision for musicians to make. Like book authors, musicians retain far more creative control than do film actors and directors, who have to answer to producers, and their corporate parents, who oversee budgets of tens of millions of dollars or more per film. Moreover, the Chinese music market is much smaller. While the pandemic helped China surpass the United States to become the world's largest film market, the music market is only the seventh largest in the world.[38] There are no known cases of executives from an American corporation calling one of its recording artists and ordering them to change the content so that it won't offend Beijing.

WILL MUSIC AND TELEVISION REMAIN AN OASIS?

Like film, the television industry has grown increasingly consolidated over the years, and the parent companies are wary that Beijing will decide to be bothered by their content.[39] In May 2019, seven months before CBS merged with Viacom, the network's show *The Good Fight* aired an episode with a China subplot. A legal drama set during the Trump era, *The Good Fight* often features musical segments satirizing current events, like the rumored Trump "pee tape." In that May episode, the showrunners had planned a musical number listing items banned in China: like Winnie-the-Pooh, an empty chair, which symbolizes the late Chinese Nobel laureate Liu Xiaobo, and Tiananmen Square. But CBS told the showrunners to delete the song. In response, they threatened to quit. As a compromise, CBS allowed them to air a placard that said, "CBS HAS CENSORED THIS CON-TENT."[40] It hangs silently on the screen for eight and a half seconds. "We had concerns with some subject matter in the episode's animated short," CBS said in a statement. "This is the creative solution that we agreed upon with the producers."[41] The moment was intensely jarring, especially because the deleted song was called "Banned in China."

Companies like Apple, Disney, and Netflix muscling into the television streaming space is also worrisome from a freedom of expression perspective. In early 2018, as Apple TV+ was building original programming, the company's head of international content development told some of the show's creators to "avoid portraying China in a poor light," according to *BuzzFeed*.[42] In 2017, Apple removed a television show from its mainland China app store—a show, backed by the banned spiritual group Falun Gong, called *China Uncensored*. As of August 2021, the show remains inaccessible in China. Tens of thousands of other active apps—from subjects ranging from American media, to gay dating, to the Dalai Lama—have also disappeared from China's Apple Store. "The two things we will never do," said Eddy Cue, Apple's senior vice president who oversees the company's content, "are hard-core nudity and China."[43]

Does Netflix censor its content to please Beijing? In September 2020, the Netflix co-founder and co-CEO Reed Hastings said, "We have not been spending any time on China in the last couple years." This seems unlikely. In April 2017, Netflix signed a licensing deal with iQiyi, one of China's largest streaming platforms.[44] Netflix's racy animated satire *BoJack Horseman* aired on iQiyi for two days, before censors removed it.[45] In March 2018, iQiyi's CEO said the deal had lapsed because "so many of Netflix's originals couldn't pass the Chinese government's regulations on content."[46] In February 2020, Netflix released an environmental, social, and corporate governance report that outlined the nine times it had removed its films from countries around the world since 2015: five were in Singapore, and the others were in Saudi Arabia, Vietnam, Germany, and New Zealand. From a public relations standpoint, this would allow Netflix to claim that it yields to censorship demands elsewhere—not just in China.[47]

What about the China content on Netflix's original films? *The Laundromat* (2019), starring Meryl Streep, Gary Oldman, and Antonio Banderas, dramatized the corruption exposed by the massive Panama Papers leak. On the one hand, *The Laundromat* aired a scene about the political scandal involving the top Chinese official Bo Xilai and his wife, Gu Kailai, and mentioned the organ harvesting of practitioners of Falun Gong, a banned spiritual sect. On the other hand, the film hewed to Beijing's political orthodoxy about Bo and Gu: that they were deeply corrupt officials who were the exception, rather than the rule. "Xi Jinping has made it clear that corruption will no longer be tolerated," Gu says in the film. Scott Z. Burns, the screenwriter for *Contagion,* also wrote and produced *The Laundromat.* When contacted for an interview, his publicist asked, "Is China being portrayed in a positive or negative light?" After being told China was being portrayed "realistically," she declined the interview request. "They didn't want to talk about China too much because it's quite a sensitive topic," said the Chinese actress Li Kunjue, who had a small role in the film.[48]

"I think entertainment companies have to make compromises over time," Hastings said in 2016, in response to a question about censoring to enter foreign markets. "Networks and studios have been navigating those waters for years," added the co-CEO Ted Sarandos, "so we'll just have to do the same." In other words, how can Netflix manage to be friendly with Beijing without losing support in the United States?

THE NBA SCANDAL OF OCTOBER 2019 BROUGHT THIS ISSUE OF friendship with China to the minds of many Americans. On October 4, the Houston Rockets' general manager, Daryl Morey, tweeted and then deleted a post supporting the protests in Hong Kong, which had been raging for six months.[49] That weekend, after Chinese sponsors fled, the Chinese Basketball Association suspended cooperation with the Rockets, and the internet giant Tencent stopped streaming Rockets games, Morey and the team's owner apologized. In Chinese, the league issued a statement saying that "we are extremely disappointed in the inappropriate remarks" made by Morey, while in

America droves of fans and politicians flayed the league for abasing itself. A few days later, the National Basketball Association's commissioner, Adam Silver, issued a statement supporting free speech, and the scandal began to subside.[50]

But the issue brought to light a difficult dichotomy about friendship for American corporations. If they publicly yielded to Beijing, Americans would excoriate them. If they didn't, Beijing might. "We, as American people, do a lot of business in China . . . but Daryl Morey was right," the former NBA star Shaquille O'Neal said in October 2019, about the Houston Rockets general manager and his tweet about Hong Kong. "We're allowed to say what we want to say and we're allowed to speak up about injustices."[51] But LeBron James, the NBA's biggest star, a progressive political icon, and a prominent Trump critic, lambasted Morey.[52] "He wasn't educated on the situation," James said.[53] "So many people could have been harmed, not only financially, but physically. Emotionally. Spiritually."[54]

It's hard to escape the conclusion that Beijing won. In October 2020, almost exactly a year to the day from his deleted tweet, Morey announced he was leaving the Rockets.[55] And just six days before Morey's announcement, Chinese state television CCTV finally aired an NBA game, ending the blackout instituted after the Morey scandal. In December 2020, Morey said that he was "comfortable with what he did," for Hong Kong, but added, "I was extremely concerned. You don't want the second most powerful government on Earth mad at you, if you can avoid it. In this case, I couldn't." "If decades of American policy regarding engagement in China were to change," NBA spokesman Mike Bass said in an emailed response to questions, "we—like other U.S. businesses operating in China—would of course adhere to that change and approach our global efforts differently."[56]

What is the strategy behind Beijing's actions? Beijing convinces foreigners and foreign institutions like the NBA that conversations on a wide range of issues will offend the country and its 1.4 billion people and that the offense will limit Americans' access to the country. "China has a long and very consistent track record of trading the real or imagined benefits of 'access'—visas, market share, joint venture approvals, research cooperation, IPO fees, and the 'honor' of being met at the Purple Light Pavilion in Beijing by someone who far outranks you—for acquiescence and/or silence on its 'red line' issues," said Lucy Hornby, a longtime China journalist.

Criticism of China's unfair treatment of American companies often focuses on technology transfers, state support of domestic businesses, and intellectual-property theft. But Beijing doesn't just want foreign companies to advance its economic interests. It wants them to advance its political ones, too. In subtle and sophisticated ways, Beijing persuades, cajoles, and cudgels American companies to promote the values of the Party, parrot the Party's views, and enshrine self-censorship about China in their corporate cultures. When it's successful, the companies advance Chinese propaganda.

Beijing makes public examples of a small number of people and institutions—like the NBA, or Mercedes-Benz, which Beijing criticized in February 2018 for quoting the Dalai Lama in an Instagram post—which it chooses by some unknown calculus.[57] And when institutions concede, whether they've been made examples of or not, Chinese representatives sometimes convince them they therefore must concede just a little more.

In January 2018, Marriott sent guests an online survey that listed Hong Kong, Taiwan, Tibet, and Macau as countries, and a U.S.-based employee of the company named Roy Jones "liked" a Twitter post about the nationhood of Tibet while manning a Marriott social media account.[58] Beijing made an example of Marriott—a company thriving in China, with nearly three hundred hotels there and growing. Because Beijing likes non-Chinese to think that acknowledging the idea of Tibetan independence is a grave offense, it required Marriott to shut down its Chinese websites and apps for seven days.

The company apologized and, parroting China's propaganda organs, said it didn't "support separatist groups that subvert the sovereignty and territorial integrity of China." And it fired the forty-nine-year-old Jones from his $14-an-hour job. "This job was all I had," Jones said in a March 2018 interview. "I'm at the age now where I don't have many opportunities."[59] Indeed, it's a tough situation for many employees. In 2019, the American stock photo provider Shutterstock began censoring its search in China.[60] After more than 180 employees signed a petition decrying the move, Shutterstock's COO told the petitioners they were free to leave if they didn't like the company's ethical choices.[61] One of the employees who decided to leave, Stefan Hayden, had less than two years before won the company's "All Around Values" award. "Obviously they didn't like those values when they conflicted" with the senior management's desire to placate Beijing, Hayden told me.

One way American companies protect the Party's view is by suppressing negative information; Morey did this when he deleted his tweet, and Hollywood films do this by removing elements the Party may find critical, like when *World War Z* deleted a reference to China. The American entertainment company Activision Blizzard did this as well when it suspended a professional gamer and required him to forfeit $10,000 in prize money for shouting, "Liberate Hong Kong, revolution of our times," in a post-match interview. (After an outcry, the company moderated the punishment.)[62] Beijing does not want to weaken these companies or push them out of China. Instead, it wants them to follow the Party's rules, both in China and globally. "China doesn't just want you to comply with its wishes," the former Singaporean ambassador Bilahari Kausikan said in June 2018. It wants you to "do what it wants without being told."[63] Although Tencent owns 5 percent of Activision Blizzard, it's unlikely that any Chinese source told the company how to act. Like some academics and Hollywood filmmakers, it had internalized Beijing's demands.[64]

And sometimes companies parrot the Party's view by amplifying positive information. After the 2018 incident, Marriott announced an "eight-point rectification plan" to "regain confidence and trust."[65] Part of the plan, according to the *Hong Kong Free Press,* included expanding "employee education globally"—that is, educating its staff on Chinese propaganda.[66] A Versace statement was even more groveling. In August 2019, after an outcry over a T-shirt that implied Hong Kong was independent, the luxury clothing brand affirmed that "we love China and resolutely respect the sovereignty of its territory."[67]

Xi calls this "discourse power"—the ability to shape the narrative and "tell China's story well."[68] Foreign companies and their employees are excellent proxies for evangelizing China's position. While the United States often gets credit for its soft power, China wins in what we could call proxy power. When the retired Chinese basketball star Yao Ming—who now runs the Chinese Basketball

Association, a government-linked organization with a strong Party presence—praises China, Americans expect it. When the then Houston Rockets star James Harden apologizes for his team and professes that "we love China" and "everything there about them," that feels more genuine.[69] (Even the actor John Cena's overwrought May 2021 video apology for implying that Taiwan is a country—"Sorry. Sorry. I'm really sorry. You have to understand that I love and respect China and Chinese people"—sounds heartfelt.[70]) Though Harden's sentiments may be sincere, his contrition advances Beijing's propaganda goals.

Sometimes, when China punishes a foreign company for violating unstated rules, no one bothers to publicly explain how to rectify the crime. The Chinese sportswear firm Anta, for example, simply canceled contract negotiations with the NBA because the league's words were "wrong."[71] To restore their good standing, executives must supplicate, with minimal guidance from the Party-state. "The NBA has been in cooperation with China for many years," the Foreign Ministry spokesman Geng Shuang said at an October 2019 news conference. "It knows clearly in its heart what to say and what to do."

Businesses don't comply because they respect or concur with Beijing's views. They do it because they don't want Beijing to punish them: the Chinese internet giant Tencent had reportedly paid the NBA $1.5 billion for the five-year contract Tencent wanted to cancel after the scandal erupted.[72] The league known for its tolerance cowered, as the sports website *Deadspin* puts it, because Beijing "actually has the ability to do what thick-necked Americans in Oakleys who like to burn shoes on their lawn wish they could: put a giant hole in the NBA's business."[73] And it did: the NBA later estimated the scandal cost them $400 million in lost revenue.[74]

Other times, Beijing communicates specific demands to foreign companies. In April 2018, the Civil Aviation Administration of China sent a letter to forty-four foreign airlines insisting that all their public-facing content clearly refer to Taiwan as part of China, or they would face punishment. Despite a surprisingly forthright statement from the Trump White House denouncing Beijing's move as "Orwellian nonsense and part of a growing trend by the Party to impose its political views on American citizens and private companies," in July

2018 the United States' three major international carriers, United, American, and Delta, bowed to the pressure and reclassified how they referenced Taiwan on their websites.[75]

Now that no major international airlines refer to Taiwan as a country, it would be newsworthy if any of their employees, advertisements, or affiliates said otherwise. It's much safer to self-censor than to risk a scandal that could cost revenue. One day in January 2018, China's Cyberspace Administration ordered the clothing retailer Zara and the world's largest medical device company, Medtronic, to post apologies by 6:00 p.m. for labeling Taiwan as a separate country on their websites.[76] It also demanded that the companies "conduct a comprehensive self-examination" to make sure there were no violations elsewhere on their sites. Both companies complied. In May 2020, Beijing asked the American videoconferencing company Zoom to block several digital events held by Chinese dissidents in the United States commemorating the anniversary of the Tiananmen Square massacre. Zoom acceded.[77] Zoom claimed that it canceled the events to "comply" with local laws.

In stating this, Zoom repeated the argument that many major tech companies make in justifying why they listen to Beijing's asks to censor their content. After LinkedIn launched a Chinese version of its platform in 2014, for example, it explained that it censored posts in America to comply with Chinese laws.[78] "When Zoom says it is obeying local law because it must," writes the George Washington University law professor Donald Clarke, "it is really saying, 'We don't think compliance is so terrible that it's worth risking our China business over.'"[79] Chinese laws are not only opaque but unevenly enforced. Zoom followed the law not because it corresponded to its understanding of China's constitution—which promises freedom of speech—but because a Chinese official *told* it that hosting the events was illegal.

The former Marriott employee Jones said, "We were never trained in any of the social graces when it came to dealing with China."[80] But even with training, it's an incredibly difficult space to navigate. The unpredictability and unevenness of how—and when and why—Beijing acts lead people and institutions to be overcautious, which only makes the strategy more effective. "There is no manual produced by the Chinese government about what we can and cannot say," said the China scholar Max Oidtmann. "The opacity of the Chinese censorship system is designed to make people self-censor to the greatest degree possible."

Beijing doesn't force corporate self-censorship because it cannot tolerate dissent or because the Party is so brittle that criticism would destroy it. Rather, it does so because it can. It's an effective strategy, honed over decades, that co-opts some foreign individuals and companies into facilitating the spread of Chinese propaganda. While there are risks of overplaying—a prolonged NBA scandal, for example, could have caused Chinese fans to direct their anger not only at the league but at Beijing—it has succeeded in creating a coterie of Western chief executives petrified of offending Beijing.

As a result, they lobby for Beijing's interests, in ways that open them up to charges of hypocrisy. After the deadly January 6 riot at the Capitol that President Trump incited, dozens of major U.S. companies said they will review or pause their political donations to Republicans who voted against certifying the election results. (If you won't lobby for the Republican Party, don't lobby for the Communist Party.)[81]

Like many companies, Disney has tried to walk the line between American values and friendship with China. The NBA scandal, which brought censure on the league from both sides of the political system, also hit Disney. "What we learned in the last week—we've learned how complicated this is," Iger said several weeks after Morey's October 2019 tweet.[82] "To take a position that could harm our company in some form would be a big mistake. I just don't believe it's something we should engage in in a public manner."

Many other American executives share Iger's misconception and think they can avoid politics in China. "We got a huge backlash, and I wanted to make clear that the organization has no political position," the Houston Rockets owner, Tilman Fertitta, told ESPN right after the scandal broke.[83] "We're here to play basketball and not to offend anybody"; he tweeted, "we are NOT a political organization."[84] In a December 2018 statement, the consultancy McKinsey said, "we do not support or engage in political activities."[85]

What Iger, Fertitta, and McKinsey all fail to understand, or choose to ignore, is that in today's China, Disney, the NBA, and McKinsey *are* political organizations. To succeed in China as they have, they've all aligned themselves with the Party. The NBA partners with the Ministry of Education. For the NBA to echo Party-speak and claim that the deleted tweet "undoubtedly seriously hurt the feelings of Chinese basketball fans" is an intensely political move. (And, like Chinese Party organizations, the NBA even delivered a different message in English and Chinese.[86] The NBA's comments in English— "the values of the league support individuals' educating themselves and sharing their views on matters important to them"—were far milder.)[87] McKinsey has advised at least twenty-two of China's hundred largest state-owned enterprises, according to *The New York Times*—companies that are literally arms of the Party-state—and in 2018 held a retreat in Xinjiang, just miles from a concentration camp.[88] In China—where McDonald's claimed to "uphold Chinese territorial sovereignty," where Marriott International apologized for supporting subversion—politics dominates.[89]

When the NBA scandal happened, Disney urged self-censorship. At the height of the NBA controversy, a senior news director at ESPN mandated that the network's coverage "avoid any political discussions about China and Hong Kong," according to *Deadspin*'s summary of a leaked memo—a shocking directive for the biggest political sports story of 2019.[90] ESPN even broadcast a map that included Taiwan as part of China and a dotted line to represent China's disputed claims in the South China Sea.[91] "I've literally never seen that map outside of China," tweeted Julian Ku, an expert on Chinese law.[92] Disney owns 80 percent of ESPN.

Television, not beholden, took Hollywood and the NBA to task. "You have to lower your ideals of freedom if you want to suck on the warm teat of China," a Hollywood producer explains to the kids of South Park as they struggle to write a biopic that Chinese censors will approve. "Now I know how Hollywood writers feel," says the ten-year-old Stan as a Chinese guard hovers over him and edits his writing. Mickey Mouse, wearing a shirt that expresses his love for Xi, berates superheroes like Thor for not sufficiently sucking up to the Chinese government. After Beijing scrubbed *South Park* from the Chinese internet, the shows' creators tweeted an "official" apology:

Like the NBA, we welcome the Chinese censors into our homes and hearts. We too love money more than freedom and democracy. Xi doesn't look just like Winnie the Pooh at all. Tune into our 300th episode this Wednesday at 10! Long Live the Great Communist Party of China! May this autumn's sorghum harvest be bountiful! We good now China?[93]

In October 2016, the NBA took over a training camp in Urumqi, the capital of the region of Xinjiang. (Disney's ESPN owns a stake in the NBA China.) The American coaches were frequently harassed; as foreigners, they couldn't rent housing and had to stay in hotels: one coach was detained three times, without cause. Far worse was how the NBA's presence in Xinjiang legitimized one of the world's worst atrocities. "One of the biggest challenges was not only the discrimination and harassment I faced," tweeted Corbin Loubert, a strength coach who worked for the NBA from June 2018 to May 2019, according to his LinkedIn, "but turning a blind eye to the discrimination and harassment that the Uyghur people around me faced."

The NBA said that it ended its involvement with the Xinjiang training camp in the first half of 2019,[94] but Disney's involvement with Xinjiang didn't end. The most devastating part of *Mulan*, Disney's much-anticipated live-action remake of the 1998 animated film, which it released in September 2020, isn't the story.[95] The film retells the ancient Chinese tale of Hua Mulan, a filial daughter who dresses as a man to join the army, honor her father, and save the emperor. While the film engenders pride for China, it does so with a subtle touch: besides a few mentions of defending the Silk Road, a favorite trading route of Xi's, little links it to the modern-day country. *The New York Times* called it "lightly funny and a little sad, filled with ravishing landscapes."[96]

The problem is in the credits. There's a dark side to those landscapes. Disney filmed *Mulan* in regions across China (among other locations).[97] In the credits, Disney offers a special thanks to more than a dozen Chinese institutions that helped with the film. These include four Party propaganda departments in the region of Xinjiang as well as the Public Security Bureau of the city of Turpan in the same region—organizations that are facilitating crimes against humanity. It's sufficiently astonishing that it bears repeating: Disney has thanked four propaganda departments and a public security bureau in Xinjiang, a region in northwest China that is the site of one of the world's worst human rights abuses happening today.[98] Actions like forced sterilization campaigns have caused the birthrate in Xinjiang to plummet more than 48 percent from 2017 to 2019—the largest known decline of any territory since the United Nations began collecting global fertility statistics more than seventy years ago. "Imposing measures intended to prevent births within the group" fits within the legally recognized definition of genocide.[99] Disney, in other words, worked with regions where genocide is occurring, and thanked government departments that are helping to carry it out.[100]

Why did Disney need to work in Xinjiang? It didn't. There are plenty of other regions in China, and countries around the world, that offer the starkly beautiful mountain scenery present in the film. But in doing so, Disney has helped normalize a crime against humanity.

It's unclear exactly what *Mulan*'s relationship with Xinjiang is; in a letter to the British government, the president of Walt Disney Studios Motion Picture Production, Sean Bailey, said that a Chinese firm it hired provided them with a list of credits to be included and that the filming in Xinjiang lasted only four days. But some of the crew members, such as the production designer, Grant Major, spent months in and around Xinjiang, while the director, Niki Caro, visited Xinjiang at least once, on a scouting mission in September 2017, according to her Instagram.[101] In 1946, Disney released *Song of the South*, which glorified life on a plantation in painfully racist terms.[102] Rightfully ashamed, Disney later pulled the film; it's now difficult to find a copy. *Mulan* is Disney's most problematic movie since then. Not because of its content, but because of the shameful compromises Disney made to shoot it.

MY FAVORITE SCENE ABOUT CHINA IN AMERICAN TELEVISION CAME from *The Office*, the satire about small-town American corporate life. "My whole life I believed that America was number one," the dim-witted boss, Michael Scott, says in a 2010 episode. "Not America is number two. England is number two. China should be like, eight."

Played by Steve Carell, Scott had read a magazine in the dentist's office and learned that "China is a sleeping dragon that is just beginning to stir."[103]

"I say we bomb 'em," says the office malcontent Dwight. "By 2020 they're gonna be the world's largest economy and they're getting a taste for protein. We'll all starve." Dwight's outrageous comments don't inspire hatred for the Chinese. Rather, they mock the fear and the ignorance of those who believe—as Malthus did in the eighteenth century, and some do today—that poorer nations' desire to consume like Americans could starve the planet; bombing them would resolve it. Satirizing ignorance is cathartic; it reduces fear, rather than raising it.

For centuries, Americans and Brits have compared China to a sleeping beast. From the nineteenth century to the present, many books and articles about China reference an immortal line often erroneously attributed to Napoleon: "Let China sleep. For when she wakes, she will shake the world." It's been a cliché for decades. "Every time during the last half-century or more that the sleeping Chinese dragon flicked his tail, there were American watchers anxiously sure that it was at last coming awake," the U.S. journalist Harold Isaacs wrote in 1958.[104] In 1997, *The Economist* bemoaned the popularity of the quotation and complained it "launched a thousand articles."[105] It has since inspired a thousand more, including a December 2017 *Financial Times* article about oil prices, an October 2020 Christian Broadcasting Network article about Xi, a January 2021 *Forbes* article about China's rise, and an October 2014 *New York Post* editorial about that year's pro-democracy protests in Hong Kong.[106] In 1994, the *New York Times* journalists Nicholas Kristof and Sheryl WuDunn published their best-selling *China Wakes;* two decades earlier, the former French diplomat Alain Peyrefitte published his best-selling *When China Awakes,* predating 2006's *China Shakes the World,* and a China chapter in the popular 2017 book *Dark Side of the Boom: The Excesses of the Art Market in the 21st Century,* titled—you guessed it—"China Wakes."[107]

There is even a Chinese version of the quotation, referring to the country as a "sleeping lion," and it may be an even bigger cliché there than in the West: China's most popular search engine, Baidu, returns roughly 1.7 million results for "sleeping lion," with the vast majority of the top results referencing the Napoleon quotation.[108] "Domestically, this expression has spread very wide," the intellectual Tian Fangmeng wrote in the Chinese edition of *The New York Times*, "from shoddy patriotic essays written by middle schoolers to weighty international affairs analyses by experts."[109] Even Xi himself used a version of the quotation, in a March 2014 speech in France.[110]

What explains its popularity? The quotation has allowed both America and China to defer reckoning with China's present importance. It allows Americans to cling to the idea of American exceptionalism, to displace into the future the anxiety about the loss of global prestige—the current weakening of the U.S. global order and the strengthening of a Chinese one.

There are three main options. Should we yield gracefully or quietly to China's dominance, as the United Kingdom did after World War II, and retreat to being China's second? To the exasperation of many American corporations, the American people are unlikely to accept that. A February 2021 survey by Pew found that 67 percent of Americans had negative feelings toward China, up from 46 percent in 2018.[111]

And frustration with China is not just an American problem. Several of the countries surveyed, including Sweden, Australia, the United Kingdom, and South Korea, feel worse about China than the United States does. And while the U.S. global reputation took a massive hit under Trump, other countries' views of America are already beginning to improve under Biden.

Should the U.S. government try to overthrow the Party? Perhaps. Forcing or even nudging revolutions and coups is a notoriously tricky business, as the United States has learned in dozens of countries across the world, from Afghanistan to Vietnam. Not only would a revolution in Beijing likely send the global economy into a tailspin, but there's no guarantee that Xi's replacement would be less authoritarian than he is. As bad as certain things are in China—especially the situation in Xinjiang—the situation can always grow far worse. A democratized China, for example, could elect a populist who taps into grassroots Chinese hatred of the Japanese, drawing the United States into a devastating third world war.

Should the United States try to weaken and contain certain elements of the Party, like its military and its security forces, while strengthening trade ties and partnering with Beijing on climate change? That's the most likely strategy for the Biden administration to embrace: as this book goes to print in September 2021, Biden has yet to elucidate his China strategy. It privileges America's economy, and it forestalls a war with China. Does that permit the two sides to reach an understanding so that they can coexist peacefully—or at least without attempting to slaughter each other's citizens—for the next several decades? Or does it merely allow Beijing to continue to strengthen its position vis-à-vis the United States so that when the two sides do eventually go to war, China is a much more formidable enemy? Many proponents of the second strategy argue that the United States should improve domestic competitiveness, streamline democracy, and invest in science and math. Naturally. That should factor into every global strategy—but it doesn't directly address China's rise.

American elite are divided on how to handle China. China's friends insist on some versions of the first and third strategies. Corporations like Disney and Apple claim to act apolitically but push America toward the first strategy. Since the George W. Bush administration, parts of the Pentagon have been preparing for the second strategy. Some officials there believe we are already fighting an undeclared war against China—and that China is already fighting an undeclared war against America.

Personally, I believe the Party poses an existential threat to the American-managed world order, an imperfect system that has nevertheless prevented a third world war. If China's political system evolves into a democracy like Taiwan, or Japan, I believe the United States can share with and yield power to China; the first strategy, in other words. I don't think that will happen, however, for decades.

I believe that the second strategy, despite its massive risks, is better for both Americans and Chinese. Indeed, the third strategy likely just forestalls the first. But—and this is an obvious point, though one rarely stated—it's not my decision to make.

It's a debate happening in countries around the world. Zambians, writes the analyst Mwansa Chalwe Snr, are wondering why China "cracks down strongly" on corruption at home but tolerates it abroad. The Australian intellectual David Brophy calls his 2021 book *China Panic* about a search for an ethical way for a middle power to handle China, "Australia's alternative to paranoia and pandering." As the pandemic finally recedes, Americans are beginning to have a raucous intellectual debate about China and their future.[112]

What do the American people want? Since Kissinger first met with Premier Zhou in 1971, a few dozen mostly old white men have steered and managed America's relationship with China. Politicians from both parties regularly talk to voters about China. But they rarely discuss it with them. "I don't know why you guys keep saying China's a threat," Secretary of the Treasury Steve Mnuchin said in an Oval Office meeting early in Trump's term. "You live in your DC bubble. Nobody outside DC thinks China is a threat."[113] But in polling conducted in February 2021, the Pew Research Center found that 89 percent of Americans consider China a competitor or an enemy, rather than a partner, while a Gallup poll from the same period showed that 45 percent of Americans consider China the greatest enemy of the United States.[114]

How do steelworkers in Pennsylvania, teachers in Mississippi, and preachers in Indiana feel about the future of their country? Ask them.

CHAPTER EIGHT

Defending the Rights of Chinese and Chinese Americans

★

QIAN XUESEN WAS A DIFFICULT MAN. "STUDENTS WERE SCARED STIFF of him," remarked a colleague of his at Caltech, where he taught in the 1940s and 1950s. "He had the bearing of a Chinese emperor." In her 1995 biography, *Thread of the Silkworm,* the journalist Iris Chang wrote that Qian in the early 1950s "was an extremely proud person to begin with and his recent string of intellectual successes had made his arrogance at times nearly intolerable." Arguably the world's top expert on jet propulsion, Qian contributed significantly to the American war effort in the 1940s. Even though he wasn't an American citizen, the U.S. military appointed him a rank equal to colonel.

But in February 1950, Senator Joseph McCarthy gave a speech claiming 105 Communists had infiltrated the State Department. Red fear swept the nation. Because Qian allegedly attended Communist meetings in the 1930s, the U.S. military removed his security clearance. It then arrested him. And in 1955, it returned him to a shambolic China eager to develop its missile program. Deporting Qian "was the stupidest thing this country ever did," the former navy secretary Dan Kimball said. "He was no more a Communist than I was, and we forced him to go."[1]

McCarthy's Red Scare damaged the careers of thousands of talented writers, actors, lawyers, and politicians, including the playwright Arthur Miller, the physicist J. Robert Oppenheimer, and the poet Langston Hughes. And yet, the fierce and proud Qian was that period's most consequential victim. He "revolutionized the whole of missile science in China—of military science, for that matter," the

Berkeley electrical engineering professor Ernest Kuh told Chang.[2] Qian was the scientist who spearheaded China's missile program in the 1960s; its controversial 1966 testing of a ballistic missile capped with a nuclear warhead sparked a major nuclear crisis similar to the 2017 U.S.–North Korea showdown. More damning, however, was a June 1958 article Qian wrote praising the science behind some of the farming techniques of the Great Leap Forward, the 1958–1962 period of famine that led to the deaths of tens of millions of people. With any catastrophe that size there are many villains; still, Qian deserves special censure. Qian "wrote this article to give Mao's programs scientific justification," said the science historian Xu Liangying.* "After this hit the newspapers, Mao followed through with his policies. This article had a terrible influence on Mao. And yes, it had an impact on the famine that followed."

How should Americans counter the pernicious aspects of the Party's influence without resorting to McCarthyite racism, counterproductive levels of vigilance, or paranoia? Americans should learn from the Qian debacle and realize that the best responses are both strategic and ethical. Qian's deportation not only contravened American values. It also helped China develop missiles that could strike the United States a decade or two earlier than they would have without his brilliance, and exacerbated a massive famine.

Trump's descriptions of China, Chinese people, and the coronavirus strengthened Beijing by allowing the Party to claim that it defends Chinese people globally from American racism. At a dinner with business executives in August 2018, Trump mentioned an unnamed country—clearly China, one of the dinner's attendees told *Politico*—and said that "almost every student that comes over to this country is a spy."[3] He has mocked Senator Dianne Feinstein for hiring an ethnically Chinese driver, whom she fired after the FBI warned her he might be a spy.[4] And he often referred to the coronavirus as the "Chinese virus" or "Kung Flu."

Sadly, Trump and Qian are in good historical company. Qian's mistreatment and Trump's comments are only two small examples of

---

* Chang, conducting interviews in China forty years after the famine, found that "numerous sources vehemently cursed Qian" for the article.

the U.S. government's tragic and horrifying history of racism toward Chinese and Chinese Americans, which began in earnest in the second half of the nineteenth century. In 1878 a California state senate investigation released a report titled *Chinese Immigration: Its Social, Moral, and Political Effect.* The report found "that California's concerns about immorality, prostitution, and unemployment all stemmed from Chinese immigrants," the historian Jean Pfaelzer writes in her 2007 book, *Driven Out: The Forgotten War Against Chinese Americans.* Several years later, Congress passed the Chinese Exclusion Act of 1882, which made the Chinese the first people specifically banned from entering America. "The Empire of China acts like a threatening cloud hanging over the virgin states of the Pacific," Senator La Fayette Grover (D-Ore.) said in March 1882. "Her people may swarm upon us like locusts." Representative Horace Page (R-Calif.) agreed with the sentiment. "How absurd would be the idea of undertaking to naturalize a Chinaman?" he asked. Congress didn't even overturn the act until 1943, and then only partially.[5] The racism lingered. In 1961, the screenwriter Robert Alan Aurthur interviewed the former president Harry S Truman about the Korean War—during which the Chinese fought with the North Koreans against the Americans—eight years after he had left office. Truman grew steadily drunker throughout the interview, Aurthur writes, and started raving about the "Yellow Chinee [*sic*]" and "Chinks."[6]

Chinese Americans weren't spared the racism sparked by the economic rise of Japan in the 1970s and 1980s, when Japan nearly dominated the U.S. car, television, and camera markets, and Representative John D. Dingell (D-Mich.) could get away with calling the Japanese "little yellow people."[7] In 1982—exactly one hundred years after the passing of the Chinese Exclusion Act—two unemployed autoworkers murdered the Chinese American man Vincent Chin, seemingly because they thought he was Japanese and responsible for their joblessness. A judge sentenced the two white men who committed the murder to only three years' probation. "These aren't the kind of men you send to jail," he said, sparking national protests and a growing awareness among Asian Americans of the need to lobby, protest, and organize.[8]

The Chinagate scandal of 1996 not only warned Americans of

the danger of Beijing's influence on the U.S. political process; it also sparked anti-Chinese racism and chilled Asian American participation in government. In 1997, the *National Review* published a cover featuring Bill and Hillary Clinton with buckteeth and slanted eyes.[9] "One of my deep regrets about this entire matter," said Johnny Chung, who donated money to the DNC that came from China's military intelligence, "has been the terrible impact that the campaign finance scandal caused in part by myself has had upon Asian Americans and, in particular, Chinese Americans."

The paranoia from the Chinagate scandal also helped engender one of the biggest counterintelligence failures in U.S. history. The Taiwanese-born American Wen Ho Lee worked as a nuclear scientist for the Los Alamos Laboratory when he was arrested in December 1999 and indicted on fifty-nine counts. He spent 278 days in solitary confinement without bail, only to be cleared of all charges except the minor one of mishandling sensitive documents. The judge apologized, and President Bill Clinton said the "whole thing was quite troubling to me," but Lee was never pardoned.[10] Some Asian scientists boycotted U.S. research labs as a result of Lee's case and of the systemic mistreatment and mistrust they felt. "I think it's hard for a white person," said Dr. Huan Lee, a Chinese American scientist at Los Alamos, "to appreciate the bias."[11]

In the late twentieth century, American cities and towns started changing derogatory place-names. In 1980 the city of Pekin, Illinois—so named because its nineteenth-century founders thought that if they dug a hole under their home and through the earth, they would come upon China's capital—decided to change the name of its high school team. The Pekin Chinks became the Pekin Dragons. Soon after, a local roller-skating arena stopped calling itself the Chink Rink.[12]

But as of August 2021, roughly two dozen other place-names in the United States still disturbingly have the word "Chinaman."[13] They include places like Chinaman Trail in Oregon, Chinaman Bayou in Louisiana, Old Chinaman, a mine in New Mexico, and Chinamans Canyon in Colorado, four hours south of Denver. In Idaho, Montana, Texas, and Oregon, hikers can still summit Chinaman Hat, probably named after the conical hat worn by Chinese laborers in the late nineteenth century. Even California, a state that prides itself on its wokeness, hosts Chinaman Creek, a stream that flows in the forests three hours outside Sacramento.

As China emerged relatively unscathed from the 2008 financial crisis, it sparked a period that the cultural critic Oliver Wang called "Fear the Chinese/Be the Chinese."[14] The Yale Law School professor Amy Chua's January 2011 op-ed in *The Wall Street Journal*, "Why Chinese Mothers Are Superior," and her best-selling book *Battle Hymn of the Tiger Mother* sparked a national debate about the possibility of Chinese cultural superiority. "The more powerful China becomes, the more Chinese Americans are perceived as vessels of such power," wrote the former White House staffer Eric Liu in 2014. "The more discomfitingly assertive China is, the more Chinese Americans are seen as discomfitingly assertive in their dealings." As worries about Chinese spying grew, the number of defendants indicted under the U.S. Economic Espionage Act with Chinese names from 2009 to 2015 grew to 52 percent, more than triple the ratio from 1997 to 2009.[15] The rate of wrongful accusations for Chinese-named defendants was almost twice as high. Just like the imagined crime of "driving while black," profiling Chinese Americans as spies may "be creating a new crime," writes the legal scholar Andrew Chongseh Kim, "researching while Asian."[16]

During the Trump era, Chinese and Chinese American researchers, professors, and students began to fall under increased suspicion. In 2018, Stephen Miller, Trump's top aide on immigration, tried to get Trump to stop providing student visas to Chinese nationals.[17] Increased tensions between the United States and China and the scourge of the coronavirus exacerbated the problem. In March 2020, a man stabbed three Asians—including a two-year-old and a six-year-old—because he thought they were "Chinese and infecting people with the coronavirus" (they were Burmese).[18] And in August 2020, Secretary of State Mike Pompeo said that Trump was considering restricting Chinese students from studying in the United States.[19] As this book goes to print, a combination of geopolitical tensions, increased scrutiny on Chinese students with military or security backgrounds, U.S. and Chinese paranoia about COVID, and Chinese fears about safety in the United States has reduced the number of Chinese students in the United States. "Nothing could be better for China," said Frank Wu, the president of Queens College in New York and author of the book *Yellow: Race in America Beyond Black and White*, "than for the United States to throw out all the Chinese immigrants."[20]

HOW CAN AMERICANS BE VIGILANT WITHOUT BEING RACIST? OR, for those who feel that the racism charge is overblown by left-leaning media, how can the movement to protect American ideals against Beijing avoid being tarnished or distracted by accusations of racism?

China's rise, and the growing global threat of the Party, sit uneasily amid two ideological stains on American history: the Yellow Scare and the Red Peril. "One of the things we're trying to do is view the China threat as not just a whole-of-government threat, but a whole-of-society threat on their end," the FBI director, Christopher Wray, said in a much-quoted February 2018 speech. "And I think it's going to take a whole-of-society response by us."[21] But to focus on collective vigilance, especially in a country that has such a devastating and recent history of anti-Chinese discrimination, is both ethically and strategically wrong. The Party delights when the U.S. government discriminates against Chinese, because it can then more credibly claim to represent the interests of Chinese people globally.

China is the only true area of bipartisan agreement. But many Americans—especially on the left—don't understand that Representative Nancy Pelosi and Senator Chuck Schumer substantially agree with Senators Ted Cruz and Marco Rubio about the need to counter Beijing's aggression. Democratic strategists must find a way to energize the isolationist arm of the Democrats—by focusing on what Beijing is doing in the United States, not in China. And Republican strategists, for national security reasons, must avoid the temptation of demonizing both Chinese people and friends like Iger and Locke. What Beijing and its friends do is bad enough. There is no need to exaggerate it.

In July 2021, a group of more than forty progressive groups sent a letter to the Biden administration, urging them to "end the New Cold War" and start cooperating with China to fight climate change. But Democrats—and especially progressives—must understand that countering China is a far more effective way of both fighting climate change AND selling it to the American people. Why? Because Beijing has far more to lose with climate change than the United States does. China is by far the world's largest polluter—it emits more greenhouse gas than the rest of the developed world combined—and that burden of substandard air and water quality falls overwhelmingly on Chinese people. Partnering with China reduces U.S. leverage to push China to reduce its emissions. It's also bad politics.[22]

The words we use when having this conversation matter greatly. While Chinese receiving overwhelmingly positive coverage in film is problematic, that doesn't mean Hollywood should return to the crude portrayals of Fu Manchu or Charlie Chan. Journalists should be careful not to employ animalistic words when describing Chinese actions. "Much of the media coverage of China and its dealings with America can be understood more clearly if you conduct a simple thought experiment: imagine that the reports are describing not people but pathogens. Or parasites," writes Liu. He cites as an example "Chinese hackers *burrowing* their way into American bank accounts and into classified US military servers" (italics mine).[23]

Removing "Chinaman" from the lexicon of appropriate place-names is a small start. Changing place-names containing the word "Chinaman" is not about ignoring local history or about censoring certain words. "Chinaman" is an appellation that Chinese Americans sometimes use for themselves. The rapper Christopher Wong Won of the pioneering hip-hop group 2 Live Crew called his solo 1992 debut *The Chinaman*.[24] Liu titled his 2014 memoir *A Chinaman's Chance*, a phrase that means "nearly impossible" and probably originates from the inability of Chinese laborers to get a fair trial—or to avoid pogroms—in late-nineteenth-century America. (Comparing "Chinaman" to the terms "Englishman" and "Irishman" isn't apt, because those words aren't wielded as insults.) As any American who has ever been called "white trash," the *n* word, or "kike" knows, the race and background of the speaker matter. "We all say things about our own family, that if someone else said that about our mother, we would punch them," Frank Wu told me. "It's about intimacy and irony."

Changing an inflammatory place-name can be an intensely local endeavor, said Mark Monmonier, a professor of geography at Syracuse University. In November, commissioners in Colorado's Chaffee County debated a proposal to rename Chinaman Gulch, a ravine 130 miles northwest of Chinamans Canyon.[25] The commissioners voted unanimously against the proposal, with one calling the name Chinaman Gulch "descriptive and evocative."

But sometimes national pressure can help. In 2001, after several years of advocacy from Asian American groups, the U.S. Board on Geographic Names changed the name of an Idaho mountain from Chinks Peak to Chinese Peak.[26] Want to help today? Share the petition that is advocating to change the name of Chinaman Lake, in northern Minnesota.[27] Call elected officials in Sacramento, California's capital, and encourage them to raise awareness about renaming nearby Chinaman Creek. Or better yet, push for the Board on Geographic Names to expand its list of prohibited names to include "Chinaman" as well.[28]

IN JUNE 2018, AFTER THE STATE DEPARTMENT CONSIDERED FURTHER limiting some Chinese student visas in fields like high-tech manufacturing, aviation, and robotics, the Chinese physicist and Cornell researcher Yangyang Cheng wrote an essay titled "Don't Close the Door on Chinese Scientists Like Me."[29] "Without being implemented, the suggestion alone of such discriminatory policies casts doubt on every Chinese citizen as a potential agent of the Chinese state, guilty until proved innocent, and inadvertently gives credence to the Chinese government's own claim that it holds not only control over a territory but also ownership of a people, including its diaspora," she wrote.

A small number of Chinese students spy on other students, some Chinese steal American technology and bring it to China to enrich themselves, and some Chinese enact and implement policies that harm Americans. But the importance of maintaining an open and free America, and the contributions of millions of Chinese Americans and future Chinese Americans to America, far outweighs the negatives. "Even though concerns about espionage are legitimate, the smart thing for the U.S. government to do amidst rising diplomatic tensions is try to win over Chinese students and scholars by leaving them alone in a free academic environment on U.S. campuses," wrote the Chinese columnist and Yale graduate Yifu Dong.[30]

The U.S. government should explicitly welcome Chinese to work, study, and grow in the United States, and affirm that it does not worry about the divided loyalty of Chinese Americans. Biden should apologize, on behalf of the Office of the President of the United States, for the grave mistreatment Chinese Americans have faced. Offering an official apology to Qian would be a good first step.

In January 2020, I met the historian Jack Tchen at Manhattan's Museum of Chinese in America, which he co-founded in 1980. That day, the Harvard professor and Trump lawyer Alan Dershowitz had just mounted an asinine rejection of the standards for impeachment. No one credible accuses Dershowitz of betraying America because of his loyalty to Israel, Tchen said, adding, "That's how the Chinese American community needs to be viewed."

In these areas George W. Bush, who always spoke ethically and honorably about Muslims, serves as a model for American behavior. Six days after the planes hit the Twin Towers, Bush spoke at the Islamic Center of Washington, D.C. "When we think of Islam we think of a faith that brings comfort to a billion people around the world," he said. "America counts millions of Muslims amongst our citizens, and Muslims make an incredibly valuable contribution to our country. Muslims are doctors, lawyers, law professors, members of the military, entrepreneurs, shopkeepers, moms and dads. And they need to be treated with respect."[31] And unlike Trump, the former secretary of state Mike Pompeo often spoke about the Party in an exemplary fashion. "I want to be sure that my language is precise today," he said in a December 2020 speech at Georgia Tech. "When I say 'China,' I'm talking about the Chinese Communist Party. I love and value, as we all do, our Chinese American community, and the Chinese people that live here in the United States and those that live in China as well." Biden has a great opportunity to echo that type of language with both Chinese people and Chinese Americans.[32]

The February 2020 arrest of the chair of the Harvard chemistry department, Charles Lieber, for allegedly lying to the U.S. government about his ties to China, helped shift the debate about racial profiling. "This wake-up call is far louder because of who this person is, his ethnicity and the institution for which he works," said Kei Koizumi, a White House science adviser during the Obama administration. Now it doesn't just affect "Chinese or other Asians like myself."[33]

The problem lies with the Party and its friends, not with Chinese people.

There are plenty of antagonists in this story, some Chinese, some not. For those upset with Beijing's influence in America, understand this: by helping to normalize corruption among our former diplomats and warping American perception of China over the last four decades, Kissinger has done more harm to American interests than every ethnically Chinese businessman, hacker, spy, whether they hold American or Chinese citizenship.

A final note: it's not nearly enough for me to say that Chinese Americans are allies in the fight against pernicious Party influence; "ally" implies an othering from the rest of America. Chinese Americans are *America,* just like Nebraskans or blacks or Jews. "America must welcome all—Chinese, Irish, German, pauper or not, criminal or not—all, all, without exceptions: become an asylum for all who choose to come," the poet Walt Whitman said, after the horrific Chinese Exclusion Act of 1882. "We may have drifted away from this principle temporarily but time will bring us back."[34]

ACKNOWLEDGMENTS

This was a difficult book to write. Throughout the process, I received great support from dozens of people: in alphabetical order, they include:

Misha Auslin, Doug Baldasare, Amanda Bennett, Christian Caryl, Nick Consonery, Robert Daly, Jeremy Dauber, Miri Pomerantz Dauber, Kwame Dougan, Julien Dumoulin-Smith, Josh Eisenmann, Sherri Ferris, Deborah Fikes, Uri Friedman, Amanda Ghanooni, Zack Hosford, Melinda Liu, David Nudo, Cara Parks, Lisa Faith Phillips, Jenny McArdle, Iskander Rehman, Orville Schell, Micah Springut, Devin Stewart, Dan Stone, Abigail Teller, Jenifer Vaughan, Jeffrey Wasserstrom, David Wertime, Minky Worden, and many others, including those who asked to remain anonymous. Thank you.

I also had a series of brilliant researchers who helped with the book, and with articles I've written, over the last several years. They include Will Cooke, Margaux Garcia, Jace Gilmore, Jin Liu, Isaac Rose-Berman, and Sophia Weng, among others.

To my pseudonymous friend David Johnson: thank you for believing in me, and in these ideas—I really appreciate and value your support.

Ann McDaniel, thank you for your advice and guidance over the years. I've learned so much from you.

There's been some fantastic journalism in this area, by people including Bethany Allen-Ebrahimian, Megha Rajagopalan, Zachary Dorfman, John Judis, Ed Wong, Mike Forsythe, and Ken Silverstein, among others.

Dozens of better books came before mine and helped inform this one. I referred often from Jon Pomfret's magisterial study of the U.S.-China relationship, *The Beautiful Country and the Middle Kingdom;* James Mann's several great books on the topic; Gordon H. Chang's *Fateful*

Ties; and Richard McGregror's *The Party.* I also leaned on great books by Julia Lovell, Aaron L. Friedberg, Josh Rogin, Evan Osnos, Clive Hamilton, Mareike Ohlberg, Bob Davis, Lingling Wei, Dexter Roberts, and many others.

My agent Kim Witherspoon is a tireless advocate and a brilliant advisor: I'm very lucky that she chose to work with me. I'm also very grateful for her wonderful team, including Maria Whelan and William Callahan.

Andrew Miller and Maris Dyer took excellent care of this book: thank you for the great editing and support.

My family has been wonderfully supportive: I love you Mom, Dad, Aarlo, Hughie, and Avery.

Uncle Josh and Uncle Steven, thanks for instilling in me a love of reading and learning.

When I was a clueless 17-year-old, my parents allowed me to travel around Xinjiang for a summer: thank you for letting me learn.

This is a grim time for activists in China. I learned from many wonderful people in my six years there, many of whom are anonymous.

Years ago, I had tea with two Chinese human rights activists, in their cramped apartment in an unfashionable part of Beijing. As we were leaving the building, a decrepit old man in a Mao suit walked by them, glaring. The activists smiled at him, and waved. "Who's that?" I asked.

"Oh, he's the neighbor who's tasked with spying on us," they said. "But he's eaten a lot of bitterness, so we try to be kind to him."

May they, and not Xi Jinping, be the future of China.

Notes

Introduction

1. Grindr, "What's Up with Grindr?"; Wang, "Chinese Web Tycoon Zhou Yahui Agrees to Pay Wife $1.1 Billion for a Divorce."
2. Rogin, "Can the Chinese Government Now Get Access to Your Grindr Profile?"; Stone Fish, "China Has Access to Grindr Activity."
3. Mozilla, "Should You Trust Your Dating App or Sex Toy?"
4. Viswanatha, "U.S. Warned Jared Kushner About Wendi Deng Murdoch."
5. Lehman, *Great American Prose Poems*.
6. Columbia Law School, "Merit Janow"; Zhang, "China's Sovereign Wealth Fund Releases Annual Report"; China Investment Corporation, "China Investment Corporation 2019 Annual Report."
7. "Global Dream Forum NYC 2019 Agenda."
8. China Development Bank, "Prospectus Supplement."
9. Bank of China, "Announcement: Appointment of Independent Non-executive Director of the Bank."
10. Zoellick, "Can America and China Be Stakeholders?"
11. Isaacson, *Kissinger*, 745.
12. Brinkley, "U.S. Finds Technology Curb Fails to Cut Flow to Russians."
13. Larkin et al., "Association Between Academic Medical Center Pharmaceutical Detailing Policies and Physician Prescribing"; Orenstein, Tigas, and Jones, "Now There's Proof."
14. Van Groningen, "Big Pharma Gives Your Doctor Gifts."

Chapter One: The History of America's Influence on China

1. Swisher, *China's Management of the American Barbarians*, 48.
2. Paine, *Theological Works*, 180.
3. Chang, *Fateful Ties*, 22–25, 47.
4. Asia for Educators, "Commodore Perry and Japan (1853–1854)."
5. Perry, *Narrative of the Expedition*, 75.

6. Abeel, *Journal of a Residence in China*, 153.
7. Spence, *God's Chinese Son*.
8. Gentry and People, *Death Blow to Corrupt Doctrines*, 31.
9. Pomfret, *The Beautiful Country and the Middle Kingdom*, 91–92.
10. Lorge, *Debating War in Chinese History*, 231.
11. Livingston, *Independent Reflector*, 52:2682.
12. Westad, *Restless Empire*.
13. Pantsov, *Mao*, 73.
14. Westad, *Restless Empire*, 139.
15. Reinsch, *American Diplomat in China*.
16. City of Honolulu, "City to Dedicate Statue and Rename Park to Honor Dr. Sun Yat-Sen."
17. Li, *China's America*.
18. Reed, *Missionary Mind*.
19. Yuan and Goodnow, "Perils of Advising the Empire."
20. Pomfret, *The Beautiful Country and the Middle Kingdom*.
21. Barth and Chen, "What Did Sun Yat-sen Really Die Of?"
22. Li and Hong, *Image, Perception, and the Making of U.S.-China Relations*, 180.
23. Pomfret, *The Beautiful Country and the Middle Kingdom*, 136.
24. Brady, *Making the Foreign Serve China*, 22.
25. Geopolitical Monitor, "Brief History of China's United Front."
26. Mahnken, Babbage, and Yoshihara, "Countering Comprehensive Coercion"; Mao, *Zhongguo shehui ge jiejie de fenxi* 中国社会各阶级的分析 [Analysis of the classes in Chinese society].
27. Beauchamp-Mustafaga and Chase, "Borrowing a Boat Out to Sea."
28. Liu Jifeng 刘戟锋, Lu Xiao 卢潇, and Liu Yangyue 刘杨钺, "Zhànlüè xinli zhan de jishu zhicheng" 战略心理战的技术支撑 [Technical support for strategic psychological warfare].
29. Kwok, " 'Real Game-changers' Needed for the Govt to Curb Violence."
30. MacFarquhar, "Made in China"; Price, *Lives of Agnes Smedley*; Brady, *Making the Foreign Serve China*.
31. Stone Fish, "Can Politico Pull Off Its New Partnership with a Chinese-Owned Paper?"
32. Marxists.org, "U.S. Neo-revisionism."
33. Mao, "Farewell, Leighton Stuart."
34. Ng, "Xi Jinping Mourns 'China's Great Friend' Sihanouk"; Lovell, *Maoism*.
35. Auerbach, "Home from China."
36. Snow, *Red China Today*, 619.
37. "Du Bois, 91, Lauds China," *New York Times*.
38. Mao, "New Storm Against Imperialism."
39. Chao, "Let One Hundred Panthers Bloom"; Kelley and Esch, "Black Like Mao."
40. Howe and Trott, *Power Peddlers*, 29.

41. Karolides, *Literature Suppressed on Political Grounds,* 96.
42. Nixon, "Asia After Viet Nam."
43. National Security Agency, "Memorandum for Henry A. Kissinger."
44. Brady, *Making the Foreign Serve China,* 196.

Chapter Two: Friends with Benefits

1. Williams, "Spinning Their Wheels in China."
2. Horne, *Kissinger,* 83.
3. Zhan 张 and Zhou 周, "Guojia Anquan Jiguan shi zenmeyang yi zhi duiwu?" 国家安全机关是怎样一支队伍? [What kind of organization is the National Security Agency?].
4. Roth, "Obituary: Melvin Lasky."
5. Wong, "How China Uses LinkedIn to Recruit Spies Abroad."
6. Xue 薛, "Renmin lingxiu Zhou Enlai" 人民领袖周恩来 [The people's leader Zhou Enlai].
7. Zhou 周, "Zhou Enlai tongzhan yishu zai qingbao gongzuo zhong de yunyong" 周恩来统战艺术在情报工作中的运用 [Zhou Enlai's art in utilizing the United Front in intelligence work].
8. Mattis and Brazil, *Chinese Communist Espionage,* 102.
9. *Disinformation* (Rid testimony).
10. Brady, *Making the Foreign Serve China.*
11. Isaacson, *Kissinger,* 365.
12. "Kissinger Bests His Chief in Poll," *New York Times.*
13. Kissinger, "Eulogy for John Whitehead."
14. Isaacson, *Kissinger,* 709; Claiborne, "Columbia Post for Kissinger Opposed."
15. Egan and Lescaze, "Kissinger, Simon: Visible, Wealthy."
16. Isaacson, *Kissinger,* 694–708.
17. Gelb, "Kissinger Means Business."
18. Isaacson, *Kissinger,* 730; "Big Business of Being Henry Kissinger," *BusinessWeek.*
19. Gelb, "Kissinger Means Business."
20. "Deng Wants More Economic Reforms for China," UPI.
21. Halberstam, "New Establishment"; Allen, Richard Allen Oral History.
22. Halberstam, "New Establishment."
23. Savranskaya and Blanton, *Last Superpower Summits,* 493.
24. Isaacson, "Booknotes, Kissinger: A Biography"; Martin, "Helmut Sonnenfeldt, Expert on Soviet and European Affairs, Is Dead at 86."
25. Isaacson, *Kissinger,* 749.
26. Groot, *Managing Transitions,* 108.
27. Kissinger, "Kissinger at China Ventures—Image 2."
28. "Rong Yiren tongzhi shengping" 荣毅仁同志生平 [The life of Comrade Rong Yiren].
29. "Biography of Rong Yiren," China Vitae.

30. Church, "China."
31. Zhu, "Inside Story of When China's State-Run TV Criticized the Party."
32. Johnson, "Jesus vs. Mao?"
33. Li, *China's America,* 132.
34. Wasserstrom, *Popular Protest and Political Culture in Modern China.*
35. Buckley, "Rise and Fall of the Goddess of Democracy."
36. Kissinger, "Turmoil on Top."
37. "George H. W. Bush, Press Conference, June 5, 1989."
38. Ibid.
39. Engel, *China Diary of George H. W. Bush,* 47.
40. Vogel, *Deng Xiaoping and the Transformation of China,* 649.
41. Reuters, "Asian Nations Pick Sides in U.S. Race."
42. Suettinger, *Beyond Tiananmen,* 69; Dowd, "2 U.S. Officials Went to Beijing Secretly in July."
43. Pincus, "Kissinger Says He Had No Role in China Mission."
44. Kissinger, *On China,* 421.
45. Tyler, *Great Wall,* 366.
46. Liu and Cai, "Waiguo yao ren mingren kan Zhongguo" 外国要人名人看中国 [How foreign dignitaries and celebrities see China].
47. Lampton, *Same Bed, Different Dreams,* 24.
48. "George H. W. Bush, Press Conference, June 5, 1989."
49. Fialka, "Mr. Kissinger Has Opinions on China—and Business Ties"; Kissinger, "Europe Returns to Center Stage as the Fulcrum for World Tension."
50. Liu, "Trading Relationship Between Taiwan and the United States"; U.S. Census Bureau Foreign Trade Division, "1995: U.S. Trade in Goods with China."
51. Mann, *About Face,* 318.
52. Taipei Economic and Cultural Representative Office in the United States, "Brief Introduction of Twin Oaks."
53. McGuire, "Tsai Ing-Wen's U.S. Transit Stops in Historical Context."
54. Mann, "China's Feelings of Betrayal on Taiwan Fed Anger at U.S."
55. Weisskopf and Richburg, "China Special Report."
56. Kaiser, *So Damn Much Money,* 243.
57. Suettinger, *Beyond Tiananmen,* 213.
58. Tucker, *China Confidential,* 481.
59. Reuters, "2 Will Leave A.I.G. Board."
60. Kovaleski, "Gingrich Backs Ties with Taiwan."
61. Sciolino, "Schooling of Gingrich, the Foreign Policy Novice."
62. Mann, "Between China and the US."
63. Tenet and Freeh, "CIA/FBI Report to Congress on Chinese Espionage Activities Against the United States."
64. Sciolino, "China, Vying with Taiwan, Explores Public Relations."
65. Gerth, "Democrat Fund-Raiser Said to Detail China Tie."

66. Johnston, "Democratic Fund-Raiser Tells of Dealings with Chinese Donors."
67. Lampton, *Same Bed, Different Dreams*, 105.
68. Friedman, "Beyond Stupid."
69. Committee on Governmental Affairs, United States Senate, *Investigation of Illegal or Improper Activities in Connection with 1996 Federal Election Campaigns Final Report*.
70. Marcus, "Dole Registers as Taiwan Foreign Agent."
71. *Late Show with David Letterman*, show 1040.
72. *Johnny Chung: Foreign Connections, Foreign Contributions*.
73. "White House Turnstile," *New York Times*.
74. Kelly, "On the White House Subway."
75. Holmes, "Boeing's Campaign to Protect a Market."
76. Silverstein, "Mandarins."
77. Christopher, *In the Stream of History*, 31.
78. Sanger, "Two Roads to China."
79. Holmes, "Boeing's Campaign to Protect a Market."
80. Areddy, "Chinese Birdman Who Got U.S. Aircraft Giant Boeing Flying"; Thomas, "Boeing and US-China Relations."
81. Pomfret, *The Beautiful Country and the Middle Kingdom*, 215–17.
82. Holmes, "How Boeing Woos Beijing."
83. Faison, "China to Buy 30 Planes for $1.5 Billion from Airbus Industries."
84. Sanger, "U.S. Blames Allies for Undercutting Its China Policy."
85. Sanger, "Two Roads to China."
86. U.S. Census Bureau Foreign Trade Division, "1996: U.S. Trade in Goods with China."
87. Bradsher, "Rallying Round the China Bill, Hungrily."
88. Dreyfuss, "New China Lobby."
89. Fritz, "Big Firms Plant Seeds of 'Grass-Roots' China Lobby."
90. Bradsher, "Rallying Round the China Bill."
91. Pincus, "Kissinger Says He Had No Role in China Mission."
92. Mufson and Kaiser, "U.S. Insurers Lavishly Court China's Market"; Caruso-Cabrera, "Greenberg on Tiananmen."
93. Quinn, "Chubb Aims for License in China."
94. Drinkard, "China's Best Lobbyist"; *Campaign Finance Investigation Day 2*.
95. All Politics, "Clinton Defends China Trip, Engagement Policy"; O'Neill, "Bush to Visit Before Clinton"; Pomfret, "Business Takes Back Seat on China Trip."
96. Studwell, *China Dream*, 120.
97. Associated Press, "China Licenses Four Foreign Insurers."
98. Miller and Pasternak, "Problems with a Globe-Trotting Father."
99. Lampton, *Same Bed, Different Dreams*, 103–4; Basken and Forsythe, "China Lobbies U.S. on the Cheap, Aided by Boeing, Ford, Chamber."
100. Public Citizen's Global Trade Watch, "Purchasing Power."
101. Dreyfuss, "New China Lobby."

102. White House, "President Bush Speaks at Tsinghua University."
103. Reuters, "Deposition Lists Lucrative Deals for Bush Brother."
104. Carlson, "Relatively Charmed Life of Neil Bush."
105. Mellor and Patterson, "China's Chip and Connections."
106. Swartz, "Cast Away."
107. Carlson, "Relatively Charmed Life of Neil Bush."
108. Ignatius, "Bush's Brother, Other Americans Are Talking Business with China."
109. Flannery, "Fast-Growing Chinese Region Forms Ties Here."
110. "China's Size, Economic Boom Lure U.S. Chains Despite Uncertainties," *Nation's Restaurant News*.
111. Staff, "Brother of Ex–US Leader Hired by Firm"; Laurence and Hiebert, "Bush Family in China," 30.
112. Crowley, "Nixon off the Record."
113. People Staff, "Eight Days in Japan Earn Ron and Nancy $2 Million."
114. "Bulletins: Bush Joining Barrick," *Globe and Mail*.
115. Wells, "Rumble in the Jungle"; "Another Queasy Experience," *Newsweek*; Miller and Pasternak, "Problems with a Globe-Trotting Father."
116. Chinese People's Association for Friendship with Foreign Countries, "About Us."
117. Ministry of Foreign Affairs of the People's Republic of China 中华人民共和国外交部, "Zhonghua renmin gongheguo waijiaobu zhuyao zhizhe" 中华人民共和国外交部主要职责 [Main responsibilities of the Ministry of Foreign Affairs of the People's Republic of China].
118. Kyodo, "Senior Chinese Official May Visit Japan Next Month."
119. Lippman, "Bush Makes Clinton's China Policy an Issue."
120. Garza, "Arms Deal Will Test Bush Ties."
121. Bush, "Letter from the Chairman."

Chapter Three: America Consents

1. Bush, *Decision Points*, 427.
2. Wallace, "Hu's Boeing Visit Is a Hit with Workers."
3. Embassy of the People's Republic of China in the United States of America, "President Hu Jintao Attends the Welcoming Ceremony Hosted by President Bush."
4. Becker, "'Side by Side Against Terrorism.'"
5. Allen and Pan, "Bush Begins China Visit."
6. Dowd, "He's Ba-a-a-ack!"
7. Buckley, "Firing Line Debate."
8. Overell, "Masters of the Great Game Turn to Business."
9. Associated Press, "Indonesia Gets an Adviser—Kissinger."
10. Turner, "Kissinger Should Disclose Clients, Albright Says"; Hancock, "Clinton Advisers Trade on Contacts."
11. "Congressman Says Kissinger Benefits from Arms Deals."

12. D'Arcy, "Kissinger Still Wears Cloak of Secrecy."
13. "Raw Data: Kissinger's Letter to the President," Fox News.
14. Woodward, *State of Denial*, 117.
15. "Kissinger in China," Yale University Library; Barron, Perlez, and Lee, "Public Lives."
16. ICEO, "Mogen Datong zai Zhongguo he Jixinge xiansheng you shenme guanxi?" 摩根大通在中国和基辛格先生有什么关系? [What is the relationship between JPMorgan Chase in China and Mr. Kissinger?].
17. "Chinese Leaders' Activities," BBC.
18. "Chinese State Councillor Calls on US to Oppose Taiwan Independence," Xinhua News Agency.
19. Pomfret, "Secret Taiwan Fund Sought Friends, Influence Abroad."
20. Knowlton, "Bush Warns Taiwan to Keep Status Quo."
21. Kahn, "Warnings by Powell to Taiwan Provoke a Diplomatic Dispute."
22. "Vanuatu Scraps Deal with Taiwan," BBC.
23. Pottinger et al., "Cnooc Drops Offer for Unocal, Exposing U.S.-Chinese Tensions."
24. Zoellick, "Whither China?"
25. Christensen, *China Challenge*, 2.
26. Kissinger, "Speech at the Graduate University of Chinese Academy of Sciences in Beijing."
27. 2006 USCBC Member Priorities Survey, "US Companies Gain in China, Still Face Hurdles."
28. Pollack and Bradsher, "China's Need for Metal Keeps U.S. Scrap Dealers Scrounging."
29. Fishman, *China Inc.*, 178.
30. Heintz, "Jobs and the Resurgent Economy / Outsourcing CEOs."
31. Buffett and Loomis, "America's Growing Trade Deficit Is Selling the Nation Out from Under Us."
32. Fuchs and Klann, "Paying a Visit."
33. Lorenz, "Courting Beijing's Wrath."
34. Wayne, "Trading on Their Names."
35. Hancock, "Clinton Advisers Trade on Contacts."
36. Li and Hwang, "Xinhua Interviews Clinton Security Advisor Sandy Berger on Promoting US-China Ties."
37. Liao Qi 廖奇, "Lao Bushi fang Hua zhong mi 30 nian qian zuji tan Beijing bianhua tai da" 老布什访华重觅30年前足迹叹北京变化太大 [Retracing his footsteps from 30 years ago, Bush senior laments that Beijing has changed too much].
38. Westcott and George, "How George H. W. Bush Became Beijing's 'Old Friend' in the White House."
39. Lanfranco, "Analysis: American Dynastic Diplomacy."
40. Xinhua, "Zhonggong Zhongyang yinfa 'Shenhua dang he guojia jigou gaige fangan'" 中共中央印发《深化党和国家机构改革方案》[The Central

Committee of the Communist Party of China issues "Deepening Party and State Institutional Reform Plan"].

41. Sun 孙, "Lao Bushi jiang xianqi di Jing Gang bao zhi neng zhu qi zi fengfu fang Hua shouhuo" 老布什将先期抵京 港报指能助其子丰富访华收获 [Bush senior will arrive early in Beijing while Hong Kong's newspapers will help enrich his son's visit to China].

42. "China's Hu Jintao, US Ex-president Bush Hail 'Progress' in Ties 7 Mar.," BBC; "President Hu Jintao Meets Former US President Bush, Hail Sino-US Ties," BBC.

43. Abramowitz, "Bush 41 in China."

44. Barboza, "China Overtakes Japan to Become No. 2 Global Economic Power"; Chang, *Fateful Ties*, 242.

45. Guarino, "Where Is Apple Headed After Steve Jobs?"

46. Aleem, "Another Kick in the Teeth."

47. Autor, "Trade and Labor Markets."

48. Aleem, "Another Kick in the Teeth."

49. Sorkin and Barboza, "China to Buy $3 Billion Stake in Blackstone."

50. Tsinghua University, "List of Advisory Board Members."

51. Bradsher and Yuan, "China's Economy Became No. 2 by Defying No. 1."

52. Paulson, *Dealing with China,* 240.

53. Isikoff, "Chinese Hacked Obama, McCain Campaigns, Took Internal Documents, Officials Say."

54. Lynas, "How Do I Know China Wrecked the Copenhagen Deal?"

55. Singel and Kravets, "Only Google Could Leave China."

56. Dinmore and Dyer, "Immelt Hits Out at China and Obama."

57. Landler, "Obama's Journey to Tougher Tack on a Rising China"; Clinton, "US Embassy Cables: Hillary Clinton Ponders US Relationship with Its Chinese 'Banker.' "

58. Landler, "Obama's Journey to Tougher Tack on a Rising China."

59. Clinton, "America's Pacific Century."

60. Calmes, "A U.S. Marine Base for Australia Irritates China."

61. Garnaut and Liu, "Stern Sentenced to 10 Years by Chinese Court."

62. Garnaut, "Henry Kissinger Paid $5M to Steer Rio Tinto Through Stern Hu Debacle and Consolidate China Links"; Garnaut and Needham, "Rio Turns to Kissinger for Help."

63. Rio Tinto, "Shanghai Employees—Update 8."

64. Barboza, "Through a Joint Venture, Rio Tinto Strives to Repair Its Relations with China."

65. Chellel, Wild, and Stringer, "When Rio Tinto Met China's Iron Hand."

66. Barr and MarketWatch, "GE Says CEO Comments Reported out of Context."

67. Powell, "How America's Biggest Companies Made China Great Again."

68. Immelt, *Hot Seat.*

69. McDonald, "Kissinger Assails 'Deplorable' Comments on China by Both U.S. Candidates."
70. Xinhua, "Kissinger's Pride in 40-Year China Experiences."
71. Embassy of the People's Republic of China in the United States of America, "Vice President Meets Kissinger to Discuss China-U.S. Ties."
72. Xinhua, "Kissinger's Pride in 40-Year China Experiences."
73. Stephens, "Henry Kissinger on China."
74. Kissinger, *On China,* 184.
75. Nathan, "What China Wants."
76. Helfand, "Mayor in East Asia."
77. Sikba and Dardick, "Chinese President Hu Jintao to Visit Chicago."
78. Tareen, "China's President to See Chicago Chinese Institute"; "Chinese President Hu Jintao Talks Business in Chicago," BBC.
79. Kapos, "Mayor Richard Daley Says Chicago's Making a Big Push into China."
80. "Daley Rides the Rails in China," NBC News.
81. U.S. Department of Justice, "FARA Quick Search—Tur Partners, LLC."
82. Tur Partners LLC, "Registration Statement"; Office of the Attorney General, "Report of the Attorney General."
83. Embassy of the People's Republic of China, "Vice-Premier Liu Yandong Meets with Mayor of Chicago Rahm Emanuel."
84. Daley, "Short Form Registration Statement."
85. "Biography of Liu Yandong," China Vitae.
86. Xi 习, "Zai Zhongguo Gongchandang di shijiu ci quanguo daibiao dahui shang de baogao" 在中国共产党第十九次全国代表大会上的报告 [Report to the 19th National Congress of the Communist Party of China].
87. Wang, "Tips from the Top."
88. Dalian Wanda Group, "Wanda Group Announces Receipt of All Necessary Approvals for AMC Acquisition."
89. Kamen, "Here's Why the Chinese Government Hated Gary Locke."
90. "40 People in 40 Years: Gary Locke," *China Daily.*
91. Stone Fish, "Why Can't Ex–Chinese Leaders Travel Abroad?"
92. "Nobel Peace Prize 2002."
93. Chin, "Beijing Aims to Blunt Western Influence in China."
94. Fan 范 and Luo 罗, "Zhuli 'xiwang yingcai' qingnian xuezhe" 助力"希望英才"青年学者 [Assisting "promising and talented" young scholars].
95. Carter Center, "China."
96. Carter Center, "Carter Center in China."
97. Brennan, "Jimmy Carter Took Call About China from Concerned Donald Trump."
98. Manevich, "Americans More Negative Toward China over Past Decade."
99. Wike, "6 Facts About How Americans and Chinese See Each Other."
100. Diamond, "Donald Trump: China Is 'Raping Our Country.'"

101. Hilsenrath and Davis, "How the China Shock, Deep and Swift, Spurred the Rise of Trump."
102. Banfield, "Democratic Party Unrest; Trump Meets Kissinger."
103. Crowley, "Kissinger Primary."
104. Zhou, "Trump Wasn't Going to Do 'a Fucking Thing' if China Invaded Taiwan."
105. Schmitz, "Kushner Family, China's Anbang End Talks over Manhattan Real Estate Deal"; Rauhala and Wan, "In a Beijing Ballroom, Kushner Family Pushes $500,000 'Investor Visa' to Wealthy Chinese."
106. Smith and Phillips, "China Hails Trump's Appointment of 'Old Friend' Terry Branstad as Ambassador."
107. Stone Fish, "Wilbur Ross Remained on Chinese Joint Venture Board While Running U.S.-China Trade War."
108. Reuters Staff, "Invesco WL Ross in JV with China's Huaneng Capital."
109. McGreal, "Sheldon Adelson."
110. Elliott, "Trump's Patron-in-Chief."
111. Shriber, "Las Vegas Sands Boss Adelson Told Trump to Tread Carefully with China."
112. WikiLeaks, "Macau Gaming Revenues Rise Sharply as Las Vegas Sands Boosts Engagement with Beijing Officials."
113. Leary, Mauldin, and O'Keeffe, "Sheldon Adelson Warned Trump About Impact of U.S.-China Trade War"; Rogin, *Chaos Under Heaven,* 245.
114. Pandey, "Trump: 'Xi and I Will Always Be Friends' Despite Trade Issues."
115. Trump, "Remarks by President Trump at Signing of the U.S.-China Phase One Trade Agreement."
116. Brady, *Making the Foreign Serve China,* 45.
117. Mirsky and Fairbank, "Mao and Snow."
118. Li, "Trump to Get 'State Visit–Plus' Experience in China."
119. Zhou, "China Shuts Down Forbidden City in Personal Welcome for Trump."
120. "Excerpts from Trump's Interview with the Times," *New York Times.*

Chapter Four: Shangri-La

1. Louison, "Richard Gere."
2. Siegel, "Richard Gere's Studio Exile."
3. Hamilton, "Text—H.R. 2333, 103rd Congress."
4. Lopez, *Prisoners of Shangri-La.*
5. van Schaik, *Tibet,* 216.
6. Woeser, "When Tibet Loved China."
7. Mishra, "Holy Man."
8. van Schaik, *Tibet,* 204.
9. Polo, *Travels.*
10. Klein, "10 Things You May Not Know About Dwight D. Eisenhower."
11. French, *Tibet, Tibet,* 111.
12. Dodin and Rather, *Imagining Tibet,* 57.

13. Oppenheim and Chicago Tribune, "Dalai Lama Making First Visit to U.S."
14. Zehme, "Eddie Murphy."
15. Sanchez, "Dalai Lama Urges Tibetan Freedom."
16. Kerr, *Eye of the Lammergeier.*
17. "Nobel Peace Prize 1989."
18. Fitzsimmons, "Inside Story"; Goldman, "Buddhism and Manhattan."
19. Sherrill, "Little Buddha, Big Ego."
20. Nigro, *Spirituality of Richard Gere.*
21. McLeod, "Richard Gere"; Daccache and Valeriano, *Hollywood's Representations of the Sino-Tibetan Conflict,* 78.
22. Higgins, "Hollywood Elite Says Hello, Dalai."
23. Ebert, "Red Corner Movie Review & Film Summary (1997)."
24. Guthmann, "Gere's 'Corner' on Saving Tibet."
25. Schell, *Virtual Tibet,* 107–9.
26. Buruma, "Found Horizon."
27. Stewart, "In Current Films on Tibet, Hold the Shangri-La."
28. Buruma, "Found Horizon."
29. Stolder, "Beastie Boys, Smashing Pumpkins Headline Tibetan Freedom Concert."
30. Schell, *Virtual Tibet,* 180.
31. Su, *China's Encounter with Global Hollywood,* 1.
32. Fung, *Asian Popular Culture,* 59; Yu, "Visual Spectacular, Revolutionary Epic, and Personal Voice."
33. Chandler, "Mickey Mao."
34. Gargan, "Donald Duck Learns Chinese."
35. Su, *China's Encounter with Global Hollywood,* 53.
36. Rosen, "Hollywood and the Great Wall."
37. Tempest, "How Do You Say 'Boffo' in Chinese?"
38. Su, *China's Encounter with Global Hollywood,* 13.
39. CITIC, "Chongfan 'Taitannike'" 重返泰坦尼克 [Returning to *Titanic*]; Bezlova, "Cinema-China: 'Titanic' Scores an Ideological Hit."
40. Elley, "Red River Valley"; Sullivan, "China One-Ups Disney with Its Own Tibet Pic."
41. Waxman, "China Bans Work with Film Studios"; Weinraub, "Dalai Lama's Tutor, Portrayed by Brad Pitt, Wasn't Just Roving Through the Himalayas."
42. Yu, "From *Kundun* to *Mulan.*"
43. Schell, *Virtual Tibet,* 298.
44. Barboza and Barnes, "How China Won the Keys to Disney's Magic Kingdom."
45. Box Office Mojo, "Top Lifetime Adjusted Grosses."
46. Biskind, *Down and Dirty Pictures,* 153.
47. Masters, "Why Did Eisner Hire Ovitz?"
48. Greene, *From Fu Manchu to Kung Fu Panda,* 183.
49. Weinraub, "Disney Will Defy China on Its Dalai Lama Film."

50. Schell, *Virtual Tibet*, 299.
51. Weinraub, "Hollywood Feels Chill of Chinese Warning to Disney."
52. Rose, "Michael Eisner, Charlie Rose."
53. Miller, *Powerhouse*, 507.
54. "Interviews—Martin Scorsese, Dreams of Tibet," *Frontline*, PBS.
55. Rose, "Michael Eisner, Charlie Rose."
56. Mathison and Scorsese, "Kundun," Box Office Mojo.
57. Mathison and Scorsese, "Kundun (1997)," British Film Institute.
58. Zhu, *Zhu Rongji on the Record*, 93.
59. Ressner, "Disney's China Policy."
60. Cohen, "(In)Justice with Chinese Characteristics."
61. Peers, "Mouse in a Pout."
62. Barnet, "Chinese Exhibs Yank U.S. Pix to Protest Bombing"; Bates and Farley, "Hollywood, China in a Chilly Embrace."
63. Yu, "From *Kundun* to *Mulan*."
64. Verrier, "Disney Seeks to Add China to Its World."
65. Lampton, *Same Bed, Different Dreams*, 336.
66. Dalai Lama, *My Land and My People*.
67. Stolder, "Beastie Boys, Smashing Pumpkins Headline Tibetan Freedom Concert."
68. Bates, "China Trade Deal Won't Be a Quick Hit for Hollywood."

Chapter Five: Hollywood Learns to Please Beijing

1. Brosnan, "It's Only a Movie!"
2. Gaylord, "Hollywood Aims to Please . . . China?"
3. "Jian zi ru mian!" 见字如面! [Read literally!], *China Daily*.
4. Dickie, "Chinese Film Maker Sees Moral Angle."
5. Eimer, "Chinese Cinema Industry."
6. Forns, "Hollywood Films in the Non-Western World," 32–33.
7. Puzzanghera and Magnier, "Studios Still Bit Actors in China."
8. Paul, "Hollywood Zooms In On China."
9. China Power Team, "Do Chinese Films Hold Global Appeal?"
10. Puzzanghera and Magnier, "Studios Still Bit Actors in China."
11. Farley, "Entertaining China."
12. McGregor, "China's Film Ban Is No Barrier for the Fan."
13. Barboza, "Citing Public Sentiment, China Cancels Release of 'Geisha.'"
14. Eimer, "Chinese Cinema Industry."
15. Adams, "Mum's the Word."
16. "China Sinks Dead Man's Chest," *Guardian*.
17. China.org, "Chow Yun Fat Visits HK Disneyland to Promote Pirates 3"; CCTV, "Chow Yun Fat Visits HK Disneyland to Promote Pirates of the Caribbean 3."
18. Associated Press, "Chow's 'Pirates' Scenes Cut in China."
19. Newswire, "Hollywood's 'Babel' Too Steamy for China's Censors."

20. Newswire, "China Approves 'The Da Vinci Code.'"
21. Frater, "Asia Seems Steamy Season"; Coonan, "'Pirates' Edited for China Release."
22. Kahn, "China Cancels 'Da Vinci' Movie"; Frater, "China Nixes Hollywood Pix"; Wang, "Authorities Deny Ban on Hollywood Movies."
23. Puzzanghera and Magnier, "Studios Still Bit Actors in China."
24. "In Wolves' Clothing," *Economist.*
25. McNary, "China to Miss Out on 'Dark Knight.'"
26. Spielberg, "Steven Spielberg to Hu Jintao on Darfur."
27. Cooper, "Spielberg Drops Out as Adviser to Beijing Olympics in Dispute over Darfur Conflict."
28. Bond, "Hollywood Assumes Crash Position"; Lang, "Hollywood's Global Expansion."
29. Tung, "Cinema Chains Ready to Cash In On Movie Boom."
30. Schwartzel, "Hollywood's New Script."
31. Fritz, *Big Picture,* 208–10; Guerrasio, "How 'Avatar' Paved the Way for the Huge Box Office Success of 'Avengers.'"
32. Nicholas and Orden, "Movie Mogul's Starring Role in Raising Funds for Obama"; Hodge, "Recap: Xi's Visit to the U.S."
33. Waxman, "How Hollywood and Joe Biden Got China to Drop a 20-Year Movie Quota."
34. Qin and Carlsen, "How China Is Rewriting Its Own Script."
35. Enav, "Hollywood Yielding to China's Growing Film Clout."
36. Evans, *Art of Persuasion,* 8.
37. Bernays, *Propaganda.*
38. *Merriam-Webster,* 11th ed., s.v. "rumor"; *Merriam-Webster,* 11th ed., s.v. "propaganda."
39. Jason, "Film and Propaganda."
40. Stein, "Famous Elbow Rub."
41. Chen, "Propagating the Propaganda Film."
42. Su, *China's Encounter with Global Hollywood,* 30.
43. Yuli, "China's Filmmakers Fine-Tune Patriotism for a New Generation."
44. Sauer, "Real America."
45. Hoad, "Looper Bridges the Cinematic Gap Between China and the US."
46. Langfitt, "How China's Censors Influence Hollywood."
47. Hoad, "Looper Bridges the Cinematic Gap Between China and the US"; Salisbury, "Fantastic Fest"; "Can Hollywood-China Co-productions Bridge the Audience Gap?," *Jing Daily.*
48. Pompliano, "Pomp Podcast #361."
49. WikiLeaks, "Sony Email 182471"; WikiLeaks, "Sony Email 189623"; WikiLeaks, "Sony Email 180113."
50. Lawson, "China Censors 'Men in Black 3' for Referring to Chinese Censorship"; Telegraph Staff, "Skyfall Heavily Edited by Chinese Government Censors."

51. Hipes, "Black List 2015 Scripts Announced with 'Bubbles' King of the Jungle."
52. Wagner, "Hollywood List Everyone Wants to Be On."
53. WikiLeaks, "Sony Email 200507."
54. Buckley and Bradsher, "China Moves to Let Xi Stay in Power by Abolishing Term Limit."
55. Xinhua, "Zhonggong Zhongyang yinfa 'Shenhua dang he guojia jigou gaige fangan'" 中共中央印发《深化党和国家机 革方案》 [The Central Committee of the Communist Party of China issues "Deepening Party and State Institutional Reform Plan"]; Buckley, "China Gives Communist Party More Control over Policy and Media."
56. Denyer and Lin, "China Sends Its Top Actors and Directors Back to Socialism School."
57. Carroll, "Be Nice to China."
58. Tuckman, "License to Shill."
59. Nikel, "Norway Lets Tom Cruise Bypass Coronavirus Quarantine to Film 'Mission: Impossible 7.'"
60. Loria, "Global Box Office Down 72%, Digital Leads Home Entertainment in 2020."
61. MacLeod and Sanderson, "New A List Star Rises in the East."
62. Davis, "China's Censors Confound Biz."
63. Asia Blog, "'Arrival' Actor Tzi Ma on Being Outspoken in Hollywood."
64. Batman Fandom, "Ra's al Ghul (Nolanverse)."
65. Rotten Tomatoes, "*Pacific Rim* Quotes."
66. The Hangover Fandom, "Leslie Chow."
67. Newby, "How Iron Man's Chief Villain Could Return."
68. Khatchatourian, "'Star Wars' China Poster Sparks Controversy After Shrinking John Boyega's Character."
69. Lo, "Chinese Disney Fans Decry Black 'Little Mermaid' Casting."
70. Perez, "Disney's Choice to Cast Halle Bailey in 'Little Mermaid' Is Mostly Well-Received, Poll Finds."
71. Lin, "Is China Really Ready for Black Stories?"
72. Reuters Staff, "Wanda Inks $1.7 Billion 'Red Tourism' Site in China's Communist Heartland."
73. "Bu wang chuxin yi zheng rong suiyue" 不忘初心忆峥嵘岁月 [Do not forget the original aspirations of those memorable years], *People's Daily*.
74. Reuters Staff, "Wanda Inks $1.7 Billion 'Red Tourism' Site in China's Communist Heartland."
75. Wang, "Speech by Chairman Wang Jianlin at the Launch of Yan'an Wanda City–Wanda Group Mobile."
76. Kuhn, "Chinese Blockbuster 'Wolf Warrior II' Mixes Jingoism with Hollywood Heroism."
77. Box Office Mojo, "Wolf Warrior 2."
78. Xiaoyou Ge Entertainment 逍遥阁娱记, "*Zhan Lang 2* hou you yi jun-

shi dazuo"《战狼2》后又一军事大作 [*Wolf Warrior 2* is another military masterpiece].

79. Shepherd, "Rowan Atkinson Is Reprising His Role as Mr. Bean for a Chinese Film."

80. McGovern, "'Great Wall' Director Addresses Matt Damon Whitewashing Controversy"; Nguyen, "With 'The Great Wall,' Hollywood Has Made Whitewashing China's Problem."

81. Denton, "Great Wall Review (1)."

82. Mattis, "China's 'Three Warfares' in Perspective."

83. Kong tian lie, "空天猎 (AKA Sky Hunter)."

84. Sohu News, "Lao shao jie yi, ren jian ren ai de 'Xueren qiyuan,' shi yong Haolaiwu de fangshi jiang le yi ge Zhongguo gushi" 老少皆宜，人见人爱的《雪人奇缘》，是用好莱坞的方式讲了一个中国故事 [Suitable for young and old, the universally appealing *Abominable* tells a Chinese story in Hollywood fashion].

85. Child, "Tilda Swinton Cast as Tibetan to Placate China, Says Doctor Strange Writer."

86. Wong, "'Doctor Strange' Writer Explains Casting of Tilda Swinton as Tibetan."

Chapter Six: Universities and Self-Censorship

1. Haas, "Whiff of Discontent as China Bans Imports of Soft European Cheese."

2. Stevenson and Ramzy, "China Defends Expulsion of American Journalists, Accusing U.S. of Prejudice."

3. Butterfield, *China*.

4. Eric Fish (@ericfish85), "Houston Rockets fan in China posted photo on Weibo wearing a James Harden jersey while holding up a Chinese flag and a lighter, with the caption: 'I live and die with my team. Come and catch me.' They caught him," Twitter, Oct. 8, 2019, 1:29 p.m.

5. Stone Fish, "Leaked Email."

6. Wong, "End of the Harvard Century."

7. Stone Fish, "Huawei's Surprising Ties to the Brookings Institution."

8. "Cambridge University Press Battles Censorship in China," *Economist*.

9. Bland, "Outcry as Latest Global Publisher Bows to China Censors."

10. Allen-Ebrahimian, "How China Managed to Play Censor at a Conference on U.S. Soil"; Alford, "Letter to the Editor: In Response to 'The End of the Harvard Century.'"

11. Zheng, "Beijing Accused of Pressuring Spanish University to Drop Taiwanese Event"; Scholars at Risk, "Obstacles to Excellence"; Mcneill, "They Don't Understand the Fear We Have."

12. Report to Congressional Requesters, "U.S. Universities in China Emphasize Academic Freedom but Face Internet Censorship and Other Challenges."

13. Wayt, "NYU Shanghai Quietly Added Pro-government Course at Behest

of Chinese Government"; Feng, "China Tightens Grip on Foreign University Joint Ventures"; Feng, "Beijing Vies for Greater Control of Foreign Universities in China"; Redden, "Question of NYU's Control over NYU Shanghai Sits at Center of Faculty Suit."

14. Vise, "U.S. Scholars Say Their Book on China Led to Travel Ban."
15. Editorial Board, "Forget It, Georgetown, It's China."
16. Mullins, "Dartmouth encourages faculty to safeguard students as Chinese law targets free speech globally."
17. *Cambridge English Dictionary,* s.v. "self-censorship," accessed April 7, 2021.
18. Diamond and Schell, *China's Influence and American Interests.*
19. Allen-Ebrahimian, "University of Minnesota Student Jailed in China for Tweets Critical of Government."
20. Qiu, "Chinese Students Protest in America, Face Danger at Home."
21. Goldberg, "Hong Kong Protests Spread to U.S. Colleges, and a Rift Grows."
22. Millward, "Open Letter to US (and Other) Universities in Light of Zoom's Revelations About Collaborating with the Chinese Communist Party."
23. William Long, "Shanxi Hanbin yi nanzi feifa jinxing guoji lianwang bei chachu" 陕西汉滨一男子非法进行国际联网被查处 [Man from Hanbin in Shanxi province punished for illegal internet usage], *China Digital Times* 中国数字时代, May 19, 2020.
24. Woolcock, "Wipe References to China to Protect Students, SOAS Lecturers Told"; Craymer, "China's National-Security Law Reaches into Harvard, Princeton Classrooms."
25. Sharma, "China Fights Back with Sanctions on Academics, Institute."
26. Wen and Belkin, "American Colleges Watch for Changes at Chinese Universities."
27. School Office, "Guanyu bao somg xinxi gongzuo fuzhe ren he xinxi yuan de tongzhi" 关于报送信息工作负责人和信息员的通知; Feng, "Chinese Universities Are Enshrining Communist Party Control in Their Charters."
28. Li, "Top Chinese University Stripped 'Freedom of Thought' from Its Charter."
29. Horwitz, "Chinese Students in the US Are Using 'Inclusion' and 'Diversity' to Oppose a Dalai Lama Graduation Speech."
30. Tie, "Sign the Petition."
31. Craymer, "China's National-Security Law Reaches into Harvard, Princeton Classrooms."
32. Walsh, "In Depth: Chinese Students at US Colleges Face Uncertain Future."
33. Robbins, "Historic Rise in Chinese Students at UC San Diego Stalls due to Sour Political Climate in US."
34. Mitchell, Leachman, and Saenz, "State Higher Education Funding Cuts Have Pushed Costs to Students, Worsened Inequality."
35. Petersen, "Outsourced to China."
36. Michael Gibbs Hill (@hillmgl), "These guys make Confucius Institutes look like they're doing it wrong. When Koch buys influence over the hir-

ing of professors who can achieve tenure, he can steer the direction of how economics, a foundational discipline, is taught for decades," Twitter, May 2, 2018, 7:22 a.m.

37. Aspinwall, "US Asks Taiwan to Fill Void as Confucius Institutes Close"; Levine, "'Deeply Alarmed'"; Petersen, "China's Confucius Institutes Might Be Closing, but They Succeeded"; Glaser and Chigas, "Decision to Close the Confucius Institute at Tufts University."

38. "As China's Power Waxes, the West's Study of It Is Waning," *Economist*.

39. Duggan, "UNH Creates an Anti-racism Plan, but Some Students Want More."

40. Link, "China: The Anaconda in the Chandelier."

41. Choate, *Hot Property*.

42. Berfield, "Business Ties of Bo Xilai"; "Xi Jinping Millionaire Relations Reveal Fortunes of Elite," Bloomberg News.

43. PEN America, "Darkened Screen."

44. O'Brien, "The Mayor vs. the Mogul."

45. Wong, "Bloomberg News Is Said to Curb Articles That Might Anger China."

46. O'Brien, "The Mayor vs. the Mogul."

47. French, "Bloomberg's Folly."

48. O'Brien, "The Mayor vs. the Mogul."

49. Picker, "Forbes Sues Integrated Whale Media over Deal."

50. Phoenix Hebei Network 凤凰网河北. "Bank of China and Forbes China Release the '2021 Forbes China International School Rankings.'"

51. Tu, "Starbucks Spends $1.3 Billion for Full Stake in Fast-Growing China Market."

52. Eavis and Appelbaum, "Last Month, Investors Seemed Too Pessimistic."

53. Schultz, "Building a Trusted and Enduring Brand in China and Around the World."

54. Kranish, "Bloomberg's Business in China Has Grown"; Dolan, Wang, and Peterson-Withorn, "Forbes Billionaires 2021: Michael Bloomberg."

55. Nicolaou, "Bloomberg Profits from Conference Business in China."

56. Shambaugh, "Coming Chinese Crackup."

57. Shambaugh, "Defining Current Challenges."

58. Marsh, "Westerners Are Increasingly Scared of Traveling to China as Threat of Detention Rises."

Chapter Seven: Friendship and Its Discontents

1. Xu, "Xu Zhicai's Interview."

2. Brooks, *World War Z*, 12.

3. Shaw, "Fearing Chinese Censors, Paramount Changes 'World War Z' (Exclusive)."

4. Anders, "*Last Ship* Is One Huge Navy Ad."

5. Last Ship Transcripts, Forever Dreaming, "03x01—the Scott Effect."

6. Weintraub, "'Last Ship' Producers on Elevating the Stakes in Seasons 4 and 5."

7. Makinen, "Episode of NBC's 'The Blacklist' Pulled from Chinese Websites."

8. "'Drew Carey' Visits Streets of China," CNN; Carey, "High Road to China."

9. "Drew Carey Films Episode of His Comedy Show in China," ITN.

10. Szalai, "Chinese Get Tough on Big Media."

11. Sisario, "For All the Rock in China."

12. Haithman, "Why China Tunes Out American TV."

13. Law & Order Wiki, "Tortured."

14. "China Probrem Script," South Park Archives.

15. D'Elia, "Made in China."

16. Mann, *Blackhat*.

17. Mr. Robot Wiki, "Whiterose."

18. Clarke, "Independence Day 2 Review."

19. "Madam Secretary Transcripts Season 3, Episode 16," TV Show Transcripts.

20. Brody, "'When Night Falls' and 'Django Unchained': Movie Censorship in China."

21. Ong, "Quentin Tarantino 'OK' with Chinese Fans Watching Illegal Versions of His Films."

22. Watt, "'Cloud Atlas' Cut by 38 Minutes for China Audience"; Zhang, "Wachowski Laments China's 'Cloud Atlas' Cut."

23. Kao, "China Censors Cut 40 Minutes off Science Fiction Epic Cloud Atlas."

24. Cieply and Barnes, "To Get Movies into China, Hollywood Gives Censors a Preview."

25. Wong, "James Cameron on Chinese Filmmakers, Censorship, and Potential Co-productions"; "Titanic 2012 3D Release," Box Office Mojo.

26. Nixey, "Hollywood's Star Rises in the East."

27. Anderson, "Chen Guangcheng, 'Homeland' Honored by Human Rights First."

28. "Batman Star Christian Bale Visits Disneyland with Blind Dissident Chen Guangcheng," *South China Morning Post*.

29. Osnos, "Future of America's Contest with China."

30. Associated Press, "Hong Kong to Amend Law to Step Up Film Censorship."

31. Iannucci, "'Veep' Camp David (TV Episode 2016)."

32. Pareles, "Rapper Conquered Music World in '80s with Beastie Boys."

33. Beastiemania, "Dechen Wangdu."

34. Flumenbaum, "China Bans Democracy, Declares War on Guns N' Roses."

35. Afp, "Kate Bush and Lorde Feature on Birthday Album for Dalai Lama"; Brzeski, "Lady Gaga's Dalai Lama Meeting Generates Backlash in China."

36. Buchanan, "Red Hot Chili Peppers Banned from China for Bizarre Reason."

37. "Board & Staff," Tibet House US.

38. Brzeski, "China, the World's Second-Largest Film Market, Moves Beyond Hollywood"; Smirke, "IFPI Global Music Report 2020."

39. Lee, "How Mega-mergers Are Changing the Way You Watch Your Favorite Shows and Movies."
40. Nussbaum, "CBS Censors 'The Good Fight' for a Musical Short About China."
41. Jacobs, "CBS Censors a 'Good Fight' Segment."
42. Kantrowitz and Paczkowski, "Apple Told Some Apple TV+ Show Developers Not to Anger China."
43. Nicas, Zhong, and Wakabayashi, "Censorship, Surveillance and Profits"; Smith, "Apple TV Was Making a Show About Gawker."
44. Brzeski, "Filmart."
45. Brzeski, "Netflix's 'BoJack Horseman' Blocked on China's iQiyi Streaming Service."
46. Bylund, "Netflix Just Started Reporting Renewable Energy Use and Content Removal."
47. Boren, "NBA's China–Daryl Morey Backlash, Explained."
48. Pape, "Kunjue Li Interview on Steven Soderbergh's The Laundromat."
49. Bonesteel, "NBA Commissioner Adam Silver Says League Supports Free Speech, Must Live with the Consequences."
50. Barrabi, "NBA's Shaquille O'Neal."
51. Feldman, "Shaquille O'Neal: 'Daryl Morey Was Right.'"
52. Osnos, "Future of America's Contest with China."
53. Rivas, "LeBron James Says Daryl Morey Was 'Misinformed' and 'Not Really Educated on the Situation' in China."
54. Ibid.
55. Deb and Stein, "Daryl Morey Steps Down as G.M. of the Houston Rockets."
56. MacMullan, "76ers' Morey Thought Tweet Might End His Career."
57. Our Foreign Staff, "Mercedes Apologises to China After Quoting Dalai Lama."
58. Ma, "Marriott Makes China Mad with Geopolitical Faux Pas."
59. Ma, "Marriott Employee Roy Jones Hit 'Like.'"
60. Ingram, "Chinese Censorship or 'Work Elsewhere.'"
61. Biddle, "Shutterstock Is Latest Tech Company to Censor Itself for China"; Ingram, "Chinese Censorship or 'Work Elsewhere.'"
62. Gonzalez, "Blizzard, Hearthstone, and the Hong Kong Protests."
63. Yong, "S'poreans Should Be Aware of China's Influence Ops."
64. Price, "U.S. Video Game Company Banned a Player During a Tournament for Supporting the Hong Kong Protests."
65. Xu, "Marriott Announces 'Rectification Plan' to Regain Trust."
66. Cheng, "Hotelier Marriott Unveils 'Eight-Point Rectification Plan' After Tibet and Hong Kong Geography 'Gaffe.'"
67. Sonnad, "Versace Is the Latest Major Brand to Express Its 'Deepest Apologies' to China."
68. Lim and Bergin, "Inside China's Audacious Global Propaganda Campaign."
69. ESPN News Services, "Harden Apologizes as Rift Grows."

70. Victor, "John Cena Apologizes to China for Calling Taiwan a Country."
71. Weibo Search: "Anta Nba."
72. Li, "Tencent, NBA Extend Partnership for Another Five Years in $1.5 Billion Deal."
73. Ley, "NBA Is Happy to Play China's Game."
74. Lashinsky and O'Keefe, "How the NBA Kept the Bubble from Bursting."
75. "Cheap Flights from San Francisco to Taipei," United Airlines.
76. McDonald, "China Rebukes Zara, Delta for Calling Taiwan 'Country.'"
77. Mozur, "Zoom Blocks Activist in U.S. After China Objects to Tiananmen Vigil."
78. Purnell and Xiao, "Facebook, Twitter, Google Face Free-Speech Test in Hong Kong."
79. Wang, "China's Zoom Bomb."
80. Ma, "Marriott Employee Roy Jones Hit 'Like.'"
81. Stone Fish, "Beijing Wants U.S. Business Leaders to Plead Its Case."
82. Palmeri, "Disney's Iger Staying Silent on Hong Kong Protests After NBA's China Row."
83. ESPN News Services, "China Suspends Work with Rockets over GM Tweet."
84. Tilman Fertitta (@TilmanJFertitta), "Listen. . . . @dmorey does NOT speak for the @HoustonRockets. Our presence in Tokyo is all about the promotion of the @NBA internationally and we are NOT a political organization," Twitter, Oct. 4, 2019, 11:54 p.m.
85. Bogdanich and Forsythe, "How McKinsey Has Helped Raise the Stature of Authoritarian Governments."
86. Stone Fish, "Stop Calling Xi Jinping 'President.'"
87. Deb and Stein, "N.B.A. Executive's Hong Kong Tweet Starts Firestorm in China."
88. Bogdanich and Forsythe, "How McKinsey Has Helped Raise the Stature of Authoritarian Governments."
89. Chen, "McDonald's Apologises for Advert Showing Taiwan as a Country"; Marriott International Newscenter (U.S.), "Statement from Arne Sorenson."
90. Wagner, "Internal Memo."
91. Crossley, "ESPN Criticised over China-NBA Coverage for Using 'Nine-Dash Line' Map."
92. Julian Ku (@julianku), Twitter, Oct. 9, 2019, 8:45 p.m.
93. South Park (@SouthPark), Twitter, Oct. 7, 2019, 2:22 p.m.
94. Deb, "Report: N.B.A.'s Academies in China Abused Athletes."
95. Cook and Bancroft, Mulan.
96. Dargis, "'Mulan' Review."
97. Harrison, "All the Breathtaking Locations Featured in Disney's New Live-Action Mulan."

98. Editorial Board, "What's Happening in Xinjiang Is Genocide," *Washington Post.*

99. Associated Press, "China Cuts Uighur Births with IUDs, Abortion, Sterilization"; United Nations, "United Nations Office on Genocide Prevention and the Responsibility to Protect"; Simon, "China Suppression of Uighur Minorities Meets U.N. Definition of Genocide, Report Says."

100. Ruser and Leibold, "Family De-planning."

101. Reinstein, "Inside the Rich and Timeless Sets of *Mulan*"; Nikicaro, "Day 5—China Scout"; Wintour, "Disney Unapologetic over Mulan Credit Thanking Chinese Communist Party."

102. Tobias, "Song of the South."

103. Sullivan and Lieberstein, "Season 7—Episode 10 'China.'"

104. Isaacs, *Scratches on Our Minds.*

105. "China's Fitful Sleep," *Economist.*

106. Crooks, "China Shakes the World"; Thomas, "China's Xi Jinping's 'Mandate of Heaven' to Rule the World"; Ochab, "'Let China Sleep, for When She Wakes, She Will Shake the World'"; Post Editorial Board, "Capitalist Tiger, Hidden Dragon," *New York Post.*

107. Kristof and WuDunn, *China Wakes.*

108. Baidu, "Baidu Search '睡狮.'"

109. Tian 田, "Napolun zui zao tichu Zhongguo shui shi lun ma?" 拿破崙最早提出中國睡獅論嗎? [Was Napoleon the first to put forth the theory of the sleeping Chinese lion?].

110. Sridharan, "China, the Sleeping Lion Has Woken Up, Says Xi Jinping."

111. Silver, Devlin, and Huang, "Most Americans Support Tough Stance Toward China on Human Rights, Economic Issues."

112. Chalwe Snr, "China Needs More Than Better Communication to Fix Its Africa Image Problem"; Brophy, *China Panic.*

113. Rogin, *Chaos Under Heaven*, 39.

114. Silver, Devlin, and Huang, "Most Americans Support Tough Stance Toward China on Human Rights, Economic Issues"; Younis, "New High in Perceptions of China as U.S.'s Greatest Enemy."

Chapter Eight: Defending the Rights
of Chinese and Chinese Americans

1. Osnos, "Two Lives of Qian Xuesen."

2. Chang, *Thread of the Silkworm*, xii–xiii.

3. Karni, "Trump Rants Behind Closed Doors with CEOs."

4. Hayes, "Trump Mocks Senator Feinstein Following Reports an Alleged Chinese Spy Worked for Her."

5. Office of the Historian, "Chinese Immigration and the Chinese Exclusion Acts."

6. Aurthur, "Wit and Sass of Harry S Truman."

7. Mathews, "Economic Invasion by Japan Revives Worry About Racism."
8. Little, "How the 1982 Murder of Vincent Chin Ignited a Push for Asian American Rights."
9. "Asian-Americans Say National Review Cover Is Offensive, Racist," Associated Press.
10. "President Clinton's Comments on Wen Ho Lee Case," Federation of American Scientists.
11. Glanz, "Fallout in Arms Research."
12. SI Staff, "Pekin Choose."
13. Kong, "Minority Groups Work to Change Names"; "Chinese Peak (Idaho)."
14. Coates, "Notes of a Native Tiger Son, Part 2."
15. Waldman, "U.S. Is Purging Chinese Cancer Researchers from Top Institutions."
16. Kim, "Prosecuting 'Chinese Spies.'"
17. Mitchell and Sevastopulo, "US Considered Ban on Student Visas for Chinese Nationals."
18. Kim, "Sam's Club Stabbing Suspect Thought Family Was 'Chinese Infecting People with Coronavirus.'"
19. Kelly, "Pompeo Says Trump Looking at Whether to Restrict Chinese Students from the US."
20. Magnier, "Fearing a New 'Red Scare,' Activists Fight Targeting of Chinese-Americans."
21. Kranz, "Director of the FBI Says the Whole of Chinese Society Is a Threat to the US."
22. Stone Fish, "Dear Progressives: You Can't Fight Climate Change by Going Soft on China."
23. Liu, *Chinaman's Chance,* 65.
24. Kay, "Christopher Wong Won, a Founding Member of 2 Live Crew, Dies at 53."
25. Wondra, "Chaffee Upholds Historical Accuracy for Chinaman Gulch."
26. Kong, "Minority Groups Work to Change Names"; Stone Fish, "America's Maps Are Still Filled with Racist Place Names."
27. James, "Rename Chinaman Lake."
28. Domestic Names Committee, "Principles, Policies, and Procedures."
29. Cheng, "Don't Close the Door on Chinese Scientists Like Me."
30. Tu et al., "How Should the U.S. Government Treat Chinese Students in America?"
31. Bush, "'Islam Is Peace' Says President."
32. Pompeo, "Chinese Communist Party on the American Campus."
33. Magnier, "US Moves In On Top Universities over Fear of Chinese Funding, IP Leaks."
34. Wineapple, "'I Have Let Whitman Alone.'"

BIBLIOGRAPHY

Abeel, David. *Journal of a Residence in China.* Bibliographical Center for Research, 2009.

Abramowitz, Michael. "Bush 41 in China: Kinda Like Old Times; Former President Is Back on Familiar, if Changed, Ground." *Washington Post,* Aug. 11, 2008. washingtonpost.com.

Adams, Guy. "Mum's the Word: Mark Causing Chaos at Thatcher's 80th Party." *Independent,* July 21, 2013. independent.co.uk.

Afp. "Kate Bush and Lorde Feature on Birthday Album for Dalai Lama." *Telegraph,* July 2, 2015. telegraph.co.uk.

Aleem, Zeeshan. "'Another Kick in the Teeth': A Top Economist on How Trade with China Helped Elect Trump." *Vox,* March 29, 2017. vox.com.

Alford, William P. "Letter to the Editor: In Response to 'The End of the Harvard Century.'" *The Harvard Crimson,* May 4, 2020, sec. Letters. "https://www.thecrimson.com/article/2020/5/4/letter-alford-response-to-the-end-of-the-harvard-century/" \t "_blank" thecrimson.com.

Allen, Mike, and Philip P. Pan. "Bush Begins China Visit." *Washington Post,* Feb. 21, 2002. washingtonpost.com.

Allen, Richard. Richard Allen Oral History. UVA Miller Center, May 28, 2002. millercenter.org.

Allen-Ebrahimian, Bethany. "How China Managed to Play Censor at a Conference on U.S. Soil." *Foreign Policy,* July 10, 2018. foreignpolicy.com.

———. "University of Minnesota Student Jailed in China for Tweets Critical of Government." *Axios,* Jan. 23, 2020. axios.com.

All Politics. "Clinton Defends China Trip, Engagement Policy." CNN, June 11, 1998. cnn.com.

Anders, Charlie Jane. "*The Last Ship* Is One Huge Navy Ad—and Your New TV Obsession." *Wired,* Sept. 4, 2016. wired.com.

Anderson, Monika. "Chen Guangcheng, 'Homeland' Honored by Human Rights First." *Wall Street Journal,* Oct. 25, 2012. wsj.com.

Annaud, Jean-Jacques 让—雅克—阿诺. "Xizang shi Zhongguo lingtu de yibufen" 西藏是中国领土的一部分 [Tibet is part of China]. *Sina Blog,* Dec. 28, 2009. blog.sina.com.cn.

Areddy, James T. "The Chinese Birdman Who Got U.S. Aircraft Giant Boeing Flying." *Wall Street Journal,* Sept. 24, 2015. wsj.com.

Asia Blog. "'Arrival' Actor Tzi Ma on Being Outspoken in Hollywood." Asia Society, Oct. 24, 2016. asiasociety.org.

Asia for Educators. "Commodore Perry and Japan (1853–1854)." Columbia University, 2021. afe.easia.columbia.edu.

Aspinwall, Nick. "US Asks Taiwan to Fill Void as Confucius Institutes Close." *Nikkei Asia,* Feb. 2, 2021. "https://asia.nikkei.com/Business/Education/US-asks-Taiwan-to-fill-void-as-Confucius-Institutes-close" \t "_blank" asia.nikkei.com

Associated Press. "Asian-Americans Say National Review Cover Is Offensive, Racist." March 20, 1997. apnews.com.

———. "China Cuts Uighur Births with IUDs, Abortion, Sterilization." June 29, 2020. apnews.com.

———. "China Licenses Four Foreign Insurers." *New York Times,* April 6, 1999. nytimes.com.

———. Associated Press. "Chow's 'Pirates' Scenes Cut in China." ABC News, June 17, 2007. abc.net.au.

———. "Hong Kong to Amend Law to Step Up Film Censorship." *AP News,* Aug. 24, 2021, sec. Entertainment. "https://apnews.com/article/entertainment-arts-and-entertainment-hong-kong-censorship-7f468deea7ab0e637b2ee58fbe28c031" \t "_blank" apnews.com.

———. "Indonesia Gets an Adviser—Kissinger." *Deseret News,* Feb. 28, 2000. deseret.com.

Atlanta Chinese Life 亚特兰大生活网. "Di er ju Kate Zhongxin-Huanqiu Shibao Zhongmei qingnian xuezhe luntan" 第二届卡特中心-环球时报中美青年学者论坛 [The Third Forum for Young Chinese and American Scholars organized by the Carter Center and the *Global Times*]. Yatelanda Shenghuo wang 亚特兰大生活网. Atlanta Chinese Life, Oct. 16, 2015. atlantachinese.net.

Auerbach, Stuart. "Home from China." *Washington Post,* April 30, 1978. washingtonpost.com.

Aurthur, Robert Alan. "The Wit and Sass of Harry S Truman." *Esquire,* Aug. 1, 1971. esquire.com.

Autor, David H. "Trade and Labor Markets: Lessons from China's Rise." IZA World of Labor, Feb. 22, 2018.

Baidu. "Baidu Search '睡狮.'" Accessed April 15, 2021. baidu.com.

Baldwin, Clare, and Kristina Cooke. "How Sony Sanitized the New Adam Sandler Movie 'Pixels' to Please China." Reuters, July 24, 2015. reuters.com.

Banfield, Ashleigh. "Democratic Party Unrest; Trump Meets Kissinger." *Legal View with Ashleigh Banfield,* CNN, May 18, 2016. cnn.com.

Bank of China. "Announcement: Appointment of Independent Non-executive Director of the Bank." MarketScreener, July 24, 2020. marketscreener.com.

Barboza, David. "China Overtakes Japan to Become No. 2 Global Economic Power." *New York Times,* Aug. 15, 2010. nytimes.com.

———. "Citing Public Sentiment, China Cancels Release of 'Geisha.'" *New York Times,* Feb. 1, 2006. nytimes.com.

———. "Through a Joint Venture, Rio Tinto Strives to Repair Its Relations with China." *New York Times,* Aug. 10, 2010. nytimes.com.

Barboza, David, and Brooks Barnes. "How China Won the Keys to Disney's Magic Kingdom." *New York Times,* June 14, 2016. nytimes.com.

Barnet, Kim. "Chinese Exhibs Yank U.S. Pix to Protest Bombing." *Variety,* May 19, 1999. variety.com.

Barr, Alistair, and MarketWatch. "GE Says CEO Comments Reported out of Context." MarketWatch, July 1, 2010. marketwatch.com.

Barrabi, Thomas. "NBA's Shaquille O'Neal: 'Daryl Morey Was Right' to Back Pro-democracy Hong Kong Protests." Fox Business, Oct. 22, 2019. foxbusiness.com.

Barron, James, Jane Perlez, and Linda Lee. "Public Lives." *New York Times,* Dec. 7, 2000. nytimes.com.

Barth, Rolf F., and Jie Chen. "What Did Sun Yat-sen Really Die Of? A Reassessment of His Illness and the Cause of His Death." *Chinese Journal of Cancer,* Sept. 2, 2016.

Basken, Paul, and Michael Forsythe. "China Lobbies U.S. on the Cheap, Aided by Boeing, Ford, Chamber." Bloomberg News, Dec. 9, 2003.

Bates, James. "China Trade Deal Won't Be a Quick Hit for Hollywood." *Los Angeles Times,* May 30, 2000. latimes.com.

Bates, James, and Maggie Farley. "Hollywood, China in a Chilly Embrace." *Los Angeles Times,* June 13, 1999. latimes.com.

BBC. "China's Hu Jintao, US Ex-president Bush Hail 'Progress' in Ties 7 Mar." BBC Monitoring Asia Pacific, March 8, 2008. bbc.com.

———. "Chinese Leaders' Activities." BBC Monitoring Asia Pacific, Dec. 5, 2003. monitoring.bbc.co.uk.

———. "Chinese President Hu Jintao Talks Business in Chicago." BBC News, Jan. 21, 2011. bbc.com.

———. "President Hu Jintao Meets Former US President Bush, Hail Sino-US Ties." BBC Monitoring Asia Pacific, Dec. 13, 2006. bbc.com.

———. "Vanuatu Scraps Deal with Taiwan." Dec. 16, 2004. news.bbc.co.uk.

Beastiemania. "Dechen Wangdu." beastiemania.com.

Beauchamp-Mustafaga, Nathan, and Michael S. Chase. "Borrowing a Boat Out to Sea." Johns Hopkins Schools of Advanced International Studies Foreign Policy Institute, 2019. fpi.sais-jhu.edu.

Beaumont-Thomas, Ben. "Paul McCartney Calls for 'Medieval' Chinese Markets to Be Banned over Coronavirus." *Guardian,* April 14, 2020. theguardian.com.

Becker, Jasper. "'Side by Side Against Terrorism'; Bush Praises Jiang for His

Backing of America's Global Campaign at Leaders' First Meeting." *South China Morning Post,* Oct. 20, 2001. scmp.com.

Benet, Lorenzo, Mary H. J. Farrell, and Janice Fuhrman. "Sure, He's Making a Box-Office Killing—but Who Is Steven Seagal?" *People,* Nov. 19, 1990. people.com.

Berfield, Susan. "The Business Ties of Bo Xilai." Bloomberg News, April 26, 2012. bloomberg.com.

Bernays, Edward L. *Propaganda.* Ig, 1928.

Bezlova, Antoaneta. "Cinema-China: 'Titanic' Scores an Ideological Hit." Inter Press Service News Agency, June 2, 1998. ipsnews.net.

Biddle, Sam. "Shutterstock Is Latest Tech Company to Censor Itself for China." *Intercept,* Nov. 6, 2019. theintercept.com.

Birnbaum, Jeffrey H. "Taking Costly Counsel from a Statesman." *Washington Post,* March 29, 2004. washingtonpost.com.

Biskind, Peter. *Down and Dirty Pictures.* Bloomsbury, 2016.

Bland, Ben. "Outcry as Latest Global Publisher Bows to China Censors." *Financial Times,* Oct. 31, 2017. ft.com.

Bloomberg News. "Xi Jinping Millionaire Relations Reveal Fortunes of Elite." June 29, 2012. bloomberg.com.

Bogdanich, Walt, and Michael Forsythe. "How McKinsey Has Helped Raise the Stature of Authoritarian Governments." *New York Times,* Dec. 15, 2018. nytimes.com.

Bond, Paul. "Hollywood Assumes Crash Position: How 'Recession Proof' Is Showbiz?" *Hollywood Reporter,* Dec. 18, 2018. hollywoodreporter.com.

Bonesteel, Matt. "NBA Commissioner Adam Silver Says League Supports Free Speech, Must Live with the Consequences." *Washington Post,* Oct. 8, 2019. washingtonpost.com.

Boren, Cindy. "The NBA's China–Daryl Morey Backlash, Explained." *Washington Post,* Oct. 7, 2019. washingtonpost.com.

Box Office Mojo. "Titanic 2012 3D Release." boxofficemojo.com.

———. "Wolf Warrior 2." boxofficemojo.com.

Bradsher, Keith. "Rallying Round the China Bill, Hungrily." *New York Times,* May 21, 2000. nytimes.com.

Bradsher, Keith, and Li Yuan. "China's Economy Became No. 2 by Defying No. 1." *New York Times,* Nov. 25, 2018. nytimes.com.

Brady, Anne-Marie. *Making the Foreign Serve China: Managing Foreigners in the People's Republic.* Rowman & Littlefield, 2003.

Brennan, David. "Jimmy Carter Took Call About China from Concerned Donald Trump: 'China Has Not Wasted a Single Penny on War.'" *Newsweek,* April 15, 2019. newsweek.com.

Brinkley, Joel. "U.S. Finds Technology Curb Fails to Cut Flow to Russians." *New York Times,* Jan. 1, 1985. nytimes.com.

Brody, Richard. "'When Night Falls' and 'Django Unchained': Movie Censorship in China." *New Yorker,* May 23, 2013. newyorker.com.

Brooks, Max. *World War Z: An Oral History of the Zombie War.* Crown, 2006.

Brophy, David. *China Panic: Australia's Alternative to Paranoia and Pandering.* Black Inc., 2021.

Brosnan, John. "It's Only a Movie!" *Starburst,* Jan. 2001. starburstmagazine.com.

Brzeski, Patrick. "China, the World's Second-Largest Film Market, Moves Beyond Hollywood." *Hollywood Reporter,* Oct. 7, 2020. hollywoodreporter.com.

———. "Filmart: iQiyi's Tim Gong Yu on Netflix, Expanding Globally, and Why the Chinese Market Is 'Unpredictable.'" *Hollywood Reporter,* March 19, 2019. hollywoodreporter.com.

———. "Lady Gaga's Dalai Lama Meeting Generates Backlash in China." *Hollywood Reporter,* June 28, 2016. hollywoodreporter.com.

———. "Netflix's 'BoJack Horseman' Blocked on China's iQiyi Streaming Service." *Hollywood Reporter,* June 27, 2017. hollywoodreporter.com.

Buchanan, Brett. "Red Hot Chili Peppers Banned from China for Bizarre Reason." *Alternative Nation,* Dec. 21, 2018. alternativenation.net.

Buckley, Chris. "China Gives Communist Party More Control over Policy and Media." *New York Times,* March 21, 2018. nytimes.com.

———. "The Rise and Fall of the Goddess of Democracy." *Sinosphere* (blog), *New York Times,* June 1, 2014. sinosphere.blogs.nytimes.com.

Buckley, Chris, and Keith Bradsher. "China Moves to Let Xi Stay in Power by Abolishing Term Limit." *New York Times,* Feb. 25, 2018. nytimes.com.

Buckley, William F., Jr. "A Firing Line Debate: Resolved: That Trade with China Should Not Be Interrupted, 2017." *Firing Line with William F. Buckley Jr.* youtube.com.

Buffett, Warren, and Carol J. Loomis. "America's Growing Trade Deficit Is Selling the Nation Out from Under Us. Here's a Way to Fix the Problem—and We Need to Do It Now." *Fortune,* Nov. 10, 2003. archive.fortune.com.

Buruma, Ian. "Found Horizon." *New York Review of Books,* June 29, 2000. nybooks.com.

Bush, George H. W. "George H. W. Bush, Press Conference, June 5, 1989." USC US-China Institute, June 5, 1989. china.usc.edu.

Bush, George W. *Decision Points.* Broadway Paperbacks, 2011.

———. "'Islam Is Peace' Says President." White House, Sept. 17, 2001. georgewbush-whitehousearchives.gov.

Bush, Prescott S. "Letter from the Chairman." United States of America–China Chamber of Commerce. web.archive.org.

BusinessWeek. "The Big Business of Being Henry Kissinger." Dec. 2, 1985.

Butterfield, Fox. *China: Alive in the Bitter Sea.* Times Books, 1982.

Bylund, Anders. "Netflix Just Started Reporting Renewable Energy Use and Content Removal." Nasdaq, Feb. 8, 2020. nasdaq.com.

Calmes, Jackie. "A U.S. Marine Base for Australia Irritates China." *New York Times,* Nov. 16, 2011. nytimes.com.

Campaign Finance Investigation Day 2. C-SPAN, 1997. c-span.org.

Carey, Drew. "The High Road to China." *The Drew Carey Show,* ABC, Nov. 18, 1998.

Carlson, Peter. "The Relatively Charmed Life of Neil Bush." *Washington Post,* Dec. 28, 2003. washingtonpost.com.

Carroll, Rory. "Be Nice to China: Hollywood Risks 'Artistic Surrender' in Effort to Please." *Guardian,* May 30, 2013. theguardian.com.

Carter Center. "The Carter Center in China." Jan. 9, 2019. cartercenter.org.

———. "China." cartercenter.org.

CCTV. "Chow Yun Fat Visits HK Disneyland to Promote Pirates of the Caribbean 3." CCTV International, May 9, 2007. cctv.com.

Chalwe Snr, Mwansa. "China Needs More Than Better Communication to Fix Its Africa Image Problem." *South China Morning Post,* Aug. 30, 2021, sec. Opinion. "http://scmp.com" \t "_blank" scmp.com.

Chandler, Clay. "Mickey Mao." *Fortune,* April 18, 2005. fortune.com.

Chang, Gordon H. *Fateful Ties: A History of America's Preoccupation with China.* Harvard University Press, 2015.

Chang, Iris. *Thread of the Silkworm.* Basic Books, 1996.

Chao, Eveline. "Let One Hundred Panthers Bloom: The Black Panthers and Mao Zedong." *ChinaFile,* Oct. 14, 2016. chinafile.com.

Chellel, Kit, Franz Wild, and David Stringer. "When Rio Tinto Met China's Iron Hand." Bloomberg, July 13, 2018. bloomberg.com.

Chen, Laurie. "McDonald's Apologises for Advert Showing Taiwan as a Country." *South China Morning Post,* Jan. 23, 2019. scmp.com.

Chen, Tina Mai. "Propagating the Propaganda Film: The Meaning of Film in Chinese Communist Party Writings, 1949–1965." *Modern Chinese Literature and Culture* 15, no. 2 (Fall 2003).

Cheng, Kris. "Hotelier Marriott Unveils 'Eight-Point Rectification Plan' After Tibet and Hong Kong Geography 'Gaffe.'" *Hong Kong Free Press,* Jan. 19, 2018. hongkongfp.com.

Cheng, Yangyang. "Don't Close the Door on Chinese Scientists Like Me." *Foreign Policy,* June 4, 2018. foreignpolicy.com.

Child, Ben. "Tilda Swinton Cast as Tibetan to Placate China, Says Doctor Strange Writer." *Guardian,* April 26, 2016. theguardian.com.

Chin, Josh. "Beijing Aims to Blunt Western Influence in China." *Wall Street Journal,* Nov. 11, 2014. wsj.com.

China Daily. "40 People in 40 Years: Gary Locke." Nov. 28, 2018. chinadaily .com.cn.

———. "Jian zi ru mian! Cong zongshuji de xin zhong 'jian ren, jian shi, jian qing'" 见字如面! 从总书记的信中'见人、见事、见情 [Read literally! "See people, see matters, see love" in the letter of the general secretary]. 中国日报, April 10, 2021. chinadaily.com.

China Development Bank. "Prospectus Supplement." Securities and Exchange Commission, Sept. 19, 2005. sec.gov.

China Investment Corporation. "China Investment Corporation 2019 Annual Report." China Investment Corporation, Sept. 25, 2020. China-inv.cn.

China.org.cn. "Chow Yun Fat Visits HK Disneyland to Promote *Pirates 3*." May 9, 2007. china.org.cn.

China Power Team. "Do Chinese Films Hold Global Appeal?" China Power, March 1, 2019. chinapower.csis.org.

China Vitae. "Biography of Liu Yandong." Feb. 2018. chinavitae.com.

———. "Biography of Rong Yiren." Accessed April 18, 2021. chinavitae.com.

Chinese People's Association for Friendship with Foreign Countries. "About Us." cpaffc.org.cn.

Choate, Pat. *Hot Property*. Knopf, 2005.

Christensen, Thomas J. *The China Challenge: Shaping the Choices of a Rising Power*. Norton, 2016.

Christopher, Warren. *In the Stream of History: Shaping Foreign Policy for a New Era*. Stanford University Press, 1998.

Church, George J. "China: Old Wounds Deng Xiaoping." *Time,* Jan. 6, 1986. content.time.com.

Cieply, Michael, and Brooks Barnes. "To Get Movies into China, Hollywood Gives Censors a Preview." *New York Times,* Jan. 15, 2013. nytimes.com.

CITIC. "Chongfan 'Taitannike': 14 nián qián de quánmín wéiguān." 重返泰坦尼克:14年前的全民围观 [Returning to *Titanic:* The moviegoers return after 14 years]. CITIC Group 中信股份. citic.com.

City of Honolulu. "City to Dedicate Statue and Rename Park to Honor Dr. Sun Yat-Sen." Honolulu Government, Nov. 7, 2007. honolulu.gov.

Claiborne, William. "Columbia Post for Kissinger Opposed." *Washington Post,* May 17, 1977. washingtonpost.com.

Clarke, Donald. "Independence Day 2 Review: A Cynical Love Song to China." *Irish Times,* June 22, 2016. irishtimes.com.

Clinton, Hillary. "America's Pacific Century." *Foreign Policy,* Oct. 11, 2011. foreignpolicy.com.

———. "US Embassy Cables: Hillary Clinton Ponders US Relationship with Its Chinese 'Banker.'" *Guardian,* March 28, 2009. theguardian.com.

CNN. "'Drew Carey' Visits Streets of China." Nov. 10, 1998. cnn.com.

Coates, Ta-Nehisi. "Notes of a Native Tiger Son, Part 2." *Atlantic,* Jan. 20, 2011. theatlantic.com.

Cohen, Jerome A. "(In)Justice with Chinese Characteristics." *Jerry's Blog,* Dec. 31, 2017. jeromecohen.net.

Columbia Law School. "Merit Janow." Accessed April 12, 2021. law.columbia.edu.

Committee on Governmental Affairs, United States Senate. *Investigation of Illegal or Improper Activities in Connection with 1996 Federal Election Campaigns Final Report*. U.S. Government Printing Office, March 10, 1998. congress.gov.

Cook, Barry, and Tony Bancroft. *Mulan*. Disney Animation, 1998. imdb.com.

Coonan, Clifford. "Pirates Edited for China Release." *Variety,* June 11, 2007. variety.com.

Cooper, Helene. "Spielberg Drops Out as Adviser to Beijing Olympics in Dispute over Darfur Conflict." *New York Times,* Feb. 13, 2008. nytimes.com.

Craymer, Lucy. "China's National-Security Law Reaches into Harvard, Princeton Classrooms." *Wall Street Journal,* Aug. 19, 2020. wsj.com.

Crooks, Ed. "China Shakes the World." *Financial Times,* Dec. 17, 2017. ft.com.

Crossley, Gabriel. "ESPN Criticised over China-NBA Coverage for Using 'Nine-Dash Line' Map." Reuters, Oct. 10, 2019. reuters.com.

Crowley, Michael. "The Kissinger Primary." *Politico,* Feb. 4, 2015. politico.com.

Crowley, Monica. "Nixon off the Record." C-SPAN, 1996. c-span.org.

Daccache, Jenny George, and Brandon Valeriano. *Hollywood's Representations of the Sino-Tibetan Conflict.* Palgrave Macmillan, 2012.

Dalai Lama. *My Land and My People.* Warner Books, 2014.

Daley, Patrick R. "Short Form Registration Statement Pursuant to the Foreign Agents Registration Act of 1938, as Amended—Patrick R. Daley." U.S. Department of Justice, Nov. 18, 2013. efile.fara.gov.

Dalian Wanda Group. "Wanda Group Announces Receipt of All Necessary Approvals for AMC Acquisition." Cision PR Newswire, July 25, 2012. prnewswire.com.

D'Arcy, Janice. "Kissinger Still Wears Cloak of Secrecy." *Hartford Courant,* March 29, 2003. courant.com.

Dargis, Manohla. " 'Mulan' Review: A Flower Blooms in Adversity (and Kicks Butt)." *New York Times,* Sept. 3, 2020. nytimes.com.

Davis, Rebecca. "China's Censors Confound Biz." *Variety,* May 14, 2019. variety.com.

———. "Embattled Huayi Brothers Announces Closer Ties to China's Communist Party." *Variety,* July 9, 2019. variety.com.

Deb, Sopan. "Report: N.B.A.'s Academies in China Abused Athletes." *New York Times,* July 30, 2020. nytimes.com.

Deb, Sopan, and Marc Stein. "Daryl Morey Steps Down as G.M. of the Houston Rockets." *New York Times,* Oct. 15, 2020. nytimes.com.

———. "N.B.A. Executive's Hong Kong Tweet Starts Firestorm in China." *New York Times,* Oct. 6, 2019. nytimes.com.

D'Elia, Bill. "Made in China." *Boston Legal,* ABC, Dec. 8, 2008.

Denton, Kirk A. "The Great Wall Review." Ohio State University Modern Chinese Literature and Culture Center, Feb. 23, 2017. u.osu.edu.

Denyer, Simon, and Luna Lin. "China Sends Its Top Actors and Directors Back to Socialism School." *Washington Post,* Dec. 1, 2017. washingtonpost.com.

Diamond, Jeremy. "Donald Trump: China Is 'Raping Our Country.' " CNN Politics, May 2, 2016. cnn.com.

Diamond, Larry, and Orville Schell. *China's Influence and American Interests: Promoting Constructive Vigilance.* Hoover Institution Press, 2019.

Dickie, Mure. "Chinese Film Maker Sees Moral Angle." *Financial Times,* Oct. 20, 2007.

Dinmore, Guy, and Geoff Dyer. "Immelt Hits Out at China and Obama." *Financial Times,* July 1, 2010. ft.com.

Disinformation: A Primer in Russian Active Measures and Influence Campaigns, Panel II, Hearing Before the Senate Select Committee on Intelligence (2017). intelligence.senate.gov.

Dodin, Thierry, and Heinz Rather, eds. *Imagining Tibet*. Simon & Schuster, 1996.

Dolan, Kerry A., Jennifer Wang, and Chase Peterson-Withorn. "Forbes World's Billionaires List: The Richest in 2021." *Forbes*. forbes.com.

Domestic Names Committee. "Principles, Policies, and Procedures." U.S. Board on Geographic Names, Jan. 2021.

Dooley, Ben. "Chinese Firms Cash In On Xinjiang's Growing Police State." *Yahoo News*, June 26, 2018. news.yahoo.com.

Dowd, Maureen. "He's Ba-a-a-ack!" *New York Times*, Dec. 1, 2002. nytimes.com.

———. "2 U.S. Officials Went to Beijing Secretly in July." *New York Times*, Dec. 19, 1989. nytimes.com.

Dreyfuss, Robert. "The New China Lobby." *American Prospect*, Dec. 19, 2001. prospect.org.

Drinkard, Jim. "China's Best Lobbyist: Corporate America amid Stir over Donors, Firms Push to Enter Market." *Akron Beacon Journal*, March 24, 1997. beaconjournal.com.

Duggan, Emily. "UNH Creates an Anti-racism Plan, but Some Students Want More." NHPR, July 1, 2020. nhpr.org.

Eavis, Peter, and Binyamin Appelbaum. "Last Month, Investors Seemed Too Pessimistic. Now, They Seem Prescient." *New York Times*, Jan. 3, 2019. nytimes.com.

Ebert, Roger. "Red Corner Movie Review & Film Summary (1997)." Roger Ebert, Oct. 31, 1997. rogerebert.com.

Economist. "As China's Power Waxes, the West's Study of It Is Waning." Nov. 26, 2020. economist.com.

———. "Cambridge University Press Battles Censorship in China." Aug. 24, 2017. economist.com.

———. "China's Fitful Sleep." July 17, 1997. economist.com.

———. "In Wolves' Clothing." Feb. 14, 2015. economist.com.

Egan, Jack, and Lee Lescaze. "Kissinger, Simon: Visible, Wealthy." *Washington Post*, Feb. 19, 1978. washingtonpost.com.

Eimer, David. "The Chinese Cinema Industry: China's Cultural Revolution." *Independent*, Jan. 6, 2006. independent.co.uk.

Elley, Derek. "Red River Valley." *Variety*, June 30, 1997. variety.com.

Elliott, Justin. "Trump's Patron-in-Chief: Casino Magnate Sheldon Adelson." ProPublica, Oct. 10, 2018. propublica.org.

Embassy of the People's Republic of China. "Vice-Premier Liu Yandong Meets with Mayor of Chicago Rahm Emanuel." States News Service, Nov. 20, 2013. gy.china-embassy.org.

Embassy of the People's Republic of China in the United States of America. "President Hu Jintao Attends the Welcoming Ceremony Hosted by President Bush." April 25, 2006. fmprc.gov.cn.

———. "Vice President Meets Kissinger to Discuss China-U.S. Ties." *Xinhua News,* June 28, 2011. china-embassy.org.

Enav, Peter. "Hollywood Yielding to China's Growing Film Clout." *Morning Call,* April 24, 2013. mcall.com.

Engel, Jeffrey A. *The China Diary of George H. W. Bush: The Making of a Global President.* Princeton University Press, 2011.

ESPN News Services. "China Suspends Work with Rockets over GM Tweet." ESPN, Oct. 6, 2019. espn.com.

———. "Harden Apologizes as Rift Grows: 'We Love China.'" ESPN, Oct. 6, 2019. espn.com.

Evans, Jane DeRose. *The Art of Persuasion: Political Propaganda from Aeneas to Brutus.* University of Michigan Press, 1992.

Faison, Seth. "China to Buy 30 Planes for $1.5 Billion from Airbus Industries." *New York Times,* May 16, 1997. nytimes.com.

Fan, Lingzhi 范凌志, and Luo Xinyi 罗欣怡. "Zhuli 'xiwang yingcai' qingnian xuezhe" 助力"希望英才"青年学者 [Assisting "promising and talented" young scholars]. *Global Times* 环球时报, July 10, 2015. china.huanqiu.com.

Farley, Maggie. "Entertaining China; Hollywood Struggles in an Ambivalent Nation." *Los Angeles Times,* June 13, 1999. latimes.com.

Farley, Robert. "Obama and 'American Exceptionalism.'" FactCheck.org, Feb. 12, 2015. factcheck.org.

Fay, Joe. "Huawei WILL Make a Comeback to US Market, Policy Wonk Predicts." *Register,* June 17, 2014. theregister.com.

Federation of American Scientists. "President Clinton's Comments on Wen Ho Lee Case; Plus Lockhart Comments; Plus More Clinton Comments." Sept. 14, 2000. fas.org.

Feldman, Dan. "Shaquille O'Neal: 'Daryl Morey Was Right.'" *Pro Basketball Talk | NBC Sports* (blog), Oct. 24, 2019. nba.nbcsports.com.

Feng, Emily. "Beijing Vies for Greater Control of Foreign Universities in China." *Financial Times,* Nov. 19, 2017. ft.com.

———. "China Tightens Grip on Foreign University Joint Ventures." *Financial Times,* Aug. 7, 2018. ft.com.

———. "Chinese Universities Are Enshrining Communist Party Control in Their Charters." NPR, Jan. 20, 2020. npr.org.

Fialka, John J. "Mr. Kissinger Has Opinions on China—and Business Ties." *Wall Street Journal,* Sept. 15, 1989.

Fishman, Ted C. *China Inc.: How the Rise of the Next Superpower Challenges America and the World.* Scribner, 2005.

Fitzsimmons, Caitlin. "Inside Story." *Independent,* Dec. 4, 2006. independent.co.uk.

Flannery, William. "Fast-Growing Chinese Region Forms Ties Here." *St. Louis Post-Dispatch.* Jan. 22, 1994.

Flumenbaum, David. "China Bans Democracy, Declares War on Guns N' Roses." *HuffPost,* Feb. 24, 2009. huffpost.com.

Forns, Marta. "Hollywood Films in the Non-Western World." IBEI Working Papers, Feb. 6, 2020. papers.ssrn.com.

Fox News. "Raw Data: George Mitchell Resignation Letter." Dec. 12, 2002. foxnews.com.

———. "Raw Data: Kissinger's Letter to the President." Dec. 14, 2002. foxnews.com.

Frater, Patrick. "Asia Sees Steamy Season." *Variety,* July 9, 2006. variety.com.

———. "China Nixes Hollywood Pix." *Variety,* Dec. 6, 2007. variety.com.

French, Howard W. "Bloomberg's Folly." *Columbia Journalism Review,* May/June 2014. cjr.org.

French, Patrick. *Tibet, Tibet: A Personal History of a Lost Land.* HarperCollins, 2003.

Friedman, Thomas L. "Beyond Stupid." *New York Times,* March 17, 1997. nytimes.com.

Fritz, Ben. *The Big Picture: The Fight for the Future of Movies.* Houghton Mifflin Harcourt, 2018.

Fritz, Sara. "Big Firms Plant Seeds of 'Grass-Roots' China Lobby; Trade: Corporate Giants Tap Suppliers to Create Image of Small-Business Support for Extending Favored-Nation Status." *Los Angeles Times,* May 11, 1997. latimes.com.

Fuchs, Andreas, and Nils-Hendrik Klann. "Paying a Visit: The Dalai Lama Effect on International Trade." *Journal of International Economics* 91, no. 1 (2013).

Fung, Anthony Y. H. *Asian Popular Culture: The Global (Dis)continuity.* Routledge, 2013.

Gargan, Edward A. "Donald Duck Learns Chinese." *New York Times,* Oct. 24, 1986. nytimes.com.

Garnaut, John. "Henry Kissinger Paid $5M to Steer Rio Tinto Through Stern Hu Debacle and Consolidate China Links." *Sydney Morning Herald,* March 27, 2015. smh.com.au.

Garnaut, John, and Sanghee Liu. "Stern Sentenced to 10 Years by Chinese Court." *Age,* March 29, 2010. theage.com.au.

Garnaut, John, and Kristy Needham. "Rio Turns to Kissinger for Help." *Sydney Morning Herald,* March 30, 2010. smh.com.au.

Garza, Paul de la. "Arms Deal Will Test Bush Ties." *Tampa Bay Times,* April 23, 2001. tampabay.com.

Gaylord, Chris. "Hollywood Aims to Please . . . China?" *Christian Science Monitor,* July 27, 2012. csmonitor.com.

Gelb, Leslie H. "Kissinger Means Business." *New York Times,* April 20, 1986. nytimes.com.

Gelder, Lawrence. "Peaceful Man with a Flair for Violence." *New York Times,* Oct. 5, 1996. nytimes.com.

Gellman, Barton. "U.S. and China Nearly Came to Blows in '96." *Washington Post,* June 21, 1998. washingtonpost.com.

The Gentry and People. *Death Blow to Corrupt Doctrines: A Plain Statement of Facts.* American Presbyterian Mission Press, 1870.

Geopolitical Monitor. "A Brief History of China's United Front." Geopolitical Monitor, March 22, 2019. geopoliticalmonitor.com.

Georgetown Voice Editorial Board. "Forget It, Georgetown, It's China." *Georgetown Voice,* April 3, 2008. georgetownvoice.com.

Gerth, Jeff. "Democrat Fund-Raiser Said to Detail China Tie." *New York Times,* May 15, 1998. nytimes.com.

Glanz, James. "Fallout in Arms Research: A Special Report; Amid Race Profiling Claims, Asian Americans Avoid Labs." *New York Times,* July 16, 2000. nytimes.com.

Glaser, James M., and Diana Chigas. "Decision to Close the Confucius Institute at Tufts University." Office of the Provost and Senior Vice President, March 17, 2021. "https://provost.tufts.edu/blog/news/2021/03/17/decision-to-close-the-confucius-institute-at-tufts-university/" \t "_blank" provost.tufts.edu.

Global Dream Forum. "Global Dream Forum NYC 2019 Agenda." Global Dream Forum. dreamforum.global.

Globe and Mail. "Bulletins: Bush Joining Barrick." May 4, 1995. theglobeandmail .com.

Goldberg, Emma. "Hong Kong Protests Spread to U.S. Colleges, and a Rift Grows." *New York Times,* Oct. 26, 2019. nytimes.com.

Goldman, Ari L. "Buddhism and Manhattan: An Unlikely Joining Together." *New York Times,* Oct. 11, 1991. nytimes.com.

Gonzalez, Oscar. "Blizzard, Hearthstone, and the Hong Kong Protests: What You Need to Know." CNET, Nov. 5, 2019. cnet.com.

Greene, Naomi. *From Fu Manchu to Kung Fu Panda: Images of China in American Film.* University of Hawai'i Press, 2014.

Grindr. "What's Up with Grindr?" *Grindr* (blog), Tumblr, May 2017. Accessed June 16, 2021. grindr.tumblr.com.

Groot, Gerry. *Managing Transitions: The Chinese Communist Party, United Front Work, Corporatism, and Hegemony.* Routledge, 2004.

Grunbaum, Rami. "Starbucks CEO Schultz Sees China Market Surpassing U.S." *Seattle Times,* Oct. 19, 2016. seattletimes.com.

Guardian. "China Sinks Dead Man's Chest." July 10, 2006. theguardian.com.

Guarino, Mark. "Where Is Apple Headed After Steve Jobs? Apple CEO Offers His Vision." *Christian Science Monitor,* Oct. 18, 2011. csmonitor.com.

Guerrasio, Jason. "How 'Avatar' Paved the Way for the Huge Box Office Success of 'Avengers: Endgame' in China." *Insider,* May 7, 2019. businessinsider.com.

Guthmann, Edward. "Gere's 'Corner' on Saving Tibet." *SFGATE,* Oct. 26, 1997. sfgate.com.

Haas, Benjamin. "Whiff of Discontent as China Bans Imports of Soft European Cheese." *Guardian,* Sept. 10, 2017. theguardian.com.

Haithman, Diane. "Why China Tunes Out American TV." *Los Angeles Business Journal,* Nov. 24, 2017. labusinessjournal.com.

Halberstam, David. "The New Establishment: The Decline and Fall of the Eastern Empire." *Vanity Fair,* April 4, 2011. vanityfair.com.

Hamilton, Lee H. "Text—H.R. 2333, 103rd Congress (1993–1994): Foreign Relations Authorization Act, Fiscal Years 1994 and 1995." U.S. Congress, 1994. congress.gov.

Hancock, Jay. "Clinton Advisers Trade on Contacts." *Baltimore Sun,* June 25, 2001. baltimoresun.com.

Hangover Wiki. "Leslie Chow." thehangover.fandom.

Harrison, Olivia. "All the Breathtaking Locations Featured in Disney's New Live-Action Mulan." *Refinery29,* Sept. 4, 2020. refinery29.com.

Hayes, Chris. "Trump Mocks Senator Feinstein Following Reports an Alleged Chinese Spy Worked for Her." *USA Today,* Aug. 4, 2018. usatoday.com.

Heintz, Rich. "Jobs and the Resurgent Economy / Outsourcing CEOs." *SFGATE,* Feb. 17, 2004. sfgate.com.

Helfand, Duke. "Mayor in East Asia; Getting the 'Grade A Treatment'—and 30 Minutes with Kissinger." *Los Angeles Times,* Oct. 11, 2006. latimes.com.

Higgins, Bill. "Hollywood Elite Says Hello, Dalai." *Los Angeles Times,* Aug. 5, 1996. latimes.com.

Hilsenrath, Jon, and Bob Davis. "How the China Shock, Deep and Swift, Spurred the Rise of Trump." *Wall Street Journal,* Aug. 11, 2016. wsj.com.

Hilzenrath, David S. "From Public Life to Private Business Former Pentagon Chief Cohen's Firm Serves Defense Contractors." *Washington Post,* May 28, 2006. washingtonpost.com.

Hipes, Patrick. "Black List 2015 Scripts Announced with 'Bubbles' King of the Jungle—Full List." *Deadline,* Dec. 14, 2015. deadline.com.

Hoad, Phil. "Looper Bridges the Cinematic Gap Between China and the US." *Guardian,* Aug. 28, 2012. theguardian.com.

Hodge, Nathan. "Recap: Xi's Visit to the U.S." *Wall Street Journal,* Feb. 14, 2012. wsj.com.

Hofstra Law. "Julian Ku—Maurice A. Deane School of Law." law.hofstra.edu.

Holmes, Stanley. "Boeing's Campaign to Protect a Market—Corporations Lobby to Save China Trade." *Seattle Times,* May 27, 1996. archive.seattletimes.com.

———. "How Boeing Woos Beijing." *Seattle Times,* May 26, 1996. seattletimes.com.

Horne, Alistair. *Kissinger: 1973, the Crucial Year.* Simon & Schuster, 2009.

Horwitz, Josh. "Chinese Students in the US Are Using 'Inclusion' and 'Diversity' to Oppose a Dalai Lama Graduation Speech." *Quartz,* Feb. 15, 2017. qz.com.

Howe, Russell Warren, and Sarah Hays Trott. *The Power Peddlers: How Lobbyists Mold America's Foreign Policy.* Doubleday, 1977.

Huawei. "Brookings Institution Releases Report Ranking Global Cities on Public Safety Innovation at Huawei Asia Pacific Innovation Day 2017." Huawei News, Nov. 9, 2017. huawei.com.

Iannucci, Armando. " 'Veep' Camp David (TV Episode 2016)." imdb.com.

ICEO. "Mogen datong zai Zhongguo he Jixinge xiansheng you she me guanxi" 摩根大通在中国和基辛格先生有什么关系 [What is the relationship between JPMorgan Chase and Mr. Kissinger in China?]. ICEO 中国企业家网, Dec. 22, 2003. iceo.com.cn.

Ignatius, Adi. "Bush's Brother, Other Americans Are Talking Business with China." *Wall Street Journal,* Sept. 18, 1989. wsj.com.

Immelt, Jeff. *Hot Seat: What I Learned Leading a Great American Company.* Simon & Schuster, 2021.

Ingram, David. "Chinese Censorship or 'Work Elsewhere': Inside Shutterstock's Free-Speech Rebellion." NBC News, Feb. 27, 2020. nbcnews.com.

Isaacs, Harold R. *Scratches on Our Minds: American Images of China and India.* John Day, 1958.

Isaacson, Walter. "Booknotes, Kissinger: A Biography." C-SPAN, Sept. 27, 1992. cspan.org.

———. *Kissinger: A Biography.* Simon & Schuster, 2005.

Isikoff, Michael. "Chinese Hacked Obama, McCain Campaigns, Took Internal Documents, Officials Say." NBC News, June 7, 2013. nbcnews.com.

ITN. "Drew Carey Films Episode of His Comedy Show in China." ITN, Nov. 3, 1998.

Jacobs, Julia. "CBS Censors a 'Good Fight' Segment. Its Topic Was Chinese Censorship." *New York Times,* May 7, 2019. nytimes.com.

James, Olivia. "Rename Chinaman Lake." change.org.

Jason, Gary James. "Film and Propaganda: The Lessons of the Nazi Film Industry." Philosophy Papers, 2013. philpapers.org.

Jiang, Steven. "'Batman' Star Bale Punched, Stopped from Visiting Blind Chinese Activist." CNN, Dec. 15, 2011. cnn.com.

Jing Daily. "Can Hollywood-China Co-productions Bridge the Audience Gap?" Aug. 28, 2012. jingdaily.com.

Johnny Chung: Foreign Connections, Foreign Contributions, Hearing Before the House Committee on Government Reform, 106th Cong. (1999). commdocs .house.gov.

Johnson, Ian. "Jesus vs. Mao?" *ChinaFile,* Sept. 4, 2012. chinafile.com.

Johnson, Tim. *Tragedy in Crimson: How the Dalai Lama Conquered the World but Lost the Battle with China.* Nation Books, 2011.

Johnston, David. "Democratic Fund-Raiser Tells of Dealings with Chinese Donors." *New York Times,* May 12, 1999. nytimes.com.

Jones, Terril Yue, and Denny Thomas. "China's Wanda to Buy U.S. Cinema Chain AMC for $2.6 Billion." Reuters, May 20, 2012. reuters.com.

Joske, Alex. "The Party Speaks for You: Foreign Interference and the Chinese Communist Party's United Front System." Australian Strategic Policy Institute, June 2020. aspi.org.au.

Kahn, Joseph. "China Cancels 'Da Vinci' Movie." *New York Times,* June 10, 2006. nytimes.com.

———. "Warnings by Powell to Taiwan Provoke a Diplomatic Dispute." *New York Times,* Oct. 28, 2004. nytimes.com.

Kaiser, Robert G. *So Damn Much Money: The Triumph of Lobbying and the Corrosion of American Government.* Vintage Books, 2010.

Kamen, Al. "Here's Why the Chinese Government Hated Gary Locke." *Washington Post,* Feb. 26, 2014. washingtonpost.com.

Kantrowitz, Alex, and John Paczkowski. "Apple Told Some Apple TV+ Show Developers Not to Anger China." *BuzzFeed News,* Oct. 11, 2019. buzzfeednews.com.

Kao, Ernest. "China Censors Cut 40 Minutes off Science Fiction Epic Cloud Atlas." *South China Morning Post,* Jan. 23, 2013. scmp.com.

Kaplan, Ilana. "Philip Glass' 80th Birthday at Tibet House Benefit Concert Was a Message to the American People." *Billboard,* March 17, 2017. billboard.com.

Kapos, Shia. "Mayor Richard Daley Says Chicago's Making a Big Push into China." *Crain's Chicago Business,* March 10, 2011. chicagobusiness.com.

Karni, Annie. "Trump Rants Behind Closed Doors with CEOs." *Politico,* Aug. 8, 2018. politico.com.

Karolides, Nicholas J. *Literature Suppressed on Political Grounds.* Facts on File, 2011.

Kay, Jennifer. "Christopher Wong Won, a Founding Member of 2 Live Crew, Dies at 53." *Washington Post,* July 15, 2017. washingtonpost.com.

Keenan, Joe. "Roz's Turn—Frasier Transcripts Season 4 Episode 17." Frasier Archives. kacl780.net.

Kelley, Robin D. G., and Betsy Esch. "Black Like Mao: Red China and Black Revolution." Columbia University, 1999.

Kelly, Kate. "After Capitol Riots, Billionaire's 'Scholars' Confront Their Benefactor." *New York Times,* Feb. 18, 2021. nytimes.com.

Kelly, Laura. "Pompeo Says Trump Looking at Whether to Restrict Chinese Students from the US." *Hill,* Aug. 21, 2020. thehill.com.

Kelly, Michael. "On the White House Subway." *Washington Post,* Aug. 22, 1997. washingtonpost.com.

Kerr, Blake. *Eye of the Lammergeier.* IMDb, 2016. imdb.com.

Khatchatourian, Maane. "'Star Wars' China Poster Sparks Controversy After Shrinking John Boyega's Character." *Variety,* Dec. 4, 2015. variety.com.

Kim, Andrew Chongseh. "Prosecuting 'Chinese Spies': An Empirical Analysis of the Economic Espionage Act." *Cardozo Law Review,* May 2017. cardozolawreview.com.

Kim, JuYeon. "Sam's Club Stabbing Suspect Thought Family Was 'Chinese Infecting People with Coronavirus.'" KTSM, April 7, 2020. ktsm.com.

Kissinger, Henry A. "Eulogy for John Whitehead." *Henry A. Kissinger* (blog), Feb. 17, 2015. henryakissinger.com.

———. "Europe Returns to Center Stage as the Fulcrum for World Tension." *Los Angeles Times,* Oct. 8, 1989.

———. "Kissinger at China Ventures—Image 2," May 3, 1989.

———. *On China.* Penguin, 2011.

———. "Speech at the Graduate University of Chinese Academy of Sciences in Beijing." April 3, 2007.

———. "Turmoil on Top: A World of Changing Leaders, Struggling Governments, and Strange Bedfellows: China: Push for Reform, Not Rupture." *Los Angeles Times,* July 30, 1989. latimes.com.

———. *White House Years.* Simon & Schuster, 1979.

Klein, Christopher. "10 Things You May Not Know About Dwight D. Eisenhower." History, Aug. 22, 2018. history.com.

Knight, Kyle, and Kanae Doi. "Global Call to Reform Japan's Law on Transgender People." Human Rights Watch, June 14, 2019. hrw.org.

Knowlton, Brian. "Bush Warns Taiwan to Keep Status Quo: China Welcomes U.S. Stance." *New York Times,* Dec. 10, 2003. nytimes.com.

Kong, Deborah. "Minority Groups Work to Change Names." *Arizona Daily Sun,* Oct. 7, 2001. azdailysun.com.

Kong tian lie. "空天猎 (AKA Sky Hunter)." Oct. 27, 2020. web.archive.org.

Kovaleski, Serge F. "Gingrich Backs Ties with Taiwan." *Washington Post,* July 10, 1995. washingtonpost.com.

Kranish, Michael. "Bloomberg's Business in China Has Grown. That Could Create Unprecedented Entanglements if He Is Elected President." *Washington Post,* Jan. 1, 2020. washingtonpost.com.

Kranz, Michal. "The Director of the FBI Says the Whole of Chinese Society Is a Threat to the US—and That Americans Must Step Up to Defend Themselves." *Insider,* Feb. 13, 2018. businessinsider.com.

Kristof, Nicholas D., and Sheryl WuDunn. *China Wakes: The Struggle for the Soul of a Rising Power.* Times Books, 1994.

Kuhn, Anthony. "Chinese Blockbuster 'Wolf Warrior II' Mixes Jingoism with Hollywood Heroism." NPR, Aug. 10, 2017. npr.org.

Kwok, Tony. "'Real Game-changers' Needed for the Govt to Curb Violence." *China Daily,* Jan. 2, 2021. chinadaily.com.

Kyodo. "Senior Chinese Official May Visit Japan Next Month." *Japan Times,* Aug. 26, 2014. japantimes.co.jp.

Lampton, David M. *Same Bed, Different Dreams: Managing U.S.-China Relations, 1989–2000.* University of California Press, 2001.

Landler, Mark. "Obama's Journey to Tougher Tack on a Rising China." *New York Times,* Sept. 20, 2012. nytimes.com.

Lanfranco, Edward. "Analysis: American Dynastic Diplomacy." *Space War,* Nov. 15, 2005. spacewar.com.

Lang, Brent. "Hollywood's Global Expansion: New Markets, More Diversity, Bigger Profits." Reuters, July 28, 2011.

Langfitt, Frank. "How China's Censors Influence Hollywood." NPR, May 18, 2015. npr.org.

Larkin, Ian, et al. "Association Between Academic Medical Center Pharmaceutical Detailing Policies and Physician Prescribing." *JAMA,* May 2, 2017.

Lashinsky, Adam, and Brian O'Keefe. "How the NBA Kept the Bubble from Bursting." *Fortune,* Oct. 15, 2020. fortune.com.

The Last Ship Transcripts, Forever Dreaming. "03x01—the Scott Effect." June 13, 2016. transcripts.foreverdreaming.org.

LaVito, Angelica. "Starbucks Is Opening a Store in China Every 15 Hours." Yahoo Finance, Dec. 5, 2017. finance.yahoo.com.

Law & Order Wiki. "Tortured." lawandorder.fandom.com.

Lawrence, Susan V., and Murray Hiebert. "The Bush Family in China." *Far Eastern Economic Review,* Oct. 12, 2000.

Lawson, Richard. "China Censors 'Men in Black 3' for Referring to Chinese Censorship." *Atlantic,* May 31, 2012. theatlantic.com.

Leary, Alex, William Mauldin, and Kate O'Keeffe. "Sheldon Adelson Warned Trump About Impact of U.S.-China Trade War." *Wall Street Journal,* Sept. 22, 2019. wsj.com.

Lee, Edmund. "How Mega-mergers Are Changing the Way You Watch Your Favorite Shows and Movies." *New York Times,* July 27, 2018. nytimes.com.

Lehman, David. *Great American Prose Poems: From Poe to the Present.* Scribner, 2008.

Levine, Alexandra S. "'Deeply Alarmed': China Now Ahead of U.S. on Privacy Law." *Politico,* July 8, 2021. "https://www.politico.com/newsletters/politico-china-watcher/2021/07/08/deeply-alarmed-china-now-ahead-of-us-on-privacy-law-493497" \t "_blank" politico.com.

Ley, Tom. "The NBA Is Happy to Play China's Game." *Deadspin,* Oct. 7, 2019. deadspin.com.

Li, Hongshan, and Zhaohui Hong, eds. *Image, Perception, and the Making of U.S.-China Relations.* University Press of America, 1998.

Li, Jane. "A Top Chinese University Stripped 'Freedom of Thought' from Its Charter." *Quartz,* Dec. 17, 2019. qz.com.

Li, Jing. *China's America: The Chinese View the United States, 1900–2000.* State University of New York Press, 2012.

Li, Ruohan. "Trump to Get 'State Visit–Plus' Experience in China." *Global Times,* Nov. 6, 2017. globaltimes.cn.

Li, Shijia, and Fuhui Hwang. "Xinhua Interviews Clinton Security Advisor Sandy Berger on Promoting US-China Ties." Beijing Xinhua Domestic Service, n.d.

Li, Xiang. "Tencent, NBA Extend Partnership for Another Five Years in $1.5 Billion Deal." CGTN, July 29, 2019. news.cgtn.com.

Liao Qi 廖奇. "Lao Bushi fang Hua zhong mi 30 nian qian zuji tan Beijing bian-hua tai da" 老布什访华重觅30年前足迹 叹北京变化太大 [Retracing his footsteps from 30 years ago, Bush Sr. laments that Beijing has changed too much]. *Beijing Star Daily* 北京娱乐信报, Sohu 搜狐, Nov. 15, 2005. news.sohu.com.

Lim, Louisa, and Julia Bergin. "Inside China's Audacious Global Propaganda Campaign." *Guardian,* Dec. 7, 2018. theguardian.com.

Lin, Yuhan. "Is China Really Ready for Black Stories?" *Sixth Tone,* March 29, 2021. sixthtone.com.

Link, Perry. "China: The Anaconda in the Chandelier." *ChinaFile*, April 11, 2002. chinafile.com.

Lippman, Thomas W. "Bush Makes Clinton's China Policy an Issue." *Washington Post*, Aug. 20, 1999. washingtonpost.com.

Liptak, Kevin. "Trump Says Americans Will Have to Learn Chinese if Biden Wins but Offers Little Condemnation of Beijing." CNN, Aug. 11, 2020. cnn.com.

Little, Becky. "How the 1982 Murder of Vincent Chin Ignited a Push for Asian American Rights." History, May 5, 2020. history.com.

Liu, Da-Nien. "The Trading Relationship Between Taiwan and the United States: Current Trends and the Outlook for the Future." Brookings, Nov. 30, 2016. brookings.edu.

Liu, Eric. *A Chinaman's Chance: One Family's Journey and the Chinese American Dream*. PublicAffairs, 2016.

Liu, Hongchao, and Cai Guangrong. "Waiguo yao ren mingren kan Zhongguo" 外国要人名人看中国 [How foreign dignitaries and celebrities see China]. Chinese Communist Party Central Party School Press 中共中央党校出版社, 1993.

Liu, Jifeng 刘戟锋, Lu Xiao 卢潇, and Liu Yangyue 刘杨钺. "Zhànlüè xinli zhan de jishu zhicheng" 战略心理战的技术支撑 [Technical support for strategic psychological warfare]. *Guofang* 国防, no. 2 (2017).

Livingston, William. *The Independent Reflector; or, Weekly Essays on Sundry Important Subjects, More Particularly Adapted to the Province of New York*. Vol. 52. Harvard University Press, 1963.

Lo, Hoi Ying. "Chinese Disney Fans Decry Black 'Little Mermaid' Casting." *Sixth Tone*, July 4, 2019. sixthtone.com.

Long, Jeff. "Searching for Superman." Rock and Ice, 2016. rockandice.com.

Long, William. "Shanxi Hanbin yi nanzi feifa jinxing guoji lianwang bei cha-chu" 陕西汉滨一男子非法进行国际联网被查处 [Man from Hanbin in Shanxi province punished for illegal internet usage]. *China Digital Times* 中国数字时代, May 19, 2020. chinadigitaltimes.net.

Lopez, Donald S., Jr. *Prisoners of Shangri-La: Tibetan Buddhism and the West*. University of Chicago Press, 2018.

Lorenz, Andreas. "Courting Beijing's Wrath: Dalai Lama Visit Jeopardizes German Business Interests." *Spiegel International*, Sept. 17, 2007. spiegel.de.

Lorge, Peter. *Debating War in Chinese History*. Brill, 2013.

Loria, Daniel. "Global Box Office Down 72%, Digital Leads Home Entertainment in 2020." Box Office Pro, March 26, 2021. boxofficepro.com.

Louison, Cole. "Richard Gere: The Lost Transcript." *GQ*, April 11, 2007. gq.com.

Lovell, Julia. *Maoism: A Global History*. Knopf, 2019.

Lynas, Mark. "How Do I Know China Wrecked the Copenhagen Deal? I Was in the Room." *Guardian*, Dec. 22, 2009. theguardian.com.

Ma, Wayne. "Marriott Employee Roy Jones Hit 'Like.' Then China Got Mad." *Wall Street Journal*, March 3, 2018. wsj.com.

———. "Marriott Makes China Mad with Geopolitical Faux Pas." *Wall Street Journal,* Jan. 12, 2018. wsj.com.

MacLeod, Calum, and David Sanderson. "A New A List Star Rises in the East." *Times* (London), Aug. 22, 2015.

MacMullan, Jackie. "76ers' Morey Thought Tweet Might End His Career." ESPN, Dec. 23, 2020. "https://www.espn.com/nba/story/_/id/30587457/philadelphia-76ers-daryl-morey-was-worried-hong-kong-tweet-end-nba-career" \t "_blank" espn.com.

Magnier, Mark. "Fearing a New 'Red Scare,' Activists Fight Targeting of Chinese-Americans." *South China Morning Post,* Aug. 27, 2019. scmp.com.

———. "US Moves In On Top Universities over Fear of Chinese Funding, IP Leaks." *South China Morning Post,* Feb. 19, 2020. scmp.com.

Mahnken, Thomas G., Ross Babbage, and Toshi Yoshihara. "Countering Comprehensive Coercion." Center for Strategic and Budgetary Assistance, 2018. csbaonline.org.

Makinen, Julie. "Episode of NBC's 'The Blacklist' Pulled from Chinese Websites." *Los Angeles Times,* April 23, 2014. latimes.com.

Manevich, Dorothy. "Americans More Negative Toward China over Past Decade." Pew Research Center (blog), Feb. 10, 2017. pewresearch.org.

Mann, James. *About Face: A History of America's Curious Relationship with China from Nixon to Clinton.* Alfred A. Knopf, 1999.

———. "Between China and the US." *Washington Post,* Jan. 10, 1999. washingtonpost.com.

———. "China's Feelings of Betrayal on Taiwan Fed Anger at U.S." *Los Angeles Times,* Sept. 9, 1996. latimes.com.

Mann, Michael. *Blackhat.* Universal Studios, 2015.

Mao Zedong. "Farewell, Leighton Stuart!" In *Selected Works of Mao Tse-tung,* Aug. 18, 1949. marxists.org.

———. "A New Storm Against Imperialism." *Peking Review,* April 19, 1968. marxists.org.

———. *Zhongguo shehui ge jiejie de fenxi* 中国社会各阶级的分析 [Analysis of the classes in Chinese society]. Character Reform Press, 1977. catalogue.nla.gov.

Marcus, Ruth. "Dole Registers as Taiwan Foreign Agent." *Washington Post,* Jan. 13, 1998. washingtonpost.com.

Marriott International Newscenter (U.S.). "Statement from Arne Sorenson, President and CEO, Marriott International, Inc.," Jan. 11, 2018. news.marriott.com.

Marsh, Jenni. "Westerners Are Increasingly Scared of Traveling to China as Threat of Detention Rises." CNN, March 9, 2021. cnn.com.

Martin, Douglas. "Helmut Sonnenfeldt, Expert on Soviet and European Affairs, Is Dead at 86." *New York Times,* Nov. 22, 2012. nytimes.com.

Marxists.org. "U.S. Neo-revisionism as the American Expression of the International Opportunist Trend of Chinese Revisionism." marxists.org.

Masters, Kim. "Why Did Eisner Hire Ovitz?" *Slate,* Aug. 16, 2004. slate.com.

Mathews, Jay. "Economic Invasion by Japan Revives Worry About Racism." *Washington Post,* May 14, 1982. washingtonpost.com.

Mathison, Melissa, and Martin Scorsese. "Kundun." Box Office Mojo, 1997. boxofficemojo.com.

———. "Kundun." British Film Institute, 1997. bfi.org.

Mattis, Peter. "China's 'Three Warfares' in Perspective." *War on the Rocks,* Jan. 30, 2018. warontherocks.com.

Mattis, Peter, and Matthew Brazil. *Chinese Communist Espionage.* Naval Institute Press, 2019.

McDonald, Joe. "China Rebukes Zara, Delta for Calling Taiwan 'Country.'" AP News, Jan. 12, 2018. apnews.com.

McDonald, Mark. "Kissinger Assails 'Deplorable' Comments on China by Both U.S. Candidates." *IHT Rendezvous* (blog), Oct. 4, 2012. rendezvous.blogs .nytimes.com.

McGovern, Joe. "'The Great Wall' Director Addresses Matt Damon Whitewashing Controversy." *Entertainment Weekly,* Aug. 4, 2016. ew.com.

McGreal, Chris. "Sheldon Adelson: The Casino Mogul Driving Trump's Middle East Policy." *Guardian,* June 8, 2018. theguardian.com.

McGregor, Richard. "China's Film Ban Is No Barrier for the Fan." *Financial Times,* Feb. 3, 2006. ft.com.

McGuire, Kristian. "Tsai Ing-Wen's U.S. Transit Stops in Historical Context." *Diplomat,* July 5, 2016. thediplomat.com.

McLeod, Melvin. "Richard Gere: My Journey as a Buddhist." *Lion's Roar,* June 9, 2016. liansroar.com.

McNary, Dave. "China to Miss Out on 'Dark Knight.'" *Variety,* Dec. 23, 2008. variety.com.

Mcneill, Sophie. "They Don't Understand the Fear We Have." Human Rights Watch, June 30, 2021. hrw.org.

Mellor, William, and Alan Patterson. "China's Chip and Connections." Mellor Media, Aug. 1, 2004. mellormedia.com.

Miller, Alan C., and Judy Pasternak. "Problems with a Globe-Trotting Father." *Los Angeles Times,* May 7, 2000. latimes.com.

Miller, James Andrew. *Powerhouse: The Untold Story of Hollywood's Creative Artists Agency.* Custom House, 2017.

Millward, James A. "Open Letter to US (and Other) Universities in Light of Zoom's Revelations About Collaborating with the Chinese Communist Party." Medium, June 16, 2020. jimmillward.medium.com.

Ministry of Foreign Affairs. "Zhonghua renmin gongheguo waijiaobu zhuyao zhizhe fuwu Zhongguo zhengfu wang" 中华人民共和国外交部主要职责_服务_中国政府网 [Main responsibilities of the Ministry of Foreign Affairs of the People's Republic of China]. Ministry of Foreign Affairs 中华人民共和国外交部, Feb. 22, 2014. gov.cn.

Mirsky, Jonathan. "Tibet: The CIA's Cancelled War." *New York Review of Books,* April 9, 2013. nybooks.com.

Mirsky, Jonathan, and John K. Fairbank. "Mao and Snow." *New York Review of Books,* April 27, 1989. nybooks.

Mishra, Pankaj. "Holy Man." *New Yorker,* March 31, 2008. newyorker.com.

Mitchell, Michael, Michael Leachman, and Matt Saenz. "State Higher Education Funding Cuts Have Pushed Costs to Students, Worsened Inequality." Center on Budget and Policy Priorities, Oct. 24, 2019. cbpp.org.

Mitchell, Tom, and Demetri Sevastopulo. "US Considered Ban on Student Visas for Chinese Nationals." *Financial Times,* Oct. 2, 2018. ft.com.

Mozilla. "Should You Trust Your Dating App or Sex Toy?" Mozilla Foundation, Feb. 9, 2021. foundation.mozilla.org.

Mozur, Paul. "Zoom Blocks Activist in U.S. After China Objects to Tiananmen Vigil." *New York Times,* June 11, 2020. nytimes.com.

Mr. Robot Wiki. "Whiterose." mrrobot.fandom.com.

Mufson, Steven, and Robert G. Kaiser. "U.S. Insurers Lavishly Court China's Market." *Washington Post,* Nov. 25, 1999.

Mullins, Kyle. "Dartmouth Encourages Faculty to Safeguard Students as Chinese Law Targets Free Speech Globally." *The Dartmouth,* Sept. 24, 2020. Thedartmouth.com.

Nathan, Andrew J. "What China Wants." *Foreign Affairs,* June 21, 2011. foreignaffairs.com.

National Security Agency. "Memorandum for Henry A. Kissinger." NSA Archive, 1973. nsaarchive.gwu.edu.

Nation's Restaurant News. "China's Size, Economic Boom Lure U.S. Chains Despite Uncertainties." Feb. 13, 1995.

NBC News. "Daley Rides the Rails in China." March 24, 2011. nbcchicago.com.

Newby, Richard. "How Iron Man's Chief Villain Could Return." *Hollywood Reporter,* May 18, 2019. hollywoodreporter.com.

Newsweek. "Another Queasy Experience." Sept. 24, 1995. newsweek.com.

Newswire. "China Approves 'The Da Vinci Code.'" Universal Pictures, April 5, 2006. upi.com.

———. "Hollywood's 'Babel' Too Steamy for China's Censors." *Metro,* March 27, 2007. metro.co.uk.

New York Times. "China Asks for Prayers." April 18, 1913. nytimes.com.

———. "Document: What Chinese Officials Told Children Whose Families Were Put in Camps." Nov. 16, 2019. nytimes.com.

———. "Du Bois, 91, Lauds China." March 5, 1959. nytimes.com.

———. "Excerpts from Trump's Interview with the Times." Dec. 29, 2017. nytimes.com.

———. "Kissinger Bests His Chief in Poll." Dec. 30, 1973. nytimes.com.

———. "The White House Turnstile." Aug. 22, 1997. nytimes.com.

Ng, Teddy. "Xi Jinping Mourns 'China's Great Friend' Sihanouk." *South China Morning Post,* Oct. 16, 2012. scmp.com.

Nguyen, Kevin. "With 'The Great Wall,' Hollywood Has Made Whitewashing China's Problem." *GQ,* Feb. 16, 2017. gq.com.

Nicas, Jack, Raymond Zhong, and Daisuke Wakabayashi. "Censorship, Surveillance and Profits: A Hard Bargain for Apple in China." *New York Times,* May 17, 2021, sec. Technology. nytimes.com.

Nicholas, Peter, and Erica Orden. "Movie Mogul's Starring Role in Raising Funds for Obama." *Wall Street Journal,* Sept. 30, 2012. wsj.com.

Nicolaou, Anna. "Bloomberg Profits from Conference Business in China." *Financial Times,* Jan. 4, 2020. ft.com.

Nigro, Nicholas. *The Spirituality of Richard Gere.* Backbeat, 2014.

Nikel, David. "Norway Lets Tom Cruise Bypass Coronavirus Quarantine to Film 'Mission: Impossible 7.'" *Forbes,* July 25, 2020. forbes.com.

Nikicaro. "Day 5—China Scout." @nikicaro Instagram post, Sept. 28, 2017. instagram.com.

Nixey, Catherine. "Hollywood's Star Rises in the East—China's Booming Movie Business Is Good News for Wayne Wang, Says Catherine Nixey." *Times* (London), Nov. 3, 2011.

Nixon, Richard. "Asia After Viet Nam." *Foreign Affairs,* Oct. 1967. foreignaffairs .com.

Nossiter, Bernard D. "Kissinger the Alchemist." *Washington Post,* May 27, 1979. washingtonpost.com.

Nussbaum, Emily. "CBS Censors 'The Good Fight' for a Musical Short About China." *New Yorker,* May 7, 2019. newyorker.com.

O'Brien, Luke. "The Mayor vs. the Mogul." *Politico,* June 19, 2015. politico.com.

Ochab, Ewelina U. "'Let China Sleep, for When She Wakes, She Will Shake the World.'" *Forbes,* Jan. 13, 2021. forbes.com.

Office of the Attorney General. "Report of the Attorney General to the Congress of the United States on the Administration of the Foreign Agents Registration Act of 1938, as Amended, for the Six Months Ending December 31, 2013." U.S. Department of Justice, Sept. 18, 2014. justice.gov.

Office of the Historian. "Chinese Immigration and the Chinese Exclusion Acts." U.S. Department of State. history.state.gov.

O'Neill, Mark. "Bush to Visit Before Clinton." *South China Morning Post,* June 1, 1998. scmp.com.

Ong, Thuy. "Quentin Tarantino 'OK' with Chinese Fans Watching Illegal Versions of His Films." ABC News, Jan. 14, 2016. abc.net.au.

Oppenheim, Carol, and Chicago Tribune. "Dalai Lama Making First Visit to U.S." *Washington Post,* Sept. 1, 1979. washingtonpost.com.

Orenstein, Charles, Mike Tigas, and Ryann Grochowski Jones. "Now There's Proof: Docs Who Get Company Cash Tend to Prescribe More Brand-Name Meds." ProPublica, March 17, 2016. propublica.org.

Osnos, Evan. "The Future of America's Contest with China." *New Yorker,* Jan. 6, 2020. newyorker.com.

———. "The Two Lives of Qian Xuesen." *New Yorker,* Nov. 3, 2009. newyorker .com.

Our Foreign Staff. "Mercedes Apologises to China After Quoting Dalai Lama." *Telegraph,* Feb. 7, 2018. telegraph.co.uk.

Overell, Stephen. "Masters of the Great Game Turn to Business." *Financial Times,* March 23, 2000. library.yale.edu.

Paine, Thomas. *The Theological Works.* J. P. Mendum, 1859.

Palmeri, Christopher. "Disney's Iger Staying Silent on Hong Kong Protests After NBA's China Row." Bloomberg, Oct. 23, 2019. bloomberg.com.

Pandey, Erica. "Trump: 'Xi and I Will Always Be Friends' Despite Trade Issues." *Axios,* April 8, 2018. axios.com.

Pantsov, Alexander V. *Mao: The Real Story.* Simon & Schuster, 2013.

Pape, Stefan. "Kunjue Li Interview on Steven Soderbergh's The Laundromat." The HotCorn, Oct. 18, 2019. hotcorn.com.

Pareles, Jon. "Rapper Conquered Music World in '80s with Beastie Boys." *New York Times,* May 5, 2012. nytimes.com.

Paul, Franklin. "Hollywood Zooms In On China." CNN, May 22, 2000. money .cnn.com.

Paulson, Hank. *Dealing with China.* Headline, 2015.

PBS. "Interviews—Martin Scorsese, Dreams of Tibet." *Frontline,* Oct. 28, 1997. pbs.org.

Peers, Martin. "Mouse in a Pout." *Variety,* Jan. 6, 1999. variety.com.

PEN America. "Darkened Screen: Constraints on Foreign Journalists in China." PEN America, Sept. 22, 2016. pen.org.

People's Daily. "Bu wang chuxin yi zheng rong suiyue: Xin Jinping de hongse zuji" 不忘初心忆峥嵘岁月：习近平的红色足迹 [Do not forget the original aspirations of those memorable years: The red footsteps of Xi Jinping]. June 12, 2019.

People Staff. "Eight Days in Japan Earn Ron and Nancy $2 Million—Now That's Reaganomics." *People,* Nov. 6, 1989. people.com.

Perez, Lexy. "Disney's Choice to Cast Halle Bailey in 'Little Mermaid' Is Mostly Well-Received, Poll Finds." *Hollywood Reporter,* July 15, 2019. hollywoodreporter.com.

Perry, Matthew. *Narrative of the Expedition of an American Squadron to the China Seas and Japan, Performed in the Years 1852, 1853, and 1854.* U.S. Navy, 1856.

Petersen, Rachelle. "China's Confucius Institutes Might Be Closing, but They Succeeded." *RealClearEducation,* March 31, 2021. "https://www.realclear education.com/articles/2021/03/31/chinas_confucius_institutes_might_be _closing_but_they_succeeded_110559.html" \t "_blank" realcleareducation.com.

———. "Outsourced to China: Confucius Institutes and Soft Power in American Higher Education." National Association of Scholars, April 6, 2017. nas.org.

Phoenix Hebei Network 凤凰网河北. "Zhongguo yinhang xieshou fubusi zhongguo zhengshi fa bu '2021 fubusi zhongguo guoji hua xuexiao paihang bang.'" 中国银行携手福布斯中国正式发布"2021福布斯中国国际化学校排行榜" [Bank of China and Forbes China Release the "2021 Forbes China International School Rankings"]. Phoenix Hebei Network 凤凰网河北, May 27, 2021.

Picker, Leslie. "Forbes Sues Integrated Whale Media over Deal." *New York Times,* Nov. 5, 2015. nytimes.com.

Pincus, Walter. "Kissinger Says He Had No Role in China Mission." *Washington Post,* Dec. 14, 1989. washingtonpost.com.

Pollack, Andrew, and Keith Bradsher. "China's Need for Metal Keeps U.S. Scrap Dealers Scrounging." *New York Times,* March 13, 2004. nytimes.com.

Polo, Marco. *The Travels.* Penguin, 1974.

Pomfret, John. *The Beautiful Country and the Middle Kingdom: America and China, 1776 to the Present.* Macmillan, 2016.

———. "Business Takes Back Seat on China Trip: U.S. Firms Find Access at Low Ebb." *Washington Post,* June 26, 1998. washingtonpost.com.

———. "Secret Taiwan Fund Sought Friends, Influence Abroad." *Washington Post,* April 5, 2002. washingtonpost.com.

Pompeo, Mike. "The Chinese Communist Party on the American Campus." U.S. Department of State, Dec. 9, 2020. state.gov.

Pompliano, Anthony. "Pomp Podcast #361: Chris Fenton on Chinese Propaganda & Censorship in Hollywood." YouTube, 2020. youtube.com.

Post Editorial Board. "Capitalist Tiger, Hidden Dragon." *New York Post,* Oct. 1, 2014. nypost.com.

Pottinger, Matt, Russell Gold, Michael Phillips, and Kate Linebaugh. "Cnooc Drops Offer for Unocal, Exposing U.S.-Chinese Tensions." *Wall Street Journal,* Aug. 3, 2005. wsj.com.

Powell, Bill. "How America's Biggest Companies Made China Great Again." *Newsweek,* June 24, 2019. newsweek.com.

Price, Dawnthea. "A U.S. Video Game Company Banned a Player During a Tournament for Supporting the Hong Kong Protests." *Slate,* Oct. 8, 2019. slate.com.

Price, Ruth. *The Lives of Agnes Smedley.* Oxford University Press, 2005.

Public Citizen's Global Trade Watch. "Purchasing Power: The Corporate–White House Alliance to Pass the China Trade Bill over the Will of the American People." Public Citizen, Oct. 2, 2000. citizen.org.

Purnell, Newley, and Eva Xiao. "Facebook, Twitter, Google Face Free-Speech Test in Hong Kong." *Wall Street Journal,* July 3, 2020. wsj.com.

Puzzanghera, Jim, and Mark Magnier. "Studios Still Bit Actors in China." *Los Angeles Times,* June 18, 2006. latimes.com.

Qin, Amy, and Audrey Carlsen. "How China Is Rewriting Its Own Script." *New York Times,* Nov. 18, 2018. nytimes.com.

Qiu, Zhongsun. "Chinese Students Protest in America, Face Danger at Home." *Foreign Policy,* June 21, 2018. foreignpolicy.com.

Quinn, William T. "Chubb Aims for License in China." *Star-Ledger,* April 24, 1996. nj.com/starledger.

Ra's al Ghul. "Ra's al Ghul (Nolanverse)." Batman Wiki. dc.fandom.com.

Rauhala, Emily, and William Wan. "In a Beijing Ballroom, Kushner Family Pushes $500,000 'Investor Visa' to Wealthy Chinese." *Washington Post,* May 6, 2017. washingtonpost.com.

Redden, Elizabeth. "Question of NYU's Control over NYU Shanghai Sits at Center of Faculty Suit." *Inside Higher Ed,* Aug. 25, 2021. "https://www .insidehighered.com/news/2021/08/25/question-nyus-control-over-nyu -shanghai-sits-center-faculty-suit" \t "_blank" insidehighered.com.

Reed, James. *The Missionary Mind and American East Asia Policy, 1911–1915.* Harvard University Press, 1983.

Reinsch, Paul S. *An American Diplomat in China.* Alpha, 1922.

Reinstein, Mara. "Inside the Rich and Timeless Sets of *Mulan*." *Architectural Digest,* Sept. 4, 2020. architecturaldigest.com.

Report to Congressional Requesters. "U.S. Universities in China Emphasize Academic Freedom but Face Internet Censorship and Other Challenges." U.S. Government Accountability Office, Aug. 2016. gao.gov.

Ressner, Jeffrey. "Disney's China Policy." *Time,* June 24, 2001. time.com.

Reuters. "Asian Nations Pick Sides in U.S. Race." *Sun Sentinel,* Oct. 2, 1988.

———. "Clinton: 'Let's Get China Right.'" *Wired,* May 10, 2001. wired.com.

———. "Deposition Lists Lucrative Deals for Bush Brother." *New York Times,* Nov. 27, 2003. nytimes.com.

———. "2 Will Leave A.I.G. Board." *New York Times,* Feb. 14, 2006. nytimes.com.

Reuters Staff. "China Censors 'Pirates' for 'Vilifying Chinese.'" Reuters, June 14, 2007. reuters.com.

———. "Invesco WL Ross in JV with China's Huaneng Capital." Reuters, Sept. 16, 2008. reuters.com.

———. "Wanda Inks $1.7 Billion 'Red Tourism' Site in China's Communist Heartland." Reuters, Dec. 15, 2018. reuters.com.

Richburg, Keith, and Zhang Jie. "Jiang Zemin, the Old Boss, Wants to Become the New Boss." *Washington Post,* Sept. 26, 2012. washingtonpost.com.

Rio Tinto. "Shanghai Employees—Update 8." March 29, 2010. riotinto.com.

Rivas, Christian. "LeBron James Says Daryl Morey Was 'Misinformed' and 'Not Really Educated on the Situation' in China." Silver Screen and Roll, Oct. 14, 2019. silverscreenandroll.com.

Robbins, Gary. "Historic Rise in Chinese Students at UC San Diego Stalls due to Sour Political Climate in US." *San Diego Union-Tribune,* Nov. 10, 2019. sandiegouniontribune.com.

Rogin, Josh. "Can the Chinese Government Now Get Access to Your Grindr Profile?" *Washington Post,* Jan. 12, 2018. washingtonpost.com.

———. *Chaos Under Heaven: Trump, Xi, and the Battle for the Twenty-First Century.* HHM Audio, 2021.

Rose, Charlie. "Michael Eisner, Charlie Rose." *Charlie Rose,* Sept. 24, 1997. charlierose.com.

Rosen, Stanley. "Hollywood and the Great Wall." *Los Angeles Times,* June 18, 2006. latimes.com.

Roth, Andrew. "Obituary: Melvin Lasky." *Guardian,* May 22, 2004. theguardian .com.

Rotten Tomatoes. "*Pacific Rim* Quotes." Rotten Tomatoes. rottentomatoes.com.

Ruser, James, and Nathan Leibold. "Family De-planning: The Coercive Campaign to Drive Down Indigenous Birth-Rates in Xinjiang." Australian Strategic Policy Institute, May 12, 2021. aspi.org.au.

Sage, Alyssa. "Marvel Responds to 'Doctor Strange' 'Whitewashing' Criticisms over Tilda Swinton Casting." *Variety* (blog), April 27, 2016. variety.com.

Salisbury, Brian. "Fantastic Fest: Rian Johnson Talks 'Looper,' 'Back to the Future,' and What Happened to France." *Film School Rejects,* Sept. 27, 2012. filmschoolrejects.com.

Salopek, Paul. "The CIA's Secret War in Tibet." *Chicago Tribune,* Jan. 26, 1997. chicagotribune.com.

Sanchez, Rene. "Dalai Lama Urges Tibetan Freedom." *Washington Post,* Sept. 22, 1987. washingtonpost.com.

Sanger, David E. "Two Roads to China: Nice, and Not So Nice." *New York Times,* June 9, 1996. nytimes.com.

———. "U.S. Blames Allies for Undercutting Its China Policy." *New York Times,* June 12, 1996. nytimes.com.

Sauer, Abe. "Real America: 'Red Dawn' Remade: China Is Coming for Our Children." *Awl,* May 27, 2010. theawl.com.

Savranskaya, Svetlana, and Thomas S. Blanton. *The Last Superpower Summits: Gorbachev, Reagan, and Bush: Conversations That Ended the Cold War.* Central European University Press, 2017.

Schell, Orville. *Virtual Tibet: Searching for Shangri-La from the Himalayas to Hollywood.* Metropolitan Books, 2000.

Schmidt, Michael S., Keith Bradsher, and Christine Hauser. "U.S. Panel Cites Risks in Chinese Equipment." *New York Times,* Oct. 8, 2012. nytimes.com.

Schmitz, Rob. "Kushner Family, China's Anbang End Talks over Manhattan Real Estate Deal." NPR, March 29, 2017. npr.org.

Scholars at Risk. "Obstacles to Excellence." Scholars at Risk, Sept. 24, 2019. scholarsatrisk.org.

School Office. "Guanyu bao song xinxi gongzuo fuzhe ren he xinxi yuan de tongzhi" 关于报送信息工作负责人和信息员的通知 [Notice regarding the person in charge of submitting work and information officer]. Shaanxi Normal University 陕西师范大学, March 28, 2018. snu.edu.cn.

Schultz, Howard. "Building a Trusted and Enduring Brand in China and Around the World." Tsinghua University, July 13, 2020. gmba.sem.tsinghua.edu.cn.

Schwartzel, Erich. "Hollywood's New Script: You Can't Make Movies Without China." *Wall Street Journal,* April 18, 2017. wsj.com.

Sciolino, Elaine. "China, Vying with Taiwan, Explores Public Relations." *New York Times,* Feb. 2, 1996.

———. "The Schooling of Gingrich, the Foreign Policy Novice." *New York Times,* July 18, 1995. nytimes.com.

Shambaugh, David. "The Coming Chinese Crackup." *Wall Street Journal,* March 6, 2015. wsj.com.

———. "Defining Current Challenges." Panel at "The End of U.S. Engagement with China?" Brookings, March 7, 2018. brookings.edu.

Shaw, Lucas. "Fearing Chinese Censors, Paramount Changes 'World War Z' (Exclusive)." *The Wrap* (blog), March 31, 2013. thewrap.com.

Shepherd, Jack. "Rowan Atkinson Is Reprising His Role as Mr. Bean for a Chinese Film." *Independent,* March 20, 2017. independent.co.uk.

Sherrill, Martha. "Little Buddha, Big Ego." *Washington Post,* May 22, 1994. washingtonpost.com.

Shriber, Todd. "Las Vegas Sands Boss Adelson Told Trump to Tread Carefully with China." *Casino.org* (blog), Sept. 23, 2019. casino.org.

Siegel, Tatiana. "Richard Gere's Studio Exile. Why His Hollywood Career Took an Indie Turn." *Hollywood Reporter,* April 18, 2017. hollywoodreporter.com.

Sikba, Katherine, and Hal Dardick. "Chinese President Hu Jintao to Visit Chicago." *Chicago Tribune,* Jan. 12, 2011. chicagotribune.com.

Silver, Laura, Kat Devlin, and Christine Huang. "Most Americans Support Tough Stance Toward China on Human Rights, Economic Issues." Pew Research Center's Global Attitudes Project, March 4, 2021. pewresearch.org.

Silverstein, Ken. "The Mandarins." *Harper's Magazine,* Aug. 2008. harpers.org.

Simon, Scott. "China Suppression of Uighur Minorities Meets U.N. Definition of Genocide, Report Says." NPR, July 4, 2020. npr.org.

Singel, Ryan, and David Kravets. "Only Google Could Leave China." *Wired,* Jan. 15, 2018. wired.com.

Sisario, Ben. "For All the Rock in China." *New York Times,* Nov. 25, 2007. nytimes.com.

SI Staff, "Pekin Choose: The Author's High School Made the Tough Decision the Redskins Haven't." *Sports Illustrated,* Nov. 23, 2015.

Smirke, Richard. "IFPI Global Music Report 2020: Music Revenues Rise for Fifth Straight Year to $20 Billion." *Billboard,* May 4, 2020. billboard.com.

Smith, Ben. "Apple TV Was Making a Show About Gawker. Then Tim Cook Found Out." *New York Times,* Dec. 13, 2020. nytimes.com.

Smith, David, and Tom Phillips. "China Hails Trump's Appointment of 'Old Friend' Terry Branstad as Ambassador." *Guardian,* Dec. 7, 2016. theguardian.com.

Snow, Edgar. *Red China Today: The Other Side of the River.* Random House, 1971.

Sohu News. "Lao shao jie yi, ren jian ren ai de 'Xueren qiyuan,' shi yong Haolaiwu de fangshi jiang le yi ge Zhongguo gushi" 老少皆宜，人见人爱的《雪

人奇缘》, 是用好莱坞的方式讲了一个中国故事 [Suitable for young and old, the universally appealing *Abominable* tells a Chinese story in Hollywood fashion]. Sohu Inc. 搜狐, Oct. 3, 2019. sohu.com.

Sonnad, Nikhil. "Versace Is the Latest Major Brand to Express Its 'Deepest Apologies' to China." *Quartz,* Aug. 11, 2019. qz.com.

Sorkin, Andrew Ross, and David Barboza. "China to Buy $3 Billion Stake in Blackstone." *New York Times,* May 20, 2007. nytimes.com.

South China Morning Post. "Batman Star Christian Bale Visits Disneyland with Blind Dissident Chen Guangcheng." Jan. 24, 2013. scmp.com.

South Park Archives. "The China Probrem Script." southpark.fandom.

Spence, Jonathan D. *God's Chinese Son: The Taiping Heavenly Kingdom of Hong Xiuquan.* W. W. Norton, 1996.

Spielberg, Steven. "Steven Spielberg to Hu Jintao on Darfur." USC US-China Institute, April 2, 2007. china.usc.edu.

Sridharan, Vasudevan. "China, the Sleeping Lion Has Woken Up, Says Xi Jinping." *International Business Times,* March 29, 2014. ibtimes.co.uk.

Staff. "Brother of Ex–US Leader Hired by Firm." *South China Morning Post,* Nov. 9, 1999. scmp.com.

Staff. "Clinton Urges U.S. Partnership with China for Brighter Future." *Dallas Morning News,* May 11, 2001. dallasnews.com.

Starbucks. "Howard Schultz Meets with the Top Leader in Shanghai." Starbucks Stories & News, Sept. 21, 2015. stories.starbucks.com.

Stause, Jackie. " 'Veep': How That 'Monstrosity' Sets Up the Series Finale." *Hollywood Reporter,* May 5, 2019. hollywoodreporter.com.

Stein, Ruthe. "The Famous Elbow Rub / In Toronto, a Crowded Schedule of Films Competes with the Crush of Celebrities." *SFGATE,* Sept. 11, 1997. sfgate .com.

Stephens, Bret. "Henry Kissinger on China. Or Not." *Wall Street Journal,* May 21, 2011. wsj.com.

Stevenson, Alexandra, and Austin Ramzy. "China Defends Expulsion of American Journalists, Accusing U.S. of Prejudice." *New York Times,* March 18, 2020. nytimes.com.

Stewart, Barbara. "In Current Films on Tibet, Hold the Shangri-La." *New York Times,* March 19, 2000. nytimes.com.

Stolder, Steven. "Beastie Boys, Smashing Pumpkins Headline Tibetan Freedom Concert." *Rolling Stone,* Aug. 8, 1996. rollingstone.com.

Stone Fish, Isaac. "American Companies in China Shouldn't Fear Tariffs. They Should Fear a Boycott." *Washington Post,* April 10, 2018. washingtonpost.com.

———. "America's Maps Are Still Filled with Racist Place Names." *Washington Post,* Sept. 28, 2020. washingtonpost.com.

———. "Beijing Wants U.S. Business Leaders to Plead Its Case. Here's Why They Shouldn't." *Washington Post,* Jan. 18, 2021. washingtonpost.com.

———. "Can Politico Pull Off Its New Partnership with a Chinese-Owned Paper?" *Washington Post,* May 23, 2018. washingtonpost.com.

———. "China Has Access to Grindr Activity. We Should All Be Worried." *Washington Post,* April 9, 2019. washingtonpost.com.

———. "Dear Progressives: You Can't Fight Climate Change by Going Soft on China." *Washington Post,* July 10, 2021, sec. Global Opinions. "https://www .washingtonpost.com/opinions/2021/07/10/pandering-to-china-isnt-the -way-to-fight-climate-change/" \t "_blank" washingtonpost.com.

———. "Howard Schultz Has a Big China Problem." *Washington Post,* Feb. 7, 2019. washingtonpost.com.

———. "Huawei's Surprising Ties to the Brookings Institution." *Washington Post,* Dec. 7, 2018. washingtonpost.com.

———. "Leaked Email: ABA Cancels Book for Fear of 'Upsetting the Chinese Government.'" *Foreign Policy,* April 15, 2016. foreignpolicy.com.

———. "Stop Calling Xi Jinping 'President.'" *Slate,* Aug. 8, 2019. slate.com.

———. "Why Can't Ex–Chinese Leaders Travel Abroad?" *Foreign Policy,* Dec. 24, 2015. foreignpolicy.com.

———. "Wilbur Ross Remained on Chinese Joint Venture Board While Running U.S.-China Trade War." *Foreign Policy,* Oct. 29, 2020. foreignpolicy.com.

Studwell, Joe. *The China Dream: The Quest for the Last Great Untapped Market on Earth.* Grove Press, 2003.

Su, Wendy. *China's Encounter with Global Hollywood: Cultural Policy and the Film Industry, 1994–2013.* University Press of Kentucky, 2016.

Suettinger, Robert L. *Beyond Tiananmen: The Politics of U.S.-China Relations, 1989–2000.* Brookings Institution Press, 2004.

Sullivan, Halsted, and Warren Lieberstein. "Season 7—Episode 10 'China.'" OfficeQuotes.Net, March 3, 2020. officequotes.

Sullivan, Maureen. "China One-Ups Disney with Its Own Tibet Pic." *Variety,* April 1, 1997. variety.com.

Sun, Zhi 孙志. "Lao Bushi jiang xianqi di Jing Gang bao zhi neng zhu qi zi fengfu fang Hua shouhuo" 老布什将先期抵京 港报指能助其子丰富访华收获 [Bush Sr. will arrive early in Beijing while Hong Kong's newspapers will help enrich his son's visit to China]. China News Network 中国新闻网, Xinhua News Agency 新华社, Nov. 11, 2005. xinhuanet.com.

Swartz, Mimi. "Cast Away." *Texas Monthly,* May 1, 2004. texasmonthly.com.

Swisher, Earl. *China's Management of the American Barbarians: A Study of Sino-American Relations, 1841–1861.* Far Eastern Association, 1953.

Szalai, George. "Chinese Get Tough on Big Media." *Billboard,* Sept. 27, 2005. billboard.com.

Taipei Economic and Cultural Representative Office in the United States 駐美 國台北經濟文化代表處. "A Brief Introduction of Twin Oaks." Dec. 31, 2020. roc-taiwan.org.

Tan, Huileng. "Bill Clinton to Lead U.S. Delegation to Lee Kuan Yew Funeral." *Wall Street Journal,* March 26, 2015. wsj.com.

Tareen, Sophia. "China's President to See Chicago Chinese Institute." *Post and Courier* (Charleston, S.C.), Jan. 20, 2011. postandcourier.com.

Telegraph Staff. "Skyfall Heavily Edited by Chinese Government Censors." *Telegraph,* Jan. 21, 2013. telegraph.co.uk.

Tempest, Rone. "How Do You Say 'Boffo' in Chinese?" *Los Angeles Times,* Nov. 29, 1994. latimes.com.

Tenet, George J., and Louis J. Freeh. "CIA/FBI Report to Congress on Chinese Espionage Activities Against the United States." Dec. 12, 1999. fas.org.

Thomas, George. "China's Xi Jinping's 'Mandate of Heaven' to Rule the World." CBN News, Oct. 26, 2020. cbn.com.

Thomas, Neil. "Boeing and US-China Relations." MacroPolo, Feb. 26, 2019. macropolo.org.

Tibet House US. "Board & Staff." tibethouse.usa.

Tie, Shizheng. "Canceling Joshua Wong and Nathan Law, in the Name of Democracy." change.org.

———. "Sign the Petition." Change.org. Accessed April 7, 2021. change.org.

Tobias, Scott. "Song of the South: The Difficult Legacy of Disney's Most Shocking Movie." *Guardian,* Nov. 19, 2019. theguardian.com.

Trump, Donald J. "Remarks by President Trump at Signing of the U.S.-China Phase One Trade Agreement." Jan. 15, 2020. trumpwhitehouse.archives.gov.

Tsinghua University. "Tsinghua University School of Economics and Management-List of Advisory Board Members." sem.tsinghua.edu.cn.

Tu, Janet I. "Starbucks Spends $1.3 Billion for Full Stake in Fast-Growing China Market." *Seattle Times,* July 27, 2017. seattletimes.com.

Tu, Siqi, et al. "How Should the U.S. Government Treat Chinese Students in America?" *ChinaFile,* Aug. 1, 2019. chinafile.com.

Tucker, Nancy Bernkopf, ed. *China Confidential: American Diplomats and Sino-American Relations, 1945–1996.* Columbia University Press, 2001.

Tuckman, Jo. "License to Shill: Mexico Pays James Bond Film Studios Millions to Shoot Its Good Side." *Guardian,* March 12, 2015. theguardian.com.

Tung, Ariel. "Cinema Chains Ready to Cash In On Movie Boom." *China Daily,* Sept. 29, 2010. chinadaily.com.cn.

Turner, Douglas. "Kissinger Should Disclose Clients, Albright Says." *Buffalo News,* Dec. 5, 2002. buffalonews.com.

Tur Partners. "Registration Statement Pursuant to the Foreign Agents Registration Act of 1938, as Amended—Tur Partners LLC." U.S. Department of Justice, Nov. 18, 2013. efile.fara.gov.

TV Show Transcripts. "Madam Secretary Transcripts Season 3, Episode 16." tvshowtranscripts.ourboard.org.

2006 USCBC Member Priorities Survey. "US Companies Gain in China, Still Face Hurdles." US-China Business Council, Aug. 30, 2006. ansi.org.

Tyler, Patrick. *A Great Wall.* PublicAffairs, 1999.

UK Parliament. "Lord Sassoon: Registered Interests." UK Parliament, 2021. members.parliament.uk.

United Airlines. "Cheap Flights from San Francisco to Taipei." united.com.

United Nations. "United Nations Office on Genocide Prevention and the Responsibility to Protect." un.org.

UPI. "Congressman Says Kissinger Benefits from Arms Deals." Aug. 26, 1983. upi.com.

——. "Deng Wants More Economic Reforms for China." May 24, 1988. upi .com.

U.S. Census Bureau. "1995: U.S. Trade in Goods with China." census.gov.

——. "1996: U.S. Trade in Goods with China." census.gov.

U.S. Department of Justice. "FARA Quick Search—Tur Partners, LLC." efile .fara.gov.

Van Groningen, Nicole. "Big Pharma Gives Your Doctor Gifts. Then Your Doctor Gives You Big Pharma's Drugs." *Washington Post,* June 12, 2017.

van Schaik, Sam. *Tibet: A History.* Yale University Press, 2013.

Verrier, Richard. "Disney Seeks to Add China to Its World." *Los Angeles Times,* Sept. 16, 2001. latimes.com.

Victor, Daniel. "John Cena Apologizes to China for Calling Taiwan a Country." *New York Times,* May 25, 2021, sec. World. nytimes.com.

Vise, Daniel de. "U.S. Scholars Say Their Book on China Led to Travel Ban." *Washington Post,* Aug. 20, 2011. washingtonpost.com.

Viswanatha, Aruna, and Kate O'Keeffe. "U.S. Warned Jared Kushner About Wendi Deng Murdoch." *Wall Street Journal,* Jan. 25, 2018. wsj.com.

Vogel, Ezra F. *Deng Xiaoping and the Transformation of China.* Harvard University Press, 2011.

Wagner, Alex. "The Hollywood List Everyone Wants to Be On." *Atlantic,* March 2017. theatlantic.com.

Wagner, Laura. "Internal Memo: ESPN Forbids Discussion of Chinese Politics When Discussing Daryl Morey's Tweet About Chinese Politics." *Deadspin,* Oct. 8, 2019. deadspin.com.

Waldman, Peter. "The U.S. Is Purging Chinese Cancer Researchers from Top Institutions." Bloomberg, Jan. 13, 2019. bloomberg.com.

Wallace, James. "Hu's Boeing Visit Is a Hit with Workers—Leader Predicts Bright Future for Firm with China." *Seattle Post-Intelligencer,* April 20, 2006. seattlepi.com.

Wall Street Journal. "Cnooc's Aug. 2 Press Release on Withdrawal of Bid for Unocal." Aug. 3, 2005. wsj.com.

Walsh, Matthew. "In Depth: Chinese Students at US Colleges Face Uncertain Future." Nikkei Asia, July 29, 2020. asia.nikkei.com.

Walters, John. "Philip Glass Talks About 26 Years of Tibet House Benefit Concerts." *Newsweek,* Feb. 18, 2016. newsweek.com.

Wang, Dan. "China's Zoom Bomb." *ChinaFile,* June 16, 2020. chinafile.com.

Wang, Jianlin. "Speech by Chairman Wang Jianlin at the Launch of Yan'an Wanda City–Wanda Group Mobile." Wanda Group, April 18, 2019. wanda -group.com.

———. "Tips from the Top: China's Richest Man Shares Insights into His Business Success at Oxford." Saïd Business School, March 1, 2016. sbs.ox.ac.uk.

Wang, Shanshan. "Authorities Deny Ban on Hollywood Movies." *China Daily*, Dec. 15, 2007. chinadaily.com.cn.

Wang, Yue. "Chinese Web Tycoon Zhou Yahui Agrees to Pay Wife $1.1 Billion in Divorce." *Forbes*, Sept. 14, 2016. forbes.com.

Ward, Vicky. "Inconvenient Sharon Bush." *Vanity Fair*, April 30, 2008. vanityfair .com.

Washington Post Editorial Board. "China's Orwellian Tools of High-Tech Repression." *Washington Post*, Sept. 17, 2018. washingtonpost.com.

———. "What's Happening in Xinjiang Is Genocide." *Washington Post*, July 6, 2020. washingtonpost.com.

Wasserstrom, Jeffrey N. *Popular Protest and Political Culture in Modern China.* 2nd ed. Routledge, 2018.

Watt, Louise. " 'Cloud Atlas' Cut by 38 Minutes for China Audience." Associated Press, Jan. 24, 2013.

Waxman, Sharon. "China Bans Work with Film Studios." *Washington Post*, Nov. 1, 1997. washingtonpost.com.

———. "How Hollywood and Joe Biden Got China to Drop a 20-Year Movie Quota." Reuters, Feb. 20, 2012. reuters.com.

Wayne, Leslie. "Trading on Their Names; Turning Government Experience into Corporate Advice." *New York Times*, May 23, 2001. nytimes.com.

Wayt, Theo. "NYU Shanghai Quietly Added Pro-government Course at Behest of Chinese Government." *Vice*, Nov. 20, 2019. vice.com.

Weibo. "Weibo Search: ANTA Nba." weibo.com.

Weinraub, Bernard. "Dalai Lama's Tutor, Portrayed by Brad Pitt, Wasn't Just Roving Through the Himalayas." *New York Times*, June 21, 1997. nytimes.com.

———. "Disney Will Defy China on Its Dalai Lama Film." *New York Times*, Nov. 27, 1996. nytimes.com.

———. "Hollywood Feels Chill of Chinese Warning to Disney." *New York Times*, Dec. 9, 1996. nytimes.com.

Weintraub, Steve. " 'The Last Ship' Producers on Elevating the Stakes in Seasons 4 and 5." Collider, Oct. 28, 2016. collider.com.

Weisskopf, Michael, and Keith B. Richburg. "China Special Report." *Washington Post*, Nov. 12, 1996. washingtonpost.com.

Wells, Jennifer. "Rumble in the Jungle." *Maclean's*, Feb. 3, 1997. archive.macleans.ca.

Wen, Philip, and Douglas Belkin. "American Colleges Watch for Changes at Chinese Universities." *Wall Street Journal*, Dec. 27, 2019. wsj.com.

West, Darrell M., and Dan Bernstein. "Benefits and Best Practices of Safe City Innovation." Brookings Institution, Oct. 2017. brookings.edu.

Westad, Odd Arne. *Restless Empire: China and the World Since 1750.* Basic Books, 2015.

Westcott, Ben, and Steve George. "How George H. W. Bush Became Beijing's 'Old Friend' in the White House." CNN, Dec. 2, 2018. cnn.com.

Wike, Richard. "6 Facts About How Americans and Chinese See Each Other." *Pew Research Center* (blog), March 30, 2016. pewresearch.org.

WikiLeaks. "Macau Gaming Revenues Rise Sharply as Las Vegas Sands Boosts Engagement with Beijing Officials." WikiLeaks Public Library of US Diplomacy, China Hong Kong, Sept. 24, 2009. wikileaks.org.

———. "Sony Email 180113." WikiLeaks, Nov. 1, 2013. wikileaks.org.

———. "Sony Email 182471." WikiLeaks, Oct. 31, 2013. wikileaks.org.

———. "Sony Email 189623." WikiLeaks, Dec. 18, 2013. wikileaks.org.

———. "Sony Email 200507." WikiLeaks, Feb. 10, 2014. wikileaks.org.

Williams, Gordon. "Spinning Their Wheels in China." *New York Times,* Nov. 19, 1989. nytimes.com.

Wineapple, Brenda. " 'I Have Let Whitman Alone.' " *New York Review of Books,* April 18, 2019. nybooks.com.

Wintour, Patrick. "Disney Unapologetic over Mulan Credit Thanking Chinese Communist Party." *Guardian,* April 28, 2021. theguardian.com.

Woeser, Tsering. "When Tibet Loved China." *Foreign Policy,* Jan. 22, 2013. foreignpolicy.com.

Wondra, Jan. "Chaffee Upholds Historical Accuracy for Chinaman Gulch." *Ark Valley Voice,* Nov. 26, 2019. arkvalleyvoice.com.

Wong, Belinda. "Partner Letters from the President of Starbucks China." *Starbucks Stories Asia,* Sept. 21, 2015.

Wong, Edward. "Bloomberg News Is Said to Curb Articles That Might Anger China." *New York Times,* Nov. 8, 2013. nytimes.com.

———. " 'Doctor Strange' Writer Explains Casting of Tilda Swinton as Tibetan." *New York Times,* April 26, 2016. nytimes.com.

———. "How China Uses LinkedIn to Recruit Spies Abroad." *New York Times,* Aug. 27, 2019. nytimes.com.

———. "James Cameron on Chinese Filmmakers, Censorship, and Potential Co-productions." *Media Decoder Blog,* May 5, 2012. mediadecoder.blogs.nytimes.com.

Wong, Matteo. "The End of the Harvard Century." *Crimson,* April 23, 2020. thecrimson.com.

Woodward, Bob. *State of Denial: Bush at War, Part III.* Simon & Schuster, 2008.

Woolcock, Nicola. "Wipe References to China to Protect Students, Soas Lecturers Told." *Times* (London), May 7, 2021. thetimes.co.uk.

Wu, Frank H. *Yellow: Race in America Beyond Black and White.* Basic Books, 2003.

Wu, Huang 吴煌. "Lu han wangjunkai tong kuang zuole 'tongxue' bai wei ying ren hangzhou shang dangke" 鹿晗王俊凯同框做了"同学" 百位影人杭州上党课 [Lu han, Wang Junkai, and other celebrities attended "Party class study" session in Xixi, Hangzhou]. Two Eggz 蛋蛋赞 and Zhejiang News 浙江新闻, Nov. 28, 2017. twoeggz.com.

Xi, Jinping. "Juesheng quanmian jiancheng xiaokang shehui duoqu xin shidai Zhongguo tese shehui zhuyi weida shengli—zai Zhongguo gongchangdang di shijiu ci quanguo daibiao dahui shang de baogao" 决胜全面建成小康社会夺取新时代中国特色社会主义伟大胜利—在中国共产党第十九次全国代表大会上的报告 [Secure a decisive victory in building a moderately prosperous society in all respects and strive for the great success of socialism with Chinese characteristics for a new era delivered at the 19th National Congress of the Communist Party of China]. Speech, Oct. 27, 2017. Phoenix Media 凤凰. news.ifeng.com.

———. "Mingji fendoulicheng dandang lishi shiming cong dang de fendou lishi zhong jiqu qianjin liliang" 铭记奋斗历程担当历史使命 从党的奋斗历史中汲取前进力量 [Remember the course of struggle, take on the historical mission, draw forward strength from the history of the Party's struggle]. *People's Daily Online* 人民网, June 18, 2021. people.com.cn.

Xi'an International Studies University. "Distinguished Alumni Lecture Series (5): Our School Hires Dr. Liu Yawei as Part-Time Professor of Xiwai University–Xi'an International Studies University." May 19, 2016. xisu.edu.cn.

Xiaoyao Ge Entertainment 逍遥扒扒影. "*Zhan Lang 2* hou you yi junshi dazuo, beijing qiangda zhen qiang shidan, 90% de yanyuan dou shi junren" 《战狼2》后又一军事大作, 背景强大真枪实弹, 90%的演员都是军人 [*Wolf Warrior 2* is another military masterpiece, powerful background effects are from real live ammunition, 90% of the actors are military personnel]. *Sina News* 新浪新闻, Jan. 3, 2021. k.sina.cn.

Xinhua. "Chinese State Councillor Calls on US to Oppose Taiwan Independence." Newswire, Nov. 11, 2003. xinhua.net.

———. "Kissinger's Pride in 40-Year China Experiences." *China Daily,* May 27, 2011. chinadaily.com.cn.

———. "Wenjiabao huijian meiguo qian zongtong Bushi ji Faguo qian zongli" 温家宝会见美国前总统布什及法国前总理 [Wen Jiabao meets with former US president Bush and former French prime minister]. *Sina News* 新浪新闻, Nov. 15, 2005. news.sina.com.cn.

———. "Zhonggong Zhongyang yinfa 'Shenhua dang he guojia jigou gaige fangan'" 中共中央印发《深化党和国家机构改革方案》 [The Central Committee of the Communist Party of China issues "Deepening Party and State Institutional Reform Plan"]. Xinhua News Agency 新华网, March 21, 2018. xinhuanet.com.

Xu, Junqian. "Marriott Announces 'Rectification Plan' to Regain Trust." *China Daily,* Jan. 18, 2018. chinadaily.com.cn.

Xu, Zhicai. "Xu Zhicai's Interview." World War Z Wiki. worldwarz.fandom.com.

Xue, Yu 薛钰. "Renmin lingxiu Zhou Enlai" 人民领袖周恩来 [The people's leader Zhou Enlai]. *People's Daily* 人民日报, April 4, 2019. zhouenlai.people.cn.

Yale University Library. "Kissinger at China Ventures—Image 2." May 3, 1989. library.yale.edu.

———. "Kissinger in China." library.yale.edu.

Yojana, Sharma. "China Fights Back with Sanctions on Academics, Institute." *University World News,* March 25, 2021. universityworldnews.com.

Yong, Charissa. "S'poreans Should Be Aware of China's Influence Ops: Bilahari." *Straits Times,* June 28, 2018. straitstimes.com.

Younis, Mohamed. "New High in Perceptions of China as U.S.'s Greatest Enemy." Gallup, March 16, 2021. news.gallup.com.

Yu, Hongmei. "From *Kundun* to *Mulan:* A Political Economic Case Study of Disney and China." Asia Network Exchange, 2015. asianetworkexchange.org.

———. "Visual Spectacular, Revolutionary Epic, and Personal Voice: The Narration of History in Chinese Main Melody Films." *Modern Chinese Literature and Culture* 25, no. 2 (Fall 2013).

Yuan, Bo 袁勃. "Xijinping zhuxi teshi, guojia fu zhuxi Liyuanchao chuxi Xinjiapo qian zongli Liguangyao guozang" 习近平主席特使、国家副主席李源潮出席新加坡前总理李光耀国葬 [Xi Jinping's special envoy and Vice President Li Yuanchao attended the state funeral of Singapore's former prime minister Lee Kuan Yew]. *People's Daily* 人民日报, March 29, 2015. politics.people.com.cn.

Yuan, Shikai, and Frank Goodnow. "The Perils of Advising the Empire." *ChinaFile,* Dec. 30, 2015. chinafile.com.

Yuli, Zeng. "China's Filmmakers Fine-Tune Patriotism for a New Generation." *Sixth Tone,* Dec. 13, 2019. sixthtone.com.

Zehme, Bill. "Eddie Murphy: Call Him Money." *Rolling Stone,* Aug. 24, 1989. rollingstone.com.

Zhang, Hao 张昊, and Zhou Bin 周斌. "Guojia Anquan Jiguan shi zenmeyang yi zhi duiwu? Guo'anbu Xinwen Ban da jizhe wen" 国家安全机关是怎样一支队伍?国安部新闻办答记者问 [What kind of organization is the National Security Agency? The Ministry of State Security's Information Office answers questions from reporters]. Zhongguo Xinwen wang 中国新闻网. Legal Daily, *Fazhi Ribao* 法治日报, Jan. 7, 2021. chinanews.com.

Zhang, Rui. "China's Sovereign Wealth Fund Releases Annual Report." China .org, Sept. 23, 2019. china.org.cn.

———. "Wachowski Laments China's 'Cloud Atlas' Cut." China.org.cn, Jan. 2013. china.org.cn.

Zhao, Shirley. "Entertaining China; Hollywood Struggles for Fans in China's Growing Film Market." Bloomberg, Feb. 15, 2021. bloomberg.com.

Zhejiang News 浙江新闻. "120 duo wei daming dingding de Zhongguo dianying ren qiju Hangzhou Xixi shang dang ke!" 120多位大名鼎鼎的中国电影人齐聚杭州西溪上党课 [Over 120 Chinese movie stars gather in Hangzhou's Xixi for Party study session]. Guancha zhe 观察者. Zhejiang News, *Zhejiang xinwen* 浙江新闻, Nov. 27, 2017. guancha.cn.

Zheng, Sarah. "Beijing Accused of Pressuring Spanish University to Drop Taiwanese Event." *South China Morning Post,* Sept. 5, 2018. "https://www.scmp.com/news/china/diplomacy/article/2162875/beijing-accused-pressuring-spanish-university-drop-taiwanese" \t "_blank" scmp.com.

Zhiyuan, Xu. "The Anaconda and the Elephant." *China Heritage,* June 28, 2017. chinaheritage.net.

Zhou, Laura. "China Shuts Down Forbidden City in Personal Welcome for Trump." *South China Morning Post,* Nov. 8, 2017. scmp.com.

Zhou, Liyin 周立银 "Zhou enlai tongzhan yishu zai qingbao gongzuo zhong de yunyong" 周恩来统战艺术在情报工作中的运用 [Zhou Enlai's Art in Utilizing the United Front in Intelligence Work]. The United Front of Huai'an 淮安市委统战部, May 5, 2019. tzb.huaian.gov.cn.

Zhou, Viola. "Trump Wasn't Going to Do 'a Fucking Thing' if China Invaded Taiwan, a New Book Says." *Vice,* March 9, 2021. vice.com.

Zhu, Rongji. *Zhu Rongji on the Record: The Road to Reform, 1998–2003.* Brookings Institution Press, 2015.

Zhu, Ying. "The Inside Story of When China's State-Run TV Criticized the Party." *Atlantic,* June 5, 2012. theatlantic.com.

Zoellick, Robert. "Can America and China Be Stakeholders?" Carnegie Endowment for International Peace, Dec. 4, 2019. carnegieendowment.org.

———. "Whither China? From Membership to Responsibility." Speech, New York City, Sept. 21, 2005. ncuscr.org.

Index

A NOTE ABOUT THE AUTHOR

Isaac Stone Fish is the founder and CEO of the research firm Strategy Risks, which quantifies corporate exposure to China. He is also a *Washington Post* Global Opinions contributing columnist, a contributor to CBSN, an adjunct at New York University's Center for Global Affairs, a visiting fellow at the Atlantic Council, a columnist on China risk at *Barron's,* and a frequent speaker at events around the United States and the world. A fluent Mandarin speaker and formerly a Beijing correspondent for *Newsweek,* Stone Fish spent six years living in China. He lives in New York.

A NOTE ON THE TYPE

This book was set in Minion, a typeface produced by the Adobe Corporation specifically for the Macintosh personal computer and released in 1990. Designed by Robert Slimbach, Minion combines the classic characteristics of old-style faces with the full complement of weights required for modern typesetting.

Typeset by Scribe, Philadelphia, Pennsylvania

Printed and bound by Berryville Graphics,
Berryville, Virginia

Design by Betty Lew